SPORT AND SUSTAINABLE DEVELOPMENT

D0873069

Sport has the potential to be a powerful platform for positive change. This is the first textbook to introduce the fundamentals of sport and sustainable development, examining how sport can be made more sustainable in terms of its social and environmental impact, and how sport can achieve more comprehensive social and ecological objectives.

Introducing key theory, and looking at how sustainability has been embedded in real-world organizations, projects, and developments, the book draws on a range of multidisciplinary perspectives including sport business and management, development studies, environmental studies, sociology, psychology, and political science. Every chapter includes international viewpoints from the voices of professionals who have been successful in achieving sustainable development goals (SDGs) in and through their work. As pressure grows on sport, business, and wider society to put sustainability and social and environmental responsibility at the center of their operations, the themes and topics examined in this book become ever more important.

This is essential reading for any course on sport and sustainable development, and important background reading for any course in sport management, sport development, event studies, environment and society, business and the environment, or social responsibility.

Stavros Triantafyllidis received his Doctor of Philosophy (Ph.D.) in Sport Management from the University of Florida, USA. His research focuses on sport and sustainable development with an emphasis on events, transportation, and consumer behavior. He served as an Assistant Professor and Program Coordinator in Sport Management at The Citadel, The Military College of South Carolina.

Cheryl Mallen is an Associate Professor in Sport Management at Brock University, Canada. Her research focuses on sport and environmental sustainability and the impacts of new technologies on sport management.

SPORT AND SUSTAINABLE DEVELOPMENT

An Introduction

Edited by Stavros Triantafyllidis and Cheryl Mallen

Routledge
Taylor & Francis Group

LONDON AND NEW YORK

Cover credit: © Catherine Ledner/Getty Images

First published 2022
by Routledge
4 Park Square, Milton Park, Abingdon, Oxon OX14 4RN

and by Routledge
605 Third Avenue, New York, NY 10158

Routledge is an imprint of the Taylor & Francis Group, an informa business

British Library Cataloguing-in-Publication Data
A catalog record for this book is available from the British Library

Library of Congress Cataloguing-in-Publication Data
A catalog record has been requested for this book

ISBN: 978-0-367-65334-7 (hbk)
ISBN: 978-0-367-65333-0 (pbk)
ISBN: 978-1-003-12895-3 (ebk)

DOI: 10.4324/9781003128953

Typeset in Bembo
by MPS Limited, Dehradun

Access the Support Material: www.routledge.com/9780367653330

CONTENTS

FIGURES

TABLE

CONTRIBUTORS

Elia Chatzigiani is an associate professor in the Department of Sport Management and Organization at the University of Peloponnese, Greece.

Lindsey Darvin is an assistant professor of Sport Management at SUNY Cortland, New York, United States.

Greg Dingle is a lecturer in the Department of Management, Sport and Tourism at La Trobe University, Australia.

Curtis Fogel is an associate professor of Sport Management at Brock University, Canada.

Marco Tortora is a research fellow in the Department of Economic Sciences at the University of Florence, Italy, and adjunct professor in International Business and European Business Program Coordinator at Kent State University in Florence, Italy, and chair of the nonprofit association FAIR Italy.

EXPERTS IN THE FIELD

Stefano Gobbi is a project manager for Sport e Salute Spa, Rome, Italy.
Scott McRoberts is director of Athletics at the University of Guelph and associate director, International Institute for Sport Business and Leadership.
Joshua Oppolot is executive director of Youth Sport Uganda.
Michalis Triantafyllidis is the business owner of Triantafyllidis Beach Arena.

PREFACE

Purpose of text

The purpose of *Sport and Sustainable Development: An Introduction* is to define a shared vision among inspired individuals who seek a bright and sustainable future for our world. Sport is a platform to aid in achieving such results.

Learning objectives

Upon completion of this textbook, learners should be able to successfully:

1. Define sport and sustainable development (S&SD)
2. Outline the critical perspectives of S&SD
3. Apply the analytical and normative concepts of sustainable development of sport (SD*o*S) and sport for sustainable development (S4SD)
4. Analyze the current state of S&SD and critically view its opportunities and challenges
5. Evaluate practices regarding SD*o*S and S4SD
6. Compare and contrast SD*o*S and S4SD
7. Synthesize the fundamental aspects of S&SD and conceptually develop frameworks that would effectively move forward this academic field
8. Produce strategic plans, address policy development opportunities, and suggest ideas and methods for developing the area of S&SD in theory and practice.

Overview of text

Sport and Sustainable Development: An Introduction is the first text to introduce sustainable development within sport (SD*o*S), and through sport (S4SD), the efforts take place worldwide for sustainability. International in scope, each chapter places sport at the center of attention concerning sustainable development in normative and analytical concepts. This text refers to sustainable development as an analytical concept that generates predictions and determines a prescriptive way forward. Additionally, the text discusses sustainable development's normative concept, which debates how we move forward collectively. S&SD, thus, involves two pathways – (1) SDoS and (2) S4SD, which are examined across the six shared perspectives of S&SD to embrace the complexity of the modern world. The six shared perspectives reflect on the most common aspects of S&SD, namely the personal, social, economic, ecological, technological, and political perspectives.

Each chapter in this text illustrates the connection between sport (as an institution in society) and sustainable development. In our modern society, the role of sport has the power to be a platform for positive interventions such as personal development, better health, more plant-based nutrition, wellness, social equity, inclusion, along with justice, peace, economic growth, prosperity, and environmental stewardship. At the local, national, and global levels, positive socio-environmental outcomes can enhance people's well-being, communities' quality of life, strengthen local economies, preserve the natural environment – and lead to sustainable development. Designed to encourage students to develop understandings concerning S&SD, it is hoped that visions of a sustainable future are generated, and steps to move toward such a future are forged – despite the current state of the world's multiple social, political, and health challenges.

Underscoring the integration of sport with sustainable development that promotes optimizing positive personal, social, economic, and environmental outcomes is good governance. Also, positive change through sport requires the promotion of the key value of "equality." Each chapter within this text supports the position that everyone on this planet should have the opportunity to elevate their position in life with their talent and skills and that sport can be a critical factor aiding to achieve such results.

With a focus on society with the SDoS as well as S4SD, this text is an essential read for students seeking to be part of an ethical way forward to sustainable societal development – despite the current state of the world's multiple social, political, and health challenges.

Organization of text

The text is divided into three parts. Part I has four chapters. Chapter 1 explains why we study S&SD. Also, it provides the definitions for sport, sustainable development, and an interpretation concerning how sport and the two sustainable development concepts (SDoS and S4SD) function together. Chapter 1 emphasizes the importance of studying S&SD in our contemporary era. Specifically, it demonstrates the crucial role of developing S&SD courses at undergraduate and graduate levels. Chapters 2 and 3 introduce the two paths of S&SD (SDoS and S4SD), and it explains how these paths are integrated into the six perspectives of our modern world, namely personal, social, economic, ecological, technological, and political. The scholars and professionals offer in-depth discussions focusing on the key learning objectives and outcomes. Chapter 4 explores the links between S&SD and the United Nations global sustainable development goals (SDGs).

Part II explores the six perspectives of S&SD and illustrates their application through the lenses of SDoS and S4SD across six chapters. Accordingly, Chapter 5 describes the benefits of sport to people's health, well-being, and quality of life (i.e., sustainable development outcomes). Additionally, Chapter 5 analyzes how sport influences our lives and how it enhances sustainable lifestyles. This chapter refers to the positive interventions of sport in our personal lives and how it influences sustainable behaviors. For example, discussions are offered on sport-related motivations and values that enhance our ecological identity and pro-environmental behaviors, as well as our socially responsible actions, such as philanthropy and charity.

Chapter 6 introduces theories that support the connection between sport, positive social change, social justice, and environmentalism. This chapter presents the power of sport as a platform for positive social changes. Specifically, Chapter 6 explores how sport influences society and people collectively; furthermore, it introduces social sustainability aspects in concert with theoretical frameworks and how they apply in the sport industry. Lastly, sport is demonstrated through experts' views and examples are provided from the field.

The economic perspective of S&SD is the central discourse of Chapter 7. This chapter analyzes the connection between sport and economic growth at the local, regional, national, and international levels. Also, sport finance and economics are discussed to understand how sustainable financial plans and strategies can be applied in sport and further developed and executed by sport organizations.

An introduction to the ecological state of our planet opens in Chapter 8. The authors explore human-induced climate change issues, and they highlight the significant problems in the natural environment. Moreover, Chapter 8 discusses the negative impacts of the sport industry on the natural environment, and the authors analyze its possible causes in detail. For example, Chapter 8 highlights sports organizations' hazardous operations and events on the planet and its ecosystems. Specifically, specific practical examples are discussed, such as the functioning of sport facilities, sport events, and sporting goods production. One section of the chapter also focuses on sport consumer behavior, habits, the consumption of sport products and services, the traveling of fans and sport participants in North America, Europe, Australia, and Asia. Lastly, Chapter 8 presents evaluation reports on waste and carbon dioxide emissions that illustrates clearly the size of the impacts that the sport industry has on the environment. The discussion posits sport as a catalyst for environmental stewardship, including as a platform for raising ecological awareness and explaining the positive influence of sport and its communication reach to advocate for change due to the ecological crisis. Accordingly, the authors refer to evidence that constitutes sport as a powerful tool for ecological change and its capability to reach many people to cultivate positive environmental identities and eco-conscious consumers. Chapter 8 sheds light on the necessary mechanisms that sport organizations and stakeholders can adopt to reduce their negative impact on the environment. Finally, theoretical frameworks and practical implications of sport and the natural environment are provided, as is an expert's views from the sport industry.

Chapter 9 discusses the past and the current trends of sustainable technologies and sport, focusing on the advance of renewable energy as well as reducing energy demand in the sport event and facility context. This includes a discussion on sustainable development in sport by referring to the techniques that the sport industry has applied to reduce its impacts on the environment by reducing fossil fuels.

Chapter 10 discusses the integration of S&SD with respect to sport governance and non-sport governance. The discussion focuses on how sport organizations' and their operations, the manufacturing of sporting goods and services, and sports influence on global government, policy development, and decision-making.

Finally, Part III focuses on the future of S&SD and discusses it throughout three chapters. Chapter 11 introduces our vision of the world through the lens of S&SD. Accordingly, Chapter 11 discusses how S&SD can transform the current state of the world in a positive direction. The discussion encompasses the importance of S&SD for the future of sport and the global world's society. Finally, Chapter 11 demonstrates and shares a vision of S&SD in practical and theoretical terms. Importantly, Chapter 12 constitutes the students' perspective regarding S&SD and its future. The optimistic side of S&SD is highlighted through the lens of Generation Z and students in sport. Finally, Chapter 13 discusses the challenges and limitations of S&SD and the opportunities and future direction of S&SD.

Summary

This introduction has outlined the structure and rationale of this text. It explained the connection between sport and sustainable development and supports the need to educate students on becoming future leaders.

Guide for supplementary readings

- Sachs, J. (2015). *The age of sustainable development*. New York: Columbia Press

Websites

- Sport Ecology Group: https://www.sportecology.org
- We Are Guarding Earth Through Sport (We Are GETS): www.wearegets.org

Online resource center

- Routledge website
- Test Bank
- Instructor's package
- PowerPoint presentations for each chapter

ACKNOWLEDGMENTS

By Stavros Triantafyllidis: To my family's unconditional love and faith, I could not be luckier to have been raised and adored by you. The mentors who have never given up on me, I am so grateful to have you on my life's journey. Thank you so much!

By Cheryl Mallen: The love and support from family have always been a huge part of my success, and it is greatly appreciated.

PART I

The foundation of sport and sustainable development

1

INTRODUCTION TO SPORT AND SUSTAINABLE DEVELOPMENT

Stavros Triantafyllidis and Cheryl Mallen

LEARNING OBJECTIVES

Upon completion of this chapter, learners should be able to successfully:

1. Define the concept of sport and sustainable development (S&SD)
2. Identify theories and practical mechanisms associated with S&SD
3. Apply the analytical and normative concepts of sustainable development to S&SD and explain how it can be used to build robust systems in sport and society through the incorporation of the six perspectives: personal, social, economic, ecological, technological, and political
4. Recognize the two stages when building S&SD – stage I: Sustainable development of sport (SDoS) and stage II: Sport for sustainable development (S4SD)
5. Contemplate and develop effective strategic plans for S&SD and its six perspectives
6. Conceptually create antifragility and global sustainability through S&SD

Overview

The world faces a range of contemporary issues impacting the sustainability of our societies today and into the future. Examples of such issues encompass social inclusion and justice, establishing environmental safeguards, and ensuring our cities'

DOI: 10.4324/9781003128953-1

economic viability. An approach used in this text to advance our understandings of sustainability involves positioning sport as a tool to highlight the contemporary problems and potential strategies for moving forward into the future. This approach helps to advance our understandings of both sport and society – as the study of sport can represent a microcosm of society.

This chapter begins by outlining the learning objectives and glossary of terms. Next, sustainability and sustainable development (SD) concepts are defined, followed by a presentation on the conceptual foundations of a relatively new field of study called sport and sustainable development (S&SD) and the two key stages for successfully implementing sustainability. The first stage is the sustainable development of sport (SDoS) that focuses on sustainability adaptions within sport, and the second stage is sport for sustainable development (S4SD), that focuses on how sport can be used as a vehicle to transition society to achieve sustainability. It is essential to emphasize that for S&SD to become an effective strategy for global sustainability, sport works to become sustainable. Throughout this process sport can advocate for sustainability which allows society to learn from the experience of sport. Each stage can be examined via an application of six shared perspectives or levels in S&SD, including the personal, social, economic, ecological, technological, and political.

Additionally, examinations of sport are promoted through the use of two theoretical concepts. The first is the analytical concept used to describe sport, outline the issues, generate predictions, and determine prescriptive ways to address our contemporary global problems. Insights can be derived by breaking sport down based on the six perspectives outlined above and examining each to generate understandings of our modern sporting society, including its benefits, flaws, and the interlinkages between the six perspectives. Second, the normative concept involves using examinations of sport to develop a universal vision of a well-functioning society and applying learning from sport to show society successful strategies on how to move forward. Notably, the concept of anti-fragility (or creating a capacity to adapt to avoid failure) underscores the topic of sustainability.

A call is made for leadership in S&SD to guide those in sport on the journey to identify, define, analyze, provide constructive criticism, along with advancing critical thinking to explain, evaluate, and resolve some of sport and the world's current issues concerning sustainability. Further, debates are encouraged related to how S&SD, including SDoS and S4SD, can effectively build robust and sustainable systems within sport and society. Debates are encouraged for applying the two analytical concepts, including how to utilize the various visions of a good society, including a good sporting society, and how to transition collectively moving forward.

Now, let's get started with the learning objectives, followed by the glossary of terms. Then we can delve into the topic of sport and sustainability.

Glossary

Antifragility

The pursuit of robust systems that help increase the capability of individuals and organizations to thrive despite stressors, shocks, volatility, noise, mistakes, faults, attacks, or failures (Taleb, 2012).

Endosustainability

The term is derived from the endo- (within) (Dictionary.com, 2021) and sustainable (able to maintain the use of the resource at a certain level that the resource is not depleted) (Mirriam-Webster.com, 2021). Endosustainability in, the SDoS involves the actions within sport to advance the sustainability of all aspects, such as the sport organizations, operations, manufacturing, and events.

Sport

"Sport means all forms of physical activity which, through casual or organized participation, aim at expressing or improving physical fitness and well-being, forming social relationships or obtaining results in competition at all levels" (Szathmári & Kocsis, 2020, p. 4).

Sport and sustainable development (S&SD)

S&SD is the process that includes two stages: SDoS and S4SD that, together, enhance the development that meets the needs of current generations without compromising future generations' ability to meet their own needs at the personal, social, economic, ecological, technological, and political levels (Millington et al., 2021; Szathmári & Kocsis, 2020; Triantafyllidis & Darvin, 2021).

Sport for sustainable development (S4SD)

S4SD refers to the contribution of sport to our global societies' viability by encouraging sustainability across the six perspectives of personal, social, economic, ecological, technological, and political worldwide (Macovei et al., 2014; Millington et al., 2021; Schulenkorf, 2012).

Sustainability

The term refers to "the integration of environmental health, social equity, and economic vitality to create thriving, healthy, diverse and resilient communities for this generation and generations to come" (University of California, Los Angeles, 2021, para. 2).

The term encompasses the initiatives and progress in pursuit of sustainability. According to the Brundtland Commission (2001), sustainable development "meets the needs of the present without compromising the ability of future generations to meet their own needs" (p. 82). This includes "the narrow notion of physical sustainability [that] implies a concern for social equity between generations, a concern that must logically be extended to equity within each generation" (p. 82).

Sustainable development of sport (SDoS)

SD*o*S refers to the sustainable practices taken by sport regarding the management of sport products, services, events, and sport consumer behaviors to achieve sustainability within the world of sport that encompasses six perspectives including the personal, social, economic, ecological, technological, and political (McCullough et al., 2020; Szathmári & Kocsis, 2020; Triantafyllidis & Darvin, 2021).

The analytical concept applied to sport and sustainable development (S&SD)

A theoretical approach for analyzing sport as a platform to understand the world as a complex interaction of personal, social, economic, ecological, technological, and political systems. Understandings from the individual parts can be combined to determine S&SD that can be applied as a microcosm of society (Millington et al., 2021; Szathmári & Kocsis, 2020; Triantafyllidis & Darvin, 2021).

The normative concept applied to sport and sustainable development (S&SD)

Examinations are completed using sport as a platform to view the world by defining the objectives of a well-functioning society that delivers well-being for its global citizens today and for future generations. The normative concept urges us to have a universal vision of a good society. These examinations lead to understandings of where we are currently and the gaps that need to be addressed moving into the future based on the six perspectives of S&SD (Millington et al., 2021; Szathmári & Kocsis, 2020; Triantafyllidis & Darvin, 2021).

Synopsis: Sustainability, sustainable development (SD), sport and sustainable development (S&SD)

Sport can be a powerful and effective vehicle for demonstrating and advancing sustainability and sustainable development (Yélamos et al., 2019). The term sustainability refers to "the integration of environmental health, social equity, and economic vitality to create thriving, healthy, diverse, and resilient communities for this generation and generations to come" (University of California, Los Angeles, 2021, para. 2). Sustainable development encompasses the initiatives and progress in pursuit of sustainability. According to the McCarthy Brundtland Commission 2001, sustainable development is defined as the "development that meets the needs of the present without compromising the ability of future generations to meet their own needs" (p. 82). This includes narrow notion of physical sustainability [that] implies a concern for social equity between generations, a concern that must logically be extended to equity within each generation" (p. 82).

An application of sustainable development gives rise to a sub-division within sport management called S&SD. The newly developed area of S&SD has grown due to sport's power to influence those within sport and society – in this case, the influence is for advancing sustainability in both sport and the culture within our global societies. S&SD encompasses meeting the needs of the present and future sporting generations – including the pursuit of sustainability. S&SD can be followed through two stages. But, before we get into reviewing these stages, some background material is needed because both stages can be examined based on six general perspectives in sport. We now present an overview of the six perspectives used when studying sport as a platform for advancing sustainable development or S&SD.

Six perspectives of S&SD

Table 1.1 identifies and describes each of the six perspectives of S&SD, including the personal, social, economic, ecological, technological, and political aspects.

Now that we have reviewed the background material on the six perspectives, we are ready to outline the two stages that are conduits to S&SD.

Two stages and six perspectives of sport and sustainable development (S&SD)

The first stage within S&SD is SDoS, and the second is S4SD within society. Both stages can exhibit and promote values through sport, such as peace, tolerance, respect, equity, health, ecology, and education (McCullough et al., 2020; Mortimer et al., 2020). Examples of additional values promoted within sport include sportsmanship, perseverance, optimism, respect, and teamwork. These values are the building blocks for establishing norms for an inclusive and progressive sport industry and society. Both stages of S&SD can be examined using all six perspectives. The two stages of S4SD across the six perspectives of S&SD are presented in Figure 1.1.

Stage I: Sustainable development of sport (SDoS)

The first stage of S&SD is the SDoS that promotes responsible, sustainable practices. These practices are to be applied to all sports, such as building facilities, manufacturing equipment, delivering sport at all levels, and sport consumption. Achieving SDoS depends on the internal actions or proceedings that sport undertakes to become sustainable – a process known as endosustainable sport

TABLE 1.1 An overview of six perspectives of sport and sustainable development (S&SD)

1. The personal perspective of S&SD	The focus is on individuals seeking to achieve personal excellence, mental, physical, and spiritual health, respect for self and others, self-belief, and determination. Strong, well-functioning individuals can lead sport and society toward sustainability.
2. The social perspective of S&SD	The focus is on macro- and micro-sociological sentiments of sport and society and how they can be applied to S&SD concepts and practices. Further, the focus encompasses collective sustainable efforts that teams, organizations, spectators, participants, and other stakeholders seek for a well-functioning social entity within both sport and global societies.
3. The economic perspective of S&SD	The focus is on the economic state, including financial and economic policies and programs that support sport and society into the future, and includes policies such as equal pay, transparency, and determining economic priorities.
4. The ecological perspective of S&SD	The focus is on sport and the natural environment based on their "bidirectional relationship" (McCullough et al., 2020, p. 1), which includes, for example policies and programs within sport that safeguard the air, water, land, flora, and fauna worldwide and can guide society as to how to transition to safeguard the natural environment.
5. The technological perspective of S&SD	The focus is on technological innovations that have permeated and impacted sport and society. It is important to understand the trends and impacts and manage each emerging technology as it arrives in the marketplace.
6. The political perspective of S&SD	The focus is on initiating, organizing, leading, controlling, and implementing sustainability principles through sport policies and decision-making processes. The emphasis is on developing sustainable organizations within each governmental, non-governmental, for-profit, and not-for-profit organization and guiding organizations in society to also transition for sustainability.

progress. For example, the personal perspective involves focusing on the individual participating in sport by pursuing personal excellence, mental, physical, and spiritual health, respect of self and others, self-belief, and determination. Therefore, a person becomes a sustainable entity. These elements advance the overall physical and psychological strength of the participants and leadership within sport.

Meanwhile, the social perspective focuses on the collective sustainability efforts that teams, organizations, spectators, participants, and other stakeholders seek to excel at with teamwork, honesty, fairness, equity, and service above oneself that contribute to a well-functioning sporting society. The economic perspective focuses on sustainable economic policies and programs that support sport's viability

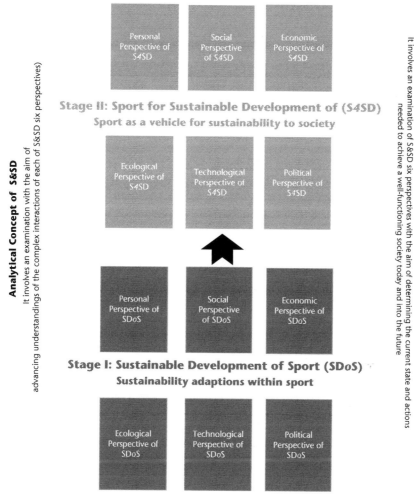

FIGURE 1.1 Conceptual illustration of six perspectives of sport and sustainable development (S&SD) across stage I: Sustainable development of sport (SDoS) and stage II: Sport for sustainable development (S4SD).

into the future. The ecological perspective includes people and an organizations' efforts to integrate environmental sustainability within sport through nature conservation, carbon-neutrality, activities safeguarding our ecology, and so on. The technological view seeks to incorporate innovations that benefit or improve the quality of sport operations, safety, performance, and the economic development of sport. And finally, the political perspective seeks to develop sustainable organizations through policies and decision-making that support organizing, leading, controlling, and implementing sustainability principles within governmental and non-governmental aspects, for-profit and not-for-profit sport.

The authors of this chapter describe endosustainable progress in sport as including effective decision-making processes and operations that seek to satisfy the safety/preservation of the natural environment while simultaneously focusing on the production and consumptive quantity of the goods and services within sport.

Stage II: S4SD

The second stage, S4SD, involves efforts related to sport as a platform for developing, promoting, and advancing sustainable development outcomes within our global society. The conversation regarding stage II, or S4SD, started with the effectiveness of a United Nations (UN) extended program called Recovering Better: Sport for Development and Peace (https://www.un.org/development/desa/dspd/wp-content/uploads/sites/22/2 020/12/Final-SDP-recovering-better.pdf). The UN has long recognized, advocated for, and supported sport's critical contributions to development and peace, with a significant record of reports and other guiding documents highlighting its unique potential (Kaufman & Wolff, 2010; Triantafyllidis & Darvin, 2021). Historically, the UN activities in this area led to the 2015 adoption of the United Nations 2030 Agenda for Sustainable Development and its stated 17 sustainable development goals (SDGs) (https://sdgs.un.org/goals), followed by the Sport for Development and Peace community involvement (https://www.un.org/development/desa/dspd/sport-development-peace.html). The latter emphasizes the global sport community's keen interest and commitment to continue using sport as a unique platform to support and promote the SDGs. Sport's potential, therefore, should be revisited to incorporate the new framework for sustainable development to encourage synergy, coherence, and the harmonization of programs to implement the SDGs. This solidly positions sport as a mechanism for promoting positive change globally. Accordingly, S4SD can offer the positive contributions of sport to the sustainable development efforts for our global society, focusing on the personal, social, ecological, technological, and political perspectives of modern world society.

Multiple examples illustrate how sport has facilitated peace and a better quality of life (Beutler, 2008; Jin, 2009; Peachey et al., 2019; Schulenkorf, 2012). For instance, sport contributes positively to people's personal well-being, regardless of gender, age, race, or ethnicity (Triantafyllidis & Kaplanidou, 2019). There is evidence that active sport participation directly impacts physical fitness, and it battles physical inactivity, obesity, and diabetes at the personal, community, and national levels (Levermore, 2008; Schulenkorf, 2012). Sport for development and peace literature has highlighted that sport plays a critical role in educating communities about environmental issues and global social issues such as racism, sexism, discrimination, and global ecological degradation (United Nations, 2019). Sport encourages balanced participation by promoting gender equality within local communities and international societies (Adriansee & Claringbould, 2016). On this matter, sport has the power to provide for and achieve equal opportunities for people of different genders, races, and socioeconomic statuses.

The analytical concept

An application of the analytical concept to S&SD involves developing understandings that the domain of sport comprises complex interactions that emerge from a complicated array of connections between personal, social, economic, ecological, technological, and political forces used in society. To understand such a world and determine how to move forward toward sustainable development, each of these forces or influences and the associated interactions can be broken down and examined to generate advanced understandings. This means applying the analytical concept of sustainable development, which encourages examining the world to develop understanding by breaking down the often complex issues and interconnected aspects as a strategy by which to solve them (Sachs, 2015).

The normative concept

The normative concept of sustainable development refers to solving global problems in an ethical manner (Sachs, 2015). A normative view of the world can help us determine the goals that need to be achieved to reach the capacity of our vision of a well-functioning society that supports individual well-being and delivers improved quality of life to future generations. The normative concept urges the establishment of an ethical and equitable global society with interlinkages between the complex social, economic, and ecological systems building antifragility by embracing good governance and positive technological change. The normative concept's primary point is the personal perspective, where we need to start the positive change at the individual level. We, as individuals, are the core element for achieveing an antifragile world by cultivating more active and sustainable habits and behaviors.

The discussion that follows advances the impact of S&SD with an overview of the concept of antifragility – or moving forward successfully despite arising stress and issues.

Defining S&SD

S&SD is viewed as the outcomes of the two stages: SDoS and S4SD that, together, enhance the development that meets the needs of current generations without compromising future generations to meet their own needs at the personal, social, economic, ecological, technological, and political levels (Millington et al., 2021; Szathmári & Kocsis, 2020; Triantafyllidis & Darvin, 2021).

According to our newly developed definition, S&SD can be interpreted as an effective strategy for global sustainability. In the following section, we explain why and how S&SD can build antifragility for worldwide sustainability, and we provide examples of the critical efforts.

S&SD as a strategy for building antifragility and achieving sustainability

S&SD is underscored by antifragility. Antifragility, is the pursuit of robust systems that help increase individuals' and organizations' capability to thrive despite stressors, shocks, volatility, noise, mistakes, faults, attacks, or failures (Taleb, 2012). Accordingly, antifragility requires leadership that promotes good governance with an openness to change. This is because people's well-being, health, and welfare depend on good governance and adapting local, regional, national, and international organizations and companies worldwide. This change promotes robust systems for survival during times of uncertainty and shocks (Taleb, 2012).

Good governance stems from a collective of governmental political bodies and non-government organizations/companies that influence societal decisions and actions. Accordingly, the UN has outlined 17 sustainable development goals (SDGs) (United Nations, 2019) that have been established to offer a global public agenda that guides political and management leaders' decisions – including the leadership in sport. Such good governance is sought to support our interconnected world trade and finance, technological innovations and progress, production and consumption flows, migration, social networks, environmental conservation programs, and services, with just laws and regulations (Broman & Robèrt, 2017).

A movement to good governance globally is needed due to threats to our communities and the planet. However, there is a lack of consensus on a single accepted conceptual vision and framework to build robust antifragile systems. To aid in developing such a framework, this chapter promotes S&SD to advance antifragile systems. Such development involves an analytical concept that describes, generates predictions, and determines a prescriptive way forward and a normative concept, whereby debates are encouraged to evaluate the path ahead collectively.

Specifically, Figure 1.1 illustrates that the analytical and normative concepts support the two stages of S&SD – stage I: SDoS and stage II: S4SD. This means that the generation of robust S&SD systems is built upon values aligned with *Sport* and *Sustainable Development*. These include sportsmanship, perseverance, optimism, respect, and teamwork in conjunction with sustainable development values alongside with freedom, equality, and sustainability (Leiserowitz et al., 2006; Szathmári & Kocsis, 2020). Ultimately, promoting ideal values such as peace and sustainability encompassed with S&SD can aid our planet's and humankind's future by building a symbiotic relationship.

Examples of efforts for antifragility through S&SD

Over the last century, the world economy has promoted actions that have threatened our planet's natural resources (Colglazier, 2015). Rapid economic growth has played a crucial role in the global climate crisis that has resulted from the devastation of human-induced climate impacts. Such impacts arise from the overuse of natural capital such as water, food, along with non-renewable energy.

The result includes environmental catastrophes (e.g., hurricanes) and epidemics (e.g., global diseases). Continuing such damaging actions is not in the best interest of human antifragility.

In this context, the UN Commission on Environment and Development Chairwoman Gro Harlem Brundtland promoted sustainable development as a definitive global definition of sustainable development. Accordingly, human actions need to transition to become responsible for safeguarding environmental resources, so that all humans can live sustainably; but how to make such a transition can involve many interpretations.

An interpretation of the UN definition of sustainable development promotes that sustainability involves modern ingenuity, which humans possess, that can be applied to advance sustainable economic welfare and social prosperity without depreciating the natural capital. Further, that sport is a crucial forum for advancing sustainable development. Support for this position includes the following announcement by the UN:

> Sport is also an important enabler of sustainable development. We recognize the growing contribution of Sport to the realization of development and peace in its promotion of tolerance and respect and the contributions it makes to the empowerment of women and young people, individuals, and communities, as well as to health, education, and social inclusion objectives. (United Nations 2030 Agenda, 2015, para. 37)

This recognition of sport as a platform for social change provides a new field of study, which investigates sport as a tool for contributing to sustainable development.

A critical examination of sport can help advance understandings related to our current state of sustainability (within sport and society), develop visions of a sustainable future, and be used as a forum to inspire a sustainable development movement. This movement can be facilitated by various groups, including individuals, communities, local businesses, and multinational companies, to achieve an envisioned sustainable future for sport and society. Each group needs to act cohesively toward achieving a sustainable future.

For instance, various group members are needed to achieve a new world order envisioned by the UN. For example, the UN promotes eliminating extreme poverty, encourages social trust through policies that strengthen the community, and safeguards the natural environment from human-induced degradation. Further, advancing this new world order can come from the different sustainability perspectives, including the personal, social, economic, ecological, technological, and political aspects. As a society, we need to learn how to move forward with such an envisioned future. Examining sport and advancing new programs/activities within sport can lead to learning about living sustainably to ensure future generations can live sustainably. Thus, sport can transition sport and society to make efficient and effective sustainable development strategies a reality. Striving to reach such a reality requires leadership.

Concluding remarks

1. S&SD includes two stages to global sustainability, including SD*o*S and S*4*SD. These stages position sport as a conduit to visions and actions toward a new world order of sustainability
2. Each stage of S&SD can be viewed using the analytical theoretical concept (that encourages breaking down sport via six perspectives or lenses) to understand the issue. Additionally, the normative theoretical concept can encourage visions of a well-functioning and sustainable world of sport – and global society
3. A call for leadership in sport is made to pursue a movement toward sustainability
4. Leadership in sport is critical so that sport and society can build antifragility for a robust future for sport and society

Future directions

1. Leadership in sport becomes a priority to develop understandings of the current state of SD*o*S and S*4*SD; for advancing visions of S&SD, for encouraging and facilitating debates that lead to a consensus on the selected vision(s) for moving forward, and for working to ensure sport builds antifragility within the system
2. Those within sport continuously advance S&SD through learning and research
3. It is now up to those in sport to give rise to the necessary leadership, to encourage the current and next generation of sporting participants to ensure a movement toward a sustainable future in sport and society
4. Government policymakers should turn their focus on establishing an S&SD policy

Review questions

1. How would you define S&SD, and how does your definition relate to the Brundtland Commission's (2001) definitive definition of sustainable development?
2. Describe the characteristics of the normative theoretical concept and outline how it applies to S&SD
3. Describe the characteristics of the analytical theoretical concept and outline how it applies to S&SD
4. List the two key stages of S&SD and outline their key characteristics.
5. What values do you conceive apply within S&SD?
6. Provide an overview of how the concept of S&SD can be used in sport strategic planning
7. Conceptually create robust systems or antifragility that strategically promote S&SD from each of the six key perspectives or lenses

Discussion questions

1. What does S&SD mean to you?
2. What is the role of sport in society? Should sport be used to advance sustainable development (or should those in sport simply focus on developing sporting activities)?
3. Discuss the value of SD*o*S without S4SD – are they separate entities or must they be linked and pursued concurrently?
4. What is your vision of the world in 30 years … and can sport help us get there?
5. How does the concept of antifragility apply to your vision?
6. How can you, as an individual, your sport organization, and your regional sporting bodies contribute to S&SD?

Learning Activities

1. Envision and write your perspective of what sustainable sport management looks like (what is your vision of a well-functioning sporting society that possesses the power to offer antifragility)? To aid in considering various aspects within your vision, see Figures 1.1 and 1.2
2. Identify three sport organizations and three non-sport organizations of any type. Use their websites as a guide to compare and contrast what they are doing regarding building organizational sustainability
3. Next, use the same three organizations' websites and analyze their vision/mission statements and core values. Do they include sustainable development within their organizational statements and values? Yes or No? What would you recommend to their executives to advance the statements and core values for sustainability?
4. If you were a leader of a sport organization, what would be your first three priorities be concerning the SD*o*S?
5. Suppose you were a leader of a non-sport organization; how would you use sport as a means for promoting sustainability outcomes to your non-sport-related consumers and employees – or S4SD?

Further reading

1. Bunds, K., McLeod, C., Barrett, M., Newman, J., & Keonigstorfer, J. (2019). The object-oriented politics of stadium sustainability: A case study of SC Freiburg. *Sustainability, 11*(23), 6712. https://doi.org/10.3390/su11236712
2. Lindsey, I. (2017). Governance in sport-for-development: Problems and possibilities of (not) learning from international development. *International Review for the Sociology of Sport, 52*(7), 801–818. https://doi.org/10.1177%2F1012690215623460
3. Moustakas, L., & Işık, A.A. (2020). Sport and sustainable development in Botswana: towards policy coherence. *Discover Sustainability, 1*(1), 1–12. https://doi.org/10.1007/s43621-020-00005-8

Sustainability
"The integration of environmental health, social equity and economic vitality in order to create thriving, healthy, diverse and resilient communities for this generation and generations to come"(UCLA Sustainability, 2021, para. 2).

Our Vision
We envision significant contributions to global sustainability through sport and sustainable development (S&SD).

Sport and Sustainable Development (S&SD)
Sport and sustainable development (S&SD) is the process that includes two stages: sustainable development of sport (SDoS) and sport for sustainable development (S4SD) that, together, enhance the development that meets the needs of current generations without compromising future generations to meet their own needs at the personal, social, economic, ecological, technological, and political levels (Millington et al., 2021; Szathmari & Kocsis, 2020; Triantafyllidis & Darvin, 2021).

STAGE 2: Sport for Sustainable Development (S4SD)
Sport for sustainable development (S4SD) refers to the contribution of sport to our global societies' viability by encouraging sustainability across the six perspectives of personal, social, economic, ecological, technological,and political worldwide (Macovei, Tufan, & Vulpe, 2014; Millington et al., 2021; Schulenkorf, 2012).

STAGE 1: Sustainable Development of Sport (SDoS)
Sustainable development of sport (SDoS) refers to the sustainable practices taken by sport regarding the management of sport products, services, and sport consumer behaviors to achieve sustainability within the world of sport that encompasses six perspectives, including the personal, social, economic, ecological, technological, and political (McCullough, Orr, & Kellison, 2020; Szathmari & Kocsis, 2020; Triantafyllidis & Darvin, 2021).

Sustainable Development (SD) Includes Antifragility

The development of robust systems that help increase individsuals and organizations' capability tio thrive despite stressors, shocks, volatility, noise, mistakes, faults, attacks, or failures (Taleb, 2012).

FIGURE 1.2 How we envision significant contributions to global sustainability through sport and sustainable development (S&SD).

4. Spaaij. R, & Schaillée (2020). Community-driven sports events as a vehicle for cultural sustainability within the context of forced migration: Lessons from the Amsterdam Futsal Tournament. *Sustainability*, *12*(3), 1020–1031. https://doi.org/10.3390/su12031020

5. Spangenberg, J. (2017). Hot air or comprehensive progress? A critical assessment of the SDGs. *Sustainable Development*, *25*(4), 311–321. https://doi.org/10.1002/sd.1657

Relevant online resources

1. Schulenkorf, N. (2012). *Sport and Sustainable Development: Designing, Managing and Leveraging Opportunities.* Retrieved from https://www.un.org/development/desa/dspd/wp-content/uploads/sites/22/2018/06/2.pdf
2. United Nations (2020). *Recovering Better: Sport for Development and Peace: Reopening, Recovery and Resilience Post-COVID-19.* Retrieved from https://www.un.org/development/desa/dspd/wp-content/uploads/sites/22/2020/12/Final-SDP-recovering-better.pdf

References

Adriansee, J., & Claringbould, I. (2016). Gender equality in sport leadership: From the Brighton Declaration to the Sydney Scoreboard. *International Review for the Sociology of Sport, 51*(5), 547–566. 110.1177/0193723521991413

Beutler, I. (2008). Sport serving development and peace: Achieving the goals of the United Nations through sport. *Sport in Society, 11*(4), 359–369. 10.1080/17430430802019227

Broman, G.I., & Robèrt, K.H. (2017). A framework for sustainable strategic development. *Journal of Cleaner Production, 140*, 17–31. 10.1016/j.jclepro.2015.10.121

Brundtland Commission. (2001). *Climate change 2001: Impacts, adaptation, and vulnerability.* In J.J. McCarthy, O.F. Canziani, N.A. Leary, D.J. Dokken, & K.S. White (Eds.), *Contributions of working group II to the third assessment report of the intergovernmental panel on climate change.* Cambridge: Cambridge University Press. Weblink: https://www.ipcc.ch/report/ar3/wg2/

Colglazier, W. (2015). Sustainable development agenda: 2030. *Science, 349*(6252), 1048–1050. 10.1126/science.aad2333

Dictionary.com. (2021, May). *Endo.* Retrieved from https://www.dictionary.com/browse/endo-

Elder, G.H. (1995). The life course paradigm: Social change and individual development. In P. Moen, G.H. Elder, Jr., & K. Lüscher (Eds.), *Examining lives in context: Perspectives on the ecology of human development* (pp. 101–139). American Psychological Association: Washington, D.C., USA. 10.1037/10176-003

Jin, H. (2009). Study on the leisure sport and the sustainable development of people. *Journal of Sustainable Development, 2*(1), 41–43. 10.5539/jsd.v2n1p44

Kaufman, P., & Wolff, E. (2010). Playing and protesting: Sport as a vehicle for social change. *Journal of Sport & Social Issues, 34*(2), 154–175. 10.1177%2F0193723509360218

Leiserowitz, A.A., Kates, R.W., & Parris, T.M. (2006). Sustainability values, attitudes, and behaviors: A review of international and global trends. *Annual Review of Environment and Resources, 31*(1), 413–444. 10.1146/annurev.energy.31.102505.133552

Levermore, R. (2008). Sport: A new engine of development? Progress in Development Studies, 8(2), 183–190. 10.1177/146499340700800204

Macovei, S., Tufan, A.A., & Vulpe, B.I. (2014). Theoretical approaches to building a healthy lifestyle through the practice of physical activities. *Procedia-Social and Behavioral Sciences, 117*, 86–91. 10.1016/j.sbspro.2014.02.183

McCullough, B.P., Orr, M., & Kellison, T. (2020). Sport ecology: Conceptualizing an emerging subdiscipline within sport management. *Journal of Sport Management, 34*(6), 509–520. 10.1123/jsm.2019-0294

Millington, R., Giles, A.R., van Luijk, N., & Hayhurst, L.M. (2021). Sport for sustainability? The extractives industry, sport, and sustainable development. *Journal of Sport and Social Issues*. -10.1177/0193723521991413

Mirriam-Webster.com. (2021). *Sustainable.* Retrieved from https://www.merriam-webster.com/dictionary/sustainable

Mortimer, H., Whitehead, J., Kavussanu, M., Gürpınar, B., & Ring, C. (2020). Values and clean sport. *Journal of Sports Sciences*, *39*(1), 1–9. 10.1080/02640414.2020.1835221

Peachey, J., Schulenkorf, N., & Spaaij, R. (2019). Sport for social change: Bridging the theory-practice divide. *Journal of Sport Management*, *33*(5), 366–378. 10.1123/jsm.2019-0291

Sachs, J.D. (2015). *The age of sustainable development.* Columbia University Press: New York City, USA. Retrieved from http://cup.columbia.edu/book/the-age-of-sustainable-development/9780231173155

Schulenkorf, N. (2012). Sustainable community development through sport and events: A conceptual framework for sport-for-development projects. *Sport Management Review*, *15*(1), 1–12. 10.1016/j.smr.2011.06.001

Szathmári, A., & Kocsis, T. (2020). Who cares about gladiators? An elite-sport-based concept of Sustainable Sport. *Sport in Society*, 1–19. 10.1080/17430437.2020.1832470

Taleb, N. (2012). *Antifragile: Things that gain from disorder* (Vol. 3). Random House Incorporated: Munich, German.

Triantafyllidis, S., & Darvin, L. (2021). Mass-participant sport events and sustainable development: Gender, social bonding, and connectedness to nature as predictors of socially and environmentally responsible behavior intentions. *Sustainability Science*, *16*(5), 239–253. 10.1007/s11625-020-00867-x

Triantafyllidis, S., & Kaplanidou, K. (2019). Marathon runners: A fertile market for "Green" donations? *Journal of Global Sport Management*, 1–14. 10.1080/24704067.2018.1561205

University of California, Los Angeles (UCLA). (2021). *What is sustainability?* Retrieved from https://www.sustain.ucla.edu/what-is-sustainability/

United Nations. (2019). *The sustainable development goals report 2019.* Retrieved from https://unstats.un.org/sdgs/report/2019/The-Sustainable-Development-Goals-Report-2019.pdf

United Nations 2030 Agenda. (2015). Transforming our world: The 2030 Agenda for sustainable development. Retrieved from https://sdgs.un.org/publications/transforming-our-world-2030-agenda-sustainable-development-17981

Yélamos, G., Carty, C., & Clardy, A. (2019). Sport: A driver of sustainable development, promoter of human rights, and vehicle for health and well-being for all. *Sport, Business and Management: An International Journal*, *9*(4), 315–327. 10.1108/SBM-10-2018-0090

2

SUSTAINABLE DEVELOPMENT OF SPORT

Stavros Triantafyllidis and Cheryl Mallen

LEARNING OBJECTIVES

Upon completion of this chapter, learners should be able to successfully:

1. Define and explain sport and sustainable development (S&SD) stage I: Sustainable development of sport (SDoS)
2. Identify the analytical and normative concepts of SDoS
3. Describe the mission, goals, and objectives of SDoS across the six perspectives of S&SD, including the personal, social, economic, ecological, technological, and political aspects
4. Discuss sustainable programs (what-is) and plans (what-if) for SDoS
5. Propose new ways for sport to strategically manage to embrace sustainable development and achieve internal sustainability (endosustainable progress)

Overview

There are many ways in which sport can become more sustainable, including advancements with respect to sport organizations and their operations, their associated stakeholders, and the production, consumption, and management of sport-related goods, services, and processes. It is important to note that there are two stages for achieving sport and sustainable development (S&SD), including

DOI: 10.4324/9781003128953-2

stage I: sustainable development of sport (S&SD) that promotes meeting the needs of current sporting participants without negatively impacting future sporting generations' abiltities to meet their own needs, and stage II: Sport for sustainable development (S4SD) that focuses on how sport can be a vehicle to aid society to transition for sustainability.

This chapter focuses on SDoS by presenting the learning objectives and glossary of terms, a discussion on its definition, key features, and suggested future directions. Accordingly, the concept of SDoS is explained with respect to how sport can adopt sustainable development practices and plans. Readers are encouraged to conceptualize mechanisms that advance sustainability within sport and the strategies and tools that aid sport in adopting sustainable development processes. Working toward sustainability supports sport today and into the future.

Glossary

Antifragility

The pursuit of robust systems that help increase individuals and organizations' capability to thrive despite stressors, shocks, volatility, noise, mistakes, faults, attacks, or failures (Taleb, 2012).

Endosustainable

The term derives from the endo- (within) (Dictionary.com, 2021) and sustainable (able to maintain the use of the resource at a certain level that the resource is not depleted) (Mirriam-Webster.com, 2021). Endosustainable progress reflected in SDoS involves all actions that advance the sustainability of sport organizations, operations, manufacturing, and events.

Sport

"Sport means all forms of physical activity which, through casual or organized participation, aim at expressing or improving physical fitness and well-being, forming social relationships or obtaining results in competition at all levels" (Szathmári & Kocsis, 2020, p. 4).

Sport and sustainable development (S&SD)

S&SD is the process that includes two stages: SDoS and S4SD that, together, enhance the development that meets the needs of current generations without compromising future generations' ability to meet their own needs at the personal, social, economic, ecological, technological, and political levels (Millington et al., 2021; Szathmari & Kocsis, 2020; Triantafyllidis & Darvin, 2021).

Sport for sustainable development (S4SD)

S4SD refers to the contribution of sport to our global societies' viability by encouraging sustainability across the six perspectives of personal, social, economic, ecological, technological, and political worldwide (Macovei et al., 2014; Millington et al., 2021; Schulenkorf, 2012).

Sustainability

The term refers to "the integration of environmental health, social equity, and economic vitality to create thriving, healthy, diverse and resilient communities for this generation and generations to come" (University of California, Los Angeles, 2021, para. 2).

The term sustainable development (SD) encompasses the initiatives and progress in pursuit of sustainability. According to the Brundtland Commission (2001), sustainable development is defined as meeting "the needs of the present without compromising the ability of future generations to meet their own needs (p. 82). This includes "the narrow notion of physical sustainability [that] implies a concern for social equity between generations, a concern that must logically be extended to equity within each generation" (p. 82)."

Sustainable development of sport (SDoS)

Sustainable development of sport (SDoS) refers to the sustainable practices taken by sport regarding the management of sport products, services, and sport consumer behaviors to achieve sustainability within the world of sport that encompasses six perspectives including the personal, social, economic, ecological, technological, and political (McCullough et al., 2020; Szathmari & Kocsis, 2020; Triantafyllidis & Darvin, 2021).

The analytical concept as applied to the sustainable development of sport (SDoS)

A theoretical approach for analyzing sport as a platform to understand the world as a complex interaction of personal, social, economic, ecological, technological, and political systems. Understandings of the individual parts can be combined to determine the overall SDoS (McCullough et al., 2020; Szathmari & Kocsis, 2020; Triantafyllidis & Darvin, 2021).

The normative concept applied to sustainable development of sport (SDoS)

Defining the objectives for a well-functioning community of sport establishes a code of ethics underscoring practices. For example, the normative concept of

SD*o*S includes guiding the production and consumption of sport events, sport organizations, and their operations to be delivered in a manner that provides for transparency, encourages well-being, and fairness for its sport-involved individuals, today and in the future. Ultimately, SD*o*S sets the foundation for a good sporting society (McCullough et al., 2020; Szathmari & Kocsis, 2020; Triantafyllidis & Darvin, 2021).

Defining and explaining SDoS

The key focus of this text is to encourage examinations of the state of SD*o*S and to promote advances in this area. The term SD*o*S refers to sustainable development that can be applied within the boundaries of sport and involves safeguarding resources to maintain sport's capacity for growth and development at a level today that can also be long lived into the future. These resources include personal human resources such as participants and game officials/referees; social resources embedded in society about the value of sport; economic resources including capital for sports facilities; the inclusion of emerging technological resources and innovations; environmental resources with respect to sport competition sites, along with clean air and water; and the political power of sport policy to influence society, such as advancing equality, and includes, but is not limited to, sport operations, stakeholder's decision-making processes and behaviors. Such progress concerns achieving synergistic outcomes for sustainability at the personal, social, economic, ecological, technological, and political perspectives of sport (McCullough et al., 2020; Szathmari & Kocsis, 2020; Triantafyllidis & Darvin, 2021).

An application of SD*o*S promotes practices that can lead the sport world to achieve many sustainability goals and objectives, including the following:

- To adopt sustainable living actions through their involvement with active and sustainable sport participation;
- To build sport communities that enhance sportsmanship and inspire healthy partnerships that improve quality of life at the personal and community levels;
- To develop opportunities for economic stability at the sport level;
- To transform the sport operations globally in a way that limit their negative impacts on the natural environment;
- To advocate for the integration of modern sport technologies with environmentally sustainable standards as the new era of practicing sport;
- To enhance long-term opportunities for those that seek careers in sport;
- To formulate new entities/agencies/organizations that measure, track, and control the unsustainable practices in sport;
- To build a sport system worldwide that encourages a transition to sustainable development.

Figure 2.1 illustates S&SD and outlines where SDoS is positioned within the concept of sustainability and our promoted vision. Next, as outlined in Figure 2.2, SDoS involves examining the current state of sustainability within sport, including the initiatives, progress, and future directions to understand the sustainable practices being employed based on the six perspectives (McCullough et al., 2020; Szathmari & Kocsis, 2020; Triantafyllidis & Darvin, 2021). Two conceptual approaches are recommended as strategies or tools to guide such an examination – the *analytical* and the *normative* concepts or viewpoints of sustainable development (Sachs, 2015). Each concept will now be described and applied to SDoS based on the six perspectives.

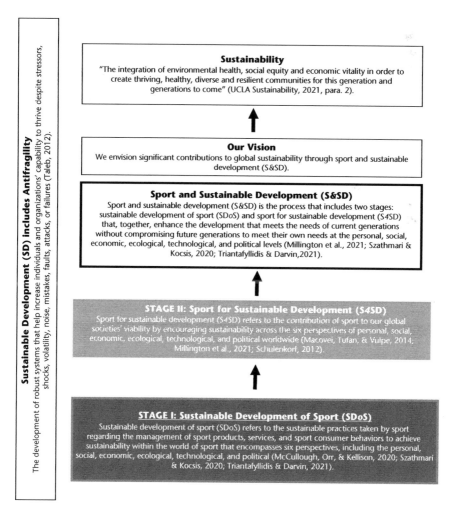

FIGURE 2.1 Sport and sustainable development (S&SD): A strategy for antifragility and global sustainability through two stages

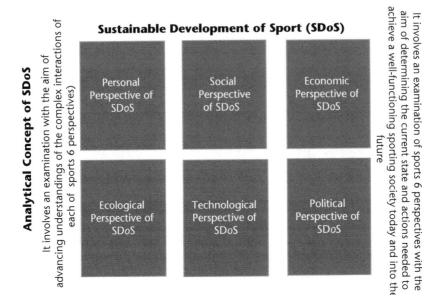

FIGURE 2.2   Conceptual illustration of sustainable development of sport (SDoS)

The analytical concept applied to SDoS

When sport is broken down into sub-sections or the six perspectives, an examination of each offers insights regarding the level of sustainability, including the current state, the issues, and barriers to successful sustainable development into the future at the multiple levels of sport, from amateur to elite and professional, and the different regions around the world. This type of examination uses the analytical viewpoint to explore the state of sport. When insights from each sub-section are pieced together, they provide a full expression of SDoS. This is because interlinkages exist between each sport's operational perspectives including the production, consumption, and delivery of sport products and services. Every sport organization, team, league, equipment producer, etc. can conduct these examinations.

Overall, an examination of SDoS using the analytical concept seeks to conclude:

• If the actions are sustainable for those in sport today and into the future?
• Or are actions today depleting resources that impact those in sport, the natural environment, etc. and cannot be sustained into the future without negatively impacting sporting participants and their opportunities?

We will now explore examples for examining SDoS based on the six perspectives with the analytical concept of SDoS.

The analytical concept and the personal perspective of SDoS

An examination focusing on the personal aspects of SDoS using the analytical concept involves a study of the opportunities that support sport participation and help advance one's health. According to Macovei et al. (2014), "the development of a healthy lifestyle should be one of the priorities of the family, school and society at large" (p. 86). Further, the World Health Organization indicates that health is a state of physical, mental, and social well-being (Macovei et al., 2014).

Psychological and social theories can guide an examination of sport and its ability to support participants' health sustainably. For example, psychological theories include frameworks that explain human behavior and outline that we can examine people's values, attitudes, perceptions, and behavioral intentions toward the given behavior (in this case, participating in sport actively). Multiple psychological theories can be utilized, for instance, attachment theory, self-determination theory, attitude-behavior paradigm, learning theory, elaboration likelihood theory, dissonance theory, identity theory, health behavior theory, and green mind theory (Petty & Cacioppo, 1986; Pretty et al., 2017; Stets & Burke, 2000; Triantafyllidis & Darvin, 2021; Triantafyllidis & Kaplanidou, 2019). Developing an understanding of the critical characteristics that make up theories and applying these characteristics when examining sport can advance our understandings of experiences from the personal perspective within multiple sports and levels, from amateur to professional sport. Such examinations shed light on sport entities and their ability to advance individuals' opportunities to promote their health through sport participation and an active lifestyle.

Consider conducting an examination related to sport's personal perspectives to advance knowledge about the situation in your community. Are sporting options available and sustainable in your community into the future? If so, what are the best practices? If not, what is needed to advance the sporting opportunities?

The analytical concept and the social perspective of SDoS

Exploring the social aspects of SDoS using the analytical concept involves focusing on sustainable community development and a sense of belonging to a group (such as a sport, team, etc.). Understandings can be advanced by determining the characteristics of social theories and applying them to examinations of sport. Social theories abound and have been utilized in sport research, such as socio-demographic, social identity, social justice, and social learning theory (Ayanadele et al., 2019; Duarte et al., 2019; Jackson et al., 2020; Oja et al., 2018). With an examination of sport based on theory, we can perceive people's social power when they are part of a sport (both solo and team). For instance, we can gain insights into the fairness and compassion found within sports communities' actions and consider trends for improving practices while moving forward into a sustainable future.

The analytical concept and the economic perspective of SDoS

Next, an overview of the economic aspects of SDoS using the analytical concept involves a focus on sport as an entity capable of continuously transforming to manage its operations, processes, and actions in an economical and financially efficient, and effective manner today and into the future. The study of sports operations can indicate their current economic policies that impact growth patterns and day-to-day financial considerations in practice. Theories can also guide an examination of sport. Such theories include the management of common pool resources, public choice theory, behavioral economics, and game theory (Bar-Eli et al., 2020; Lin, 2017; McSweeny & Safai, 2020). Examinations can help advance insights into the impacts of each economic policy and the effects of day-to-day financial decisions, along with understandings concerning the supply and demands within sport operations, costs and benefits, and financial incentives. These insights can be applied to explain how sport's economic growth can positively impact local, regional, national, and international sport and, at the time, global economies. Sustainable economic solutions and practical financial actions are required for sport organizations to be sustainable into the future. Has sport's current economic and financial position set it up to be feasible into the future?

The analytical concept and the ecological perspective of SDoS

The ecological aspects of SDoS involve ensuring sport is acting to encourage environmentally sustainable development into the future. An application of the analytical concept consists of generating insights from an examination guided by sustainability theory and its characteristics (Trendafilova et al., 2014). This theory involves "the pursuit of sustainability [that] is oriented toward long-term treatment of natural resources" [as well as a] "focus on human well-being" (Harrington, 2016, p. 4). An examination can concentrate on any of the multiple directions in ecological sustainability. For instance, one direction entails examining the sustainability of sport itself in times of climate change. This includes the impacts of climate change on the conduct of sport that requires access to snow. Another direction entails the effects of climate change on athletes' health. For instance, is sport ensuring athletes compete in pristine natural conditions for air and water – or are they polluted and impacting athlete health? Also, are conditions of extreme heat and drought affecting athletic performances and athlete health?

Further, what are the athlete impacts of changing competition schedules due to extreme weather conditions? Participants' behaviors are another area that could be examined based on their treatment of the natural environment and the effect of sport's sustainability based on their actions. These examples illustrate that the ecological perspective is embedded within the sport system and is a critical component in SDoS today and into the future. Where are your community sport and elite programs with respect to safeguarding the ecological conditions for sport sustainability into the future?

The analytical concept and the technological perspective of SDoS

Emerging technologies abound and are instrumental in the SDoS. Applying the analytical concept involves understanding the world as a complex combination of perspectives impacted by emerging technologies used within sport. An examination with the application of theories can bring forth insights into integrating technologies and their impact on sport sustainability. Examples of theories include the rational choice theory, the idea of disruptive technology, and the diffusion of innovation (Laukyte, 2020; Yim et al., 2020). The examination can be multi-pronged as technologies advance on numerous fronts, such as sports facilities management with renewable energy and snowmaking technology, three-dimensional printing of clothing, footwear, sporting equipment, and new technologies related to athlete training programs.

Further, understandings can be developed regarding technologies and their influence on advancing social and economic issues. This includes the divide between those with access to emerging sport-applicable technologies and their associated impacts to aid sport performance compared to those who do not have such access. Those in sport are being pushed to consider the ethical way forward for the integration of emerging technologies. Examinations that reconsider rules and regulations traditionally applied within sport are needed to ensure the SDoS into the future with emerging technologies. How sustainable is your sporting community from the analytical, technological perspective?

The analytical concept and the political perspective of SDoS

Leaders can influence sport governance with their decisions that establish policy and directions within the sporting system (Chatzigianni, 2018). This includes influential political power that can be wielded by sport organizations and their associated groups, such as their membership, governments, and non-governmental organizations involved in shaping policy for sport. An application of the analytical concept in SDoS promotes examinations on several intertwined perspectives using the political lens. For instance, investigations can generate insights on sport organizations and their political power to influence other sport organizations to transition to sustainability and elite athletes and their political ability to influence sustainable trends in sport.

Further, examinations can understand the power brokers and directions, impacts, and success of sports social issues such as gender equality, education, and health. Insights can also be offered based on political power and the economic perspective of sport concerning international development or the politics within elite athlete financial support programs. And a final example is that an examination of leaders in sport and their political power to integrate – or deny – the use of emerging technologies in sport can offer further understandings of SD*o*S.

The results of an analytical examination (as outlined above) can provide data on the current state of sustainability found within each of the six perspectives. Further, this data can shed light on the issues and barriers to success in achieving sustainability. Such can be used to underscore the development of ideas, initiatives, implementation tactics, and collaborations designed to advance progress in SD*o*S. Additionally, the data can aid in recognizing the limitations of sustainable sport across the six perspectives.

As seen from the examples above, SD*o*S is a complex concept that can be examined from an analytical viewpoint. The complexity continues as we move to discuss an application of the normative concept of SD*o*S.

Normative concept applied to SD*o*S

Another way to examine the current state and trends in SD*o*S involves using the normative concept to determine how to optimize the ethical, moral, ecological, and humanitarian actions within sport. We offer a vision as a starting point to encourage debate to generate a movement toward building options and a consensus on the topic.

A vision of SD*o*S

The vision presented is framed with a focus on the leadership implications for moving forward with SD*o*S. From our perspective, a current key challenge for implementing sustainability in sport involves a need for leaders who have developed (a) an awareness regarding SD*o*S and (b) the knowledge and wisdom to design and combine strategies that interlink sport's ability to be profitable and sustainable into the future.

First, our vision encourages those in sport leadership positions to immediately establish linkages with sport management researchers and disseminate information to raise awareness for students and those in the sport industry. Second, multiple examinations need to be conducted to determine the current sustainability of sport based on the six perspectives of personal, social, economic, ecological, technological, and political in their particular community, including identifying the processes in sport that act as barriers toward achieving sustainable development. Third, working groups need to be established to review the research results and strategize on how to enhance the SDoS into the future, and in particular, to determine how to fill the gaps found. Debates within these working groups are critical, and thus, the leadership needs the skill to manage debates and build consensus to make this transition a reality. Specifically, an agenda for SDoS needs to be designed with achievable goals and measurable objectives. Most importantly, this work is necessary to handle every key challenge within the six perspectives of SDoS, leading to complex and daunting tasks. Essentially, there is lots of room for many leaders to tackle different sustainability issues.

Concurrently, the leadership of sport needs to learn to design strategies and tools, establish partnerships, integrate technological innovations, push for education on the topic, and mobilize the media, clubs, etc. for the SDoS. Building the skill set within sport leadership for this role is a monumental but necessary task. Programs are needed to educate leaders about the benefits of SDoS, including its positive impacts on sport, people, society, the economy, and the natural environment. The leaders can then educate those participating in sport.

Who is responsible for developing such critical programming? One proposal is that higher education sport management programs need to take the lead on this endeavor. They can advocate for SDoS and have a meaningful impact on young people, such as Generation Z (*Gen Z*), to shape their habits and lifestyles in a healthy, pro-environmental, and philanthropic manner. This group is a critical resource, and key leadership capacity may rise from this group. However, higher education leaders need to extend a hand to those in the industry; additionally, those in the sport industry must also take the lead. This dual-directional educational strategy facilitates the building of a framework for improving SDoS as quickly as possible. Good leadership and education are the cornerstones for a transition to advance sustainable programs throughout sport.

Where can we end up? Sustainable programs can include, for example, standardized services that support SDoS, policy development embedded with the tenets of SDoS, the leveraging of partnerships established for advancing the characteristics of SDoS for effectiveness across for-profit and not-for-profit, governmental, and non-governmental organizations and foundations. Additionally, the sustainable management of human and natural resources that improve performance and set an example can advance overall sustainable development in sport.

Sport is not starting from scratch. Our vision includes following the guidance found in a key effort that is currently being conducted.

From theory to practice: Achieving SDoS

Academia has illustrated an effort to bridge the span between theory to practice. A recent publication discussed how the partnering of universities and colleges could occur worldwide to support the successful completion of projects that require the involvement of both scholars and practitioners (Darling-Hammond et al., 2020). Our vision suggests that leadership in sport builds on previous research and collaborations. Accordingly, our vision encourages sustainability planning to establish goals and programs designed to implement an SDoS plan of action.

Sustainable strategic planning for SDoS: A framework

Our vision involves embedding the following foundational framework from which to operate:

- That sports accept that the task of transitioning to sustainable development is complex and that they agree to avoid working in silos. The goal of joint efforts will see the sharing of data and plans become commonplace to guide all sectors within sport to transition. This is necessary as sport organizations should not transition to sustainable practices alone for all six perspectives, that is, personal, social, economic, ecological, technological, and political. Sharing, supporting, and cooperating within particular sports and between sports offer synergies that can lead to efficient and effective progress
- That reaching our capacity in SDoS involves embedding the concept of sustainability, or the safeguarding of sport for participants today and into the future, into all aspects of sport. This includes all sport levels from the amateur to professional and elite levels of sport, infrastructure development, competitions/events throughout the youth to the senior ranks, and programming, including human resource development (such as game officials/referees and volunteers). Capacity means all aspects of sport are saturated with the characteristics of SDoS

Concluding remarks

1. Sport is challenged to ensure mechanisms are in place that advances sustainability into the future. This includes sustainable sport organizations' operations, production practices, and consumption behaviors
2. SDoS involves focusing on the internal growth of sport toward a sustainable and prosperous future for multiple sports
3. The analytical concept is used to explain the potential of sport practices to embrace their operations across the six perspectives of personal, social, economic, ecological, technological, and political aspects that can be used to establish a good sporting society
4. The normative concept supports that sport can link across the six perspectives to help the world grow sustainably. This transition is encouraged to be well developed within the next decade to meet the deadline established in the 2030 Agenda
5. Scholars and practitioners can apply SDoS concepts within research, teaching, program designs, and strategic plans to enhance sport's ability to achieve sustainability outcomes

6. Learners should be creative and productive and can be leaders within sport that promote the values of SDoS throughout the sporting realm and the world
7. The advance of leadership and education is critical for success in SDoS

Future directions

1. Leaders need to rise to take on the challenge of SDoS
2. Research should be conducted across all levels of sport throughout the world to examine, measure, and scale the potential performance and the potential risk of moving to sustainable practices
3. Working groups need to be established to debate the way forward for the SDoS
4. Partnerships and agreements need to be advanced to encourage innovative ideas and proposals for a sustainable future
5. Education on SDoS is critical for higher education sport management programs and industry, including the media, service clubs, donors, and humanitarians

Review questions

1. In your own words, define the SDoS
2. What is the purpose of exploring the analytical concept of SDoS across the six common perspectives (i.e., personal, social, economic, ecological, technological, and political) of S&SD?
3. What are the implications of the normative concept of SDoS across the six common perspectives of S&SD? How does the analytical concept influence the normative concept of SDoS? Why?
4. List five goals derived from the SDoS
5. Provide a synopsis of the vision outlined in the chapter for achieving SDoS

Discussion questions

1. How would you introduce SDoS to a friend or family member? How would you justify the rationale that SDoS might be a solution for our sustainable future?
2. Why do the authors of this chapter suggest that sport can be developed to be fully sustainable? Please provide three examples.
3. Please identify three current and key SDoS challenges (i.e., problems) within the global sport industry. By applying your constructive criticism to these three challenges, how would you evaluate the opportunities offered in this chapter? What would be three solutions that you would provide beyond the suggestions of this chapter?

4. Discuss the role of the leadership in the SDoS. Does the current leadership have the skills or tools to help sport to transition for sustainability? If so, what skills are key? If not, what can be done to advance such skills?
5. If you were tasked with completing an evaluation of the current state of sustainability for a local sport of your choice, what would you evaluate? Who could aid with the assessment?

Learning activities

1. Using two groups of students, one group is tasked with supporting a given sport organization's sustainable transformation. The second group argues that moving to sustainable practices will cost money and bring problems concerning sport affordability in the future. For this activity, the instructor can act as the moderator, and the two groups will role-play in a political debate for each side
2. If sport is a business tool, what are your perspectives for transforming other businesses (industrial sectors – non-sport related) more sustainably? Please indicate three examples that you specify how this transformation can occur. You are the chief executive officer of a sport organization. As a concerned and responsible leader of your people, community, and sport organization, you decide to make a radical decision concerning your agency's traditional operations. After studying this chapter, what changes would you make in your organization, and what procedures would you change to establish a foundation for your sport entity's sustainable development?
3. Based on your response to learning activity #2,, write a two-page business plan about the goal and measurable objectives for the sustainability of your sport organization's critical operations for next season
4. You are part of the management group of a sports team that does not incorporate sustainable practices. The government has instituted new policies for SDoS, and you disagree with the policy changes. Write a one-page rebuttal about the new state law that mandates sustainable practices in your sport business
5. Work in groups and identify three sport organizations. For each sport organization, please visit its website and explore their involvement in sustainability, if any. Please notice that actions of sustainability are considered the sustainable development process of the sport organization
6. Again, make two groups of students – one group represents a sustainable sport organization in a developed country. The second group of students represents a sustainable sport organization in a developing country. Generate open dialogue on the different issues (and determine the problems and impacts) in applying sustainability in a developed country and sport versus a developing country and sport

7. You have just acquired a new role at the Sustainable Athletic Union (SAU) that requires you to write a sustainable plan for the minor league soccer team named "Kentavros." As a planner, you have to develop the goal (the overall result you are seeking to achieve) and multiple objectives to reach the goal (the objectives should be S.M.A.R.T. [Specific, Measurable, Attainable, Relevant, and Time-bound]). Next, design the strategies and outline any tactics that you believe will help make the team succeed concerning sustainability. This team is located in two places: (a) A city/town in a developing country and (b) in a city/town in a developed country. Accordingly, your employer asks you to write a two-page proposal of a sustainable sport plan for Kentavros based on each team location. Outline the SDoS utilizing the six perspectives (personal, social, economic, ecological, technical, and political); what is your team's normative concept (your vision of a well-functioning sustainable team)?

8. How can sport eliminate working in silos? Will new applications with technology be the key to sharing successes and missteps in the transition to sustainable development? How can sport ensure a process of sharing is established to aid all sporting bodies to learn from each other in the process of transitioning to SDoS?

9. Generate a graphic to visually illustrate the objectives outlined in #5 above based on how they relate to the six sports perspectives including the personal, social, economic, ecological, technological, and political perspectives. The graphic should illustrate the priorities and the gaps in the plan. Evaluate the leadership skills needed for achieving the goal and objectives. How can you advance your leadership skills to aid in achieving the goal and objectives?

Further reading

1. Ličen, S., & Jedlicka, S.R. (2020). Sustainable development principles in US sport management graduate programs. *Sport, Education and Society*, 1–14. https://doi.org/10.1080/13573322.2020.1816541

2. O'Brien, D., & Gardiner, S. (2006). Creating sustainable mega-event impacts: Networking and relationship development through pre-event training. *Sport Management Review*, *9*(1), 25–47. https://doi.org/10.1016/S1441-3523(06)70018-3

3. Smart, D.L., & Wolfe, R.A. (2000). Examining sustainable competitive advantage in intercollegiate athletics: A resource-based view. *Journal of Sport Management*, *14*(2), 133–153. https://doi.org/10.1123/jsm.14.2.133

4. Pfahl, M.E. (2010). Strategic issues associated with developing internal sustainability teams in sport and recreation organizations: A framework for action and sustainable environmental performance. *International Journal of Sport Management, Recreation, and Tourism*, *6*, 37–61. http://ijsmart.eu/onlinepic/vol6_3%20Pfahl.pdf

Relevant online resources

1. Sport and Development: https://www.sportanddev.org/en
2. Green Sports Alliance: https://greensportsalliance.org
3. Sport Sustainability: https://www.sportsustainability.org
4. Sustainable Surf: https://sustainablesurf.org
5. We Are Golf: https://wearegolf.org/sustainability/
6. Sustainable Golf: https://sustainable.golf
7. Sustainability Report: https://www.sustainabilityreport.com/tag/volleyball/
8. Adidas: https://www.adidas.com/us/sustainable-soccer
9. Sierra Club: https://www.sierraclub.org/sierra/green-life/2014/02/amazing-ways-nba-going-green

References

Ayanadele, O., Popoola, O., & Obosi, A. (2019). Influence of demographic and psychological factors on attitudes towards sport betting among young adults in Southwest Nigeria. *Journal of Gambling, 36*(3), 343–354. Retrieved from https://link.springer.com/article/10.1007/s10899-019-09882-9

Bar-Eli, M., Krumer, A., & Morgulev, E. (2020, December). Ask not what economics can do for sports – Ask what sport can do for economics. *Journal of Behavioral and Experimental Economics, 89*, 101597. 10.1016/j.socec.2020.101597

Brundtland Commission. (2001). *Climate change 2001: Impacts, adaptation and vulnerability.* In J.J. McCarthy, O.F. Canziani, N.A. Leary, D.J. Dokken, and K.S. White (Eds.), *Contributions of working group II to the third assessment report of the Intergovernmental Panel on Climate Change.* Cambridge: Cambridge University Press. Retrieved from https://www.ipcc.ch/report/ar3/wg2/

Chatzigianni, E. (2018). Global sport governance: Globalizing the globalized. *Sport in Society, 21*(9), 1454–1482. 10.1080/17430437.2017.1390566

Darling-Hammond, L., Flook, L., Cook-Harvey, C., Barron, B., & Osher, D. (2020). Implications for educational practice of the science of learning and development. *Applied Developmental Science, 24*(2), 97–140. 10.1080/10888691.2018.1537791

Dictionary.com. (2021, May). *Endo.* Retrieved from https://www.dictionary.com/browse/endo-

Duarte, T., Culver, D., & Paquetter, K. (2019). Framing a social learning space for wheelchair curling. *International Sport Coaching Journal, 8*(2), 197–209. 10.1123/iscj.2019-0095

Harrington, L. (2016). Sustainability theory and conceptual considerations: A review of critical ideas for sustainability and the rural context. *Papers in Applied Geography, 2*(4), 365–382. 10.1080/23754931.2016.1239222

Jackson, D., Trevisan, F., Pullen, E., & Silk, M. (2020). Towards a social justice disposition in communication and sport scholarship. *Communication and Sport, 8*(4–5), 435–451. 10.1177%2F2167479520932929

Laukyte, M. (2020). Disruptive technologies and the sport ecosystem: A few ethical questions. *Philosophies, 5*(4), 24. Retrieved from https://www.mdpi.com/2409-9287/5/4/24

Lin, K. (2017). Applying game theory to volleyball strategy. *International Journal of Performance Analysis in Sport, 14*(3), 761–774. 10.1080/24748668.2014.11868756

Macovei, S., Tufan, A.A., & Vulpe, B.I. (2014). Theoretical approaches to building a healthy lifestyle through the practice of physical activities. *Procedia-Social and Behavioral Sciences, 117*, 86–91. 10.1016/j.sbspro.2014.02.183

McCullough, B.P., Orr, M., & Kellison, T. (2020). Sport ecology: Conceptualizing an emerging subdiscipline within sport management. *Journal of Sport Management, 1*(a), 1–12. 10.1123/jsm.2019-0294

McSweeny, M., & Safai, P. (2020). Innovating Canadian sport policy: Toward new public management and public entrepreneurship? *International Journal of Sport Policy and Politics, 12*(3), 405–421. 10.1080/19406949.2020.15678

Millington, R., Giles, A.R., van Luijk, N., & Hayhurst, L.M. (2021). Sport for sustainability? The extractives industry, sport, and sustainable development. *Journal of Sport and Social Issues.* 10.1177%2F0193723521991413

Mirriam-Webster.com. (2021). *Sustainable.* Retrieved from https://www.merriam-webster.com/dictionary/sustainable

Oja, B., Bass, J., & Gordon, B. (2018). Identities in the sport workplace: Development of an instrument to measure sport employee identification. *Journal of Global Sport Management, 5*(3), 262–284. 10.1080/247004067.2018.1477521

Petty, R.E., & Cacioppo, J.T. (1986). The elaboration likelihood model of persuasion. In *Communication and persuasion* (pp. 1–24). New York, NY: Springer. Retrieved from https://link.springer.com/chapter/10.1007/978-1-4612-4964-1_1

Pretty, J., Rogerson, M., & Barton, J. (2017). Green mind theory: How brain-body-behavior links into natural and social environments for healthy habits. *International Journal of Environmental Research and Public Health, 14*(7), 706. 10.3390/ijerph14070706

Sachs, J.D. (2015). *The age of sustainable development.* New York City, New York, United States: Columbia University Press. Retrieved from http://cup.columbia.edu/book/the-age-of-sustainable-development/9780231173155

Schulenkorf, N. (2012). Sustainable community development through sport and events: A conceptual framework for sport-for-development projects. *Sport Management Review, 15*(1), 1–12. 10.1016/j.smr.2011.06.001

Stets, J.E., & Burke, P.J. (2000). Identity theory and social identity theory. *Social Psychology Quarterly, 63*(3), 224–237. 10.2307/2695870

Szathmári, A., & Kocsis, T. (2020, November). Who cares about gladiators? An elite-sport-based concept of Sustainable Sport. *Sport in Society,* 1–19.10.1080/17430437.2020.1832470

Taleb, N. (2012). *Antifragile: Things that gain from disorder* (Vol. 3). Random House Incorporated.

Trendafilova, S., McCullough, B.P., Phafl, M., Nguyen, S., Casper, J., & Picariello, M. (2014). Environmental sustainability in sport: Current state and future trends. *Global Journal on Advances in Pure & Applied Sciences, 3*, 9–14. Retrieved from https://www.researchgate.net/publication/281207006_Environmental_sustainability_in_sport_Current_state_and_future_trends

Triantafyllidis, S. (2018). Carbon dioxide emissions research and sustainable transportation in the sports industry. *C—Journal of Carbon Research, 4*(4), 57. 10.3390/c4040057

Triantafyllidis, S. & Darvin, L. (2021). Mass-participant sport events and sustainable development: gender, social bonding, and connectedness to nature as predictors of socially and environmentally responsible behavior intentions. *Sustainable Science, 16*(5), 239–253. 10.1007/s11625-020-00867-x

Triantafyllidis, S., & Kaplanidou, K. (2019). Marathon runners: A fertile market for "Green" donations?. *Journal of Global Sport Management*, 1–14. 10.1080/24704067.201 8.1561205

University of California, Los Angeles (UCLA). (2021). *What is sustainability?* Retrieved from https://www.sustain.ucla.edu/what-is-sustainability/

Yim, B., Byon, K., Baker, T., & Zhang, J. (2020). Identifying critical factors in sport consumption decision making of millennial sport fans: Mixed-methods approach. *European Sport Management Quarterly. 21*(2), 11–20. 10.1080/16184742.2020.1755713

3

SPORT FOR SUSTAINABLE DEVELOPMENT

Stavros Triantafyllidis and Cheryl Mallen

LEARNING OBJECTIVES

Upon completion of this chapter, learners should be able to successfully:

1. Define and explain stage II: sport for sustainable development (S4SD)
2. Identify the analytical and normative concepts of S4SD
3. Describe the strategic management for S4SD and apply it across the six perspectives of sport and sustainable development (S&SD) including the personal, social, economic, ecological, technological, and political aspects
4. Discuss sustainable programs (what is) and plans (what if) for S4SD
5. Propose new ways to manage sport strategically for achieving global sustainability

---

Overview

Our world members need to continuously work towards the development of a well-functioning society that works for all – and is sustainable into the future. Sport can assist by being a driving force for achieving sustainability globally. This is because sport is a platform that can advocate sustainable development practices to the world's societies. Sport emulates what is reflected within society, including the

DOI: 10.4324/9781003128953-3

global challenges we face and can address the issues and illustrate effective ways for moving forward.

This chapter outlines the learning objectives and glossary of terms, followed by an overview of S4SD – or the use of sport to promote or model changes in society. The analytical and normative concepts are applied to sport within our discussion. The analytical concept offers an opportunity to understand how sport can positively impact the complex world's systems across the six perspectives including personal, social, economic, ecological, technological, and political aspects (Macovei et al., 2014; Millington et al., 2021; Schulenkorf, 2012). The normative concept refers to how sport can showcase an ability to overcome sustainability issues and communicate practices for achieving sustainable development goals (SDGs) and extend these practices throughout our global society (Sachs, 2015; Triantafyllidis & Darvin, 2021). This application offers a strategy for highlighting current approaches, opportunities, challenges, and gaps within society. Readers are encouraged to discuss future directions for S4SD and determine the necessary leadership and strategies for the way forward. This is an important area of focus as sport's contributions today can contribute to efforts that aid communities worldwide to be sustainable for a well-functioning modern-world society into the future.

Glossary

Sport

"Sport means all forms of physical activity which, through casual or organized participation, aim at expressing or improving physical fitness and well-being, forming social relationships or obtaining results in competition at all levels" (Szathmári & Kocsis, 2020, p. 4).

Sport and sustainable development (S&SD)

S&SD is the process that includes two stages: Sustainable development of sport (SDoS) and S4SD that, together, enhance the development that meets the needs of current generations without compromising future generations' ability to meet their own needs at the personal, social, economic, ecological, technological, and political levels (Millington et al., 2021; Szathmári & Kocsis, 2020; Triantafyllidis & Darvin, 2021).

Sport for sustainable development (S4SD)

S4SD refers to the contribution of sport to our global societies' viability by encouraging sustainability across the six perspectives of personal, social, economic, ecological, technological, and political worldwide (Macovei et al., 2014; Millington et al., 2021; Schulenkorf, 2012).

Sustainability

The term refers to "the integration of environmental health, social equity, and economic vitality to create thriving, healthy, diverse and resilient communities for this generation and generations to come" (University of California, Los Angeles, 2021, para. 2).

The term sustainable development (SD) encompasses the initiatives and progress in pursuit of sustainability. According to the Brundtland Commission (2001), sustainable development meets the needs of the present without compromising the ability of future generations to "meet their own needs" (p.82). This includes "the narrow notion of physical sustainability [that] implies a concern for social equity between generations, a concern that must logically be extended to equity within each generation" (p. 82).

The analytical concept applied to sport for sustainable development (S4SD)

A theoretical approach for analyzing sport as a platform to understand the world as a complex interaction of personal, social, economic, ecological, technological, and political systems. Understandings of the individual perspectives can be combined to determine how sport can help society move forward for sustainable development (Macovei et al., 2014; Millington et al., 2021; Schulenkorf, 2012).

The normative concept of S4SD

Examinations are completed using sport as a platform to view the world by defining the objectives of a well-functioning society that delivers well-being for its global citizens today and for future generations. The normative concept urges us to have a universal vision toward a good society. These examinations lead to an understanding of where we are currently and the gaps that need to be addressed in the future based on the six perspectives. Sport can showcase to global societies how to overcome sustainability issues and communicate practices for achieving SDGs (Macovei et al., 2014; Millington et al., 2021; Schulenkorf, 2012).

Defining and explaining S4SD

Sport has a proven powerful ability to communicate messages worldwide. As a context, this ability stems from the attention sport gets from multiple media platforms. The publicity from these platforms can, for example, promote events/games, competition results, and the glamorization or demonization of the participating athletes, coaches, teams, and owners, as well as encourage intense sport spectatorship and fandom. This means that sport is communicated throughout the world to the masses – particularly with the rise of social media (Filo et al., 2015).

Given its role in society, its popularity globally, and mass communication capability, sport has a demonstrated ability to be a vehicle for presenting concepts or messages that have impacts beyond sport, such as social development messages (Bas et al., 2020). This includes concepts that promote change – including the transition to positive social and environmental actions – or S4SD. This is a vital role for sport as our global society needs to find ways to work through modern complexities and uncertainties in life – and sport can lead the way.

Sport's powerful communication capabilities have already been used for S4SD through a plethora of interventions. Examples include sport promoting initiatives that advance personal development, mental and physical health, active living, plant-based nutrition, wellness, social equity, inclusion, justice, peace, economic growth, prosperity, environmental stewardship, and sustainability (Beutler, 2008). The promotion of these notions has spanned the local, regional, national, and global levels. The results can, for example, generate positive socio-economic and environmental outcomes to enhance people's well-being, communities' quality of life and strengthen local economies. Consequently, sport contributes to the sustainable development of a global society.

Leadership encouraging good governance in S4SD is needed to build understandings of the current state of societies and the world of sport. This leadership can articulate the gaps found in sporting society (i.e., gender equality and social justice) and encourage strategies for filling such gaps in sport and beyond. Further, this leadership is vital for ensuring the successful implementation, evaluation, reporting recommendations, and renewal of effective strategies (Broman & Robèrt, 2017). The ongoing leadership role also encompasses the facilitation of debates on ideas and initiatives that propose how the gaps found in sporting society can be filled, obtaining consensus on the way forward, and using sport as a springboard to contribute to a well-functioning community effectively.

Technology is critical in facilitating innovative efforts and communicating successful initiatives in S4SD worldwide because it assists in spreading the need for interventions within our sporting society and how sport can fill this need. Such communication can also help communities replicate proven advances in S4SD and expand the progress as we move through the 21st century (Giulianotti et al., 2018). This means that leadership in S4SD needs to engage with emerging technologies in the process of pursuing good governance in order to communicate messages encouraging positive change. Other strategies that foster leadership and action in S4SD are also needed. Figure 3.1 outlines how the authors envision significant contributions to global sustainability through S4SD. Further, figure 3.2) offers a visual representation of S4SD with respect to the analytical and normative concepts that will now be discussed.

Sustainable Development (SD) includes Antifragility

The development of robust systems that help increase individuals and organization' capability to thrive despite stressors, shocks, volatility, noise, mistakes, faults, attacks, or failures (Taleb, 2012).

Sustainability
"The integration of environmental health, social equity and economic vitality in order to create thriving, healthy, diverse and resilient communities for this generation and generations to come"(UCLA Sustainability, 2021, para.2).

Our Vision
We envision significant contributions to global sustainability through sport and sustainable development (S&SD).

Sport and Sustainable Development (S&SD)
Sport and sustainable development (S&SD) is the process that includes two stages: sustainable development of sport (SDoS) and sport for sustainable development (S4SD) that, together, enhance the development that meets the needs of current generations without compromising future generations to meet their own needs at the personal, social, economic, ecological, technological, and political levels (Millington et al., 2021; Szathmari & Kocsis, 2020; Triantafyllidis & Darvin, 2021).

STAGE 2: Sport for Sustainable Development (S4SD)
Sport for sustainable development (S4SD) refers to the contribution of sport to our global societies' viability by encouraging sustainability across the six perspectives of personal, social, economic, ecological, technological, and political worldwide (Macovei, Tufan, & Vulpe, 2014; Millington et al., 2021; Schulenkorf, 2012).

STAGE 1: Sustainable Development of Sport (SDoS)
Sustainable development of sport (SDoS) refers to the sustainable practices taken by sport regarding the management of sport products, services, and sport consumer behaviors to achieve sustainability within the world of sport that encompasses six perspectives, including the personal, social, economic, ecological, technological, and political (McCullough, Orr, & Kellison, 2020; Szathmari & Kocsis, 2020; Triantafyllidis & Darvin, 2021).

FIGURE 3.1 How we envision significant contributions to global sustainability through sport and sustainable development (S&SD)

The analytical concept applied to sport for sustainable development (S4SD)

The analytical concept involves breaking sport down into sub-sections that can be further examined. In this case, the sub-sections encompass six perspectives within sport, including the personal, social, economic, ecological, technical, and political perspectives. An examination of each sub-section advances knowledge regarding the complex issues within our global communities reflected in sport. The knowledge derived from examining each sub-section – along with the collective wisdom from the pooled understandings – can generate strategies for solving issues in sport and society. The logic is that if issues are articulated and resolved within sport, then the way they were resolved can be applied to assist in resolving problems within society.

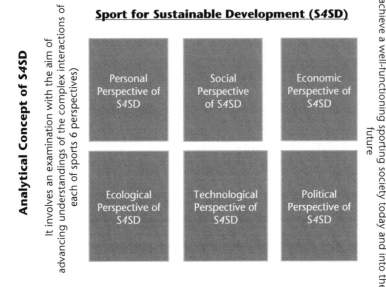

FIGURE 3.2 Conceptual illustration of sport for sustainable development (S4SD)

This positions sport as being able to demonstrate to communities the way forward. Below are examples of the analytical concept as applied to S4SD based on the six perspectives.

The analytical concept and the personal perspective of sport for sustainable development (S4SD)

From a personal perspective, sport is seen as a tool for promotions and interventions related to healthy and active living (Funk et al., 2011). Research in sport management purports that sport can help individuals reach a pillar of health and active living through sustainable behavioral actions (Sharma-Brymer et al., 2018; Triantafyllidis & Kaplanidou, 2019; Wicker, 2019). Sport can essentially encourage people to live a less sedentary life and engage in an active lifestyle (Macovei et al., 2014). The cultivation of an active lifestyle can be accomplished through many strategies, such as using the communication power of sport through mass media, appealing to all age groups (e.g., youth up to seniors), to promote positive mental and physical health impacts/associations, and social interaction through sport (Smith & Westerbeek, 2007). An application of the analytical concept to S4SD with the personal perspective involves improving understandings that sport can enhance an "Active Living" agenda that is supported by the United Nations global goal for sustainable development which aims to ensure healthy lives and promote well-being for all at all ages (UNOSDP, n.d.). For example, a goal for the personal perspective of S4SD is: **To ensure active living and enhance well-being for all ages through sport.**

The analytical concept and the social perspective of sport for sustainable development (S4SD)

From a social standpoint, sport is positioned as a platform for encouraging positive social change. The global sport industry has long-held power to drive social change for years and perhaps decades before substantial shifts are seen throughout society. Social changes are often the result of decades of behind-the-scenes work completed by numerous activists who see sport as agent for social change.

For instance, there is a new wave of activism through sport with a focus on social justice. Recently, during the playoffs in 2020, the National Basketball Association (NBA) and professional athletes used social media technology to advocate for the Black Lives Matter (BLM) movement (Wired, 2021). Specifically, players expressed their position on social issues and, for instance, were seen wearing a social change message on the back of their jerseys instead of their names (Terrill, 2020). Examples of the messages included "Equality," Justice," and "Peace." Other messages provided by the NBA platform were "Reform Education," and "Fairness," "Vote," and "Equal Rights." The need for justice and peace promoted by sport reflects the current discrimination of some athletes as minorities. Such discrimination in sport reflects the broader bias found in society.

Another example of social change through sport involves Sport for Development and Peace. One key activity is that the United Nations (UN) has designated April 6 as the International Day of Sport for Development and Peace (https://www.un.org/en/observances/sport-day). This program supports under-resourced youth sports programs, along with efforts to encourage such youth to overcome conflict, act to advance solutions for community issues, such as inclusion, and become community leaders.

These examples show that sport has encouraged social change. Sport, therefore, is positioned well to continue contributing to the pursuit of a well-functioning and inclusive global society.

The analytical concept and the economic perspective of sport for sustainable development S4SD

Further, sport can be used as a platform to review economic diversities in global societies. For example, sport products (equipment and apparel), events, and services should be produced in line with labor standards free from forced and child labor and discrimination of all forms. Decent jobs can be created by sport-based employment and entrepreneurship initiatives by complying with labor standards throughout their value chain and aligning with business policies and practices. Also, creating new jobs can reflect sustainable economic development with the appropriate policies, procedures, and standards. Sport events are considered the primary sport product, and it has been proven that such events can increase the number of new jobs and provide economic growth in the host cities. Also, sport events promote local cultures and socio-economic networks through the local workforce's involvement in the sport events.

The analytical concept and the ecological perspective of sport for sustainable development S4SD

Sport can be utilized as a platform to reveal understandings related to the state of our world ecology. This positions sport at the forefront of environmental stewardship by being a conduit that advances awareness of community-specific and global ecological issues. Understanding the state of ecological sustainability is the first step in acting to mitigate such problems.

Sport has numerous ways to bring awareness of environmental conditions forward to those in sport and the community. For instance, the conditions in which athletes must compete can be disseminated using media attention afforded to sport. This includes the state of our water systems relative to pollution for athletes competing in open water events, such as triathlons and waterskiing; our air pollution and the impacts on athletes in a marathon and other athletics events; as well as the state of our land, including flora and fauna, for athletes in cross country skiing and other ski competitions.

Further, and importantly, applying the analytical theoretical concept to sport can be used to advance understandings of climate change (Dingle & Stewart, 2018). This includes where sport events have to be adapted in specific communities due to climate change impacts. Such impacts can include extreme weather, such as prolonged droughts, devastating fires, and rising water levels, and floods, along with unusual seasonal weather. Overall, the conditions in which athletes must compete can highlight communities' ecological perspectives worldwide.

The analytical concept and the technological perspective of sport for sustainable development (S4SD)

Sport is a platform that can reveal emerging technologies that have come into the marketplace. Utilizing such technology in sport helps to advance understandings within communities about what is available, how it works, and the respective advantages or disadvantages. Technologies used in sport demonstrate to those within our global communities the latest technological innovations as options for sport and society.

Sport has numerous avenues within which to exhibit the use of new technology. Examples include sport facilities with renewable energy, green walls, air quality testing technology, in-house video communication displays, and advertisements for adapting ecological activities. Additionally, new technology can be implemented when hosting athletic competitions, such as new timing systems and artificial intelligence adapted to judge events. Individual athletes can utilize emerging technologies, such as the ever-advancing abilities of watches with features to aid athletes in monitoring their training progress. Each use of technology in sport can help those within sport communities, and individuals throughout our global society become aware of the advances happening technologically throughout the world. Understandings of what is available can expand applications for technologies that may support a well-functioning global society.

The analytical concept and the political perspective of sport for sustainable development S4SD

An application of the analytical concept of S4SD using the political perspective captures the relationship between sport and non-sport organizations, such as the intergovernmental UN and the International Olympic Committee (IOC). This recognition was formally achieved in 2009 as the IOC was given the Observer status and gained the right to participate in the UN General Assemblies (International Olympic Committee Press Release, 2009). In 2015, the UN SDGs that promoted a well-functioning society were adopted to include sport within the Agenda 2030 (UNOSDP, n.d.). This recognized sport for its powerful role in promoting peace, education, social inclusion, and a healthy lifestyle.

An application of the analytical concept involves breaking sport into sub-sections including the personal, social, economic, ecological, technical, and political perspectives. Each sub-section can be examined to foster knowledge concerning complex issues within our global societies reflected within sport – the knowledge assists in articulating and resolving such issues in sport and society. We now move to discuss an application of the *normative concept of S4SD* that focuses on determining a vision of a well-functioning society.

The normative concept and sport for sustainable development S4SD)

Examining sport using the normative concept as a tool can help achieve positive advances related to what is encompassed within a well-functioning global sustainable society. To achieve this state within society, we must establish the values and objectives of a highly functioning society – with the hope that we can reach a universal vision in our complex world. These values can be illustrated through the society of sport.

Sport is positioned to promote a social code of conduct for a well-functioning society (Sachs, 2015; Triantafyllidis & Darvin, 2021). This code needs to be open for personal influences on what it means to have a well-functioning society. This is exemplified in sport as there are available universally accepted codes of conduct for sport (i.e., fair play and the safeguarding of game officials). Simultaneously, there are variances regarding the regulation of behavior depending on where you are on a topic (i.e., cultural variances). For instance, it is acceptable to fake an injury as a strategy, yet this is unacceptable in some sports and cultures.

An examination of sport can illustrate society's economic impacts by demonstrating where sport products are manufactured (which countries), where the distribution and consumption of manufactured sporting goods are most prominent, and the implications of sporting services and events. Sport can, thus, reveal economic disparities. Further, sport is positioned to help those impacted by economic inequality by using programs that share resources. Examples include the re-distribution of used sports equipment that benefits the disadvantaged and programs that offset fees to allow participation in sport (Tyler, 2019). This shows that sport can help the disadvantaged and can encourage such actions in society.

Another examination of sport using the normative concept of S4SD involves an ecological focus. Sport can establish what a well-functioning sporting society can look like by seeking practices that advance environmental sustainability. For instance, sport teams have promoted recycling; and, in turn, hope to influence sports fans to improve the recycling rates within their communities (McCullough, 2012). Additionally, sport facilities have transitioned to alternative clean energy sources, such as solar energy (Chard & Mallen, 2013). In turn, they have furthered learning as to how to adapt to other community buildings. And finally, the environmental footprint of major and mega-sized sport events has been determined (Broder-Nemeth & Parshley, 2020); and this exhibits to those in sport, and those in communities, how to reduce such impacts.

Further, sport has embraced the advance of emerging technologies. Examples include technologies for clothing and shoes for sport participation, timing equipment for sport events, improvements in sporting equipment, along with emerging technologies for repairing/rebuilding injured athletes. Sport can tout that other technological developments are not acceptable, such as using performance enhancements banned in sport (Crouse, 2009). For a well-functioning society, this positions sport as exemplifying what is fair or acceptable – or prohibited – concerning technology use. Taking a position can help those in society debate and determine what is best for society.

An examination of sport and the political perspective can facilitate understandings of a well-functioning, contemporary society. Policies in sport reflect support for ideologies such as gender equality and opportunities, gay rights, apartheid, and multiple other social justice issues. These policies and the following implementation issues can help teach how to integrate all people into our society.

Overall, S4SD utilizes sport as a platform to encourage a well-functioning society. This platform can function as the antidote to adverse outcomes derived from human practices, global pandemics, climate crises, and financial and political corruption. In whole or in part, the current challenges can be solved with the appropriate use of sport as a vehicle for promoting positive change.

Building programs for sport for sustainable development S4SD

Our vision for achieving sustainable development through sport requires excellent leadership in both the sport management academy and the industry. Therefore, we begin by proposing the building of programs to educate leaders about the benefits of S4SD, including the positive impacts on people, society, the economy, and the natural environment.

One proposal is that higher educators in sport management programs take the lead on this endeavor. They can advocate for S4SD within every course taught and have a meaningful impact on young people, such as Generation Z (*Gen Z*), to shape their work and life habits in a healthy, pro-environmental, and philanthropic manner.

This education can facilitate the building of a framework for improving sport and society for long-term sustainability. With good leadership and the support of emerging and advanced technology, education for S4SD can be the cornerstone for a transition to advance sustainable programs throughout sport and society.

Importantly, sport leaders do not need to develop sustainability goals – as sport can simply adopt the already fully developed United Nations (UN) seventeen (17) Sustainable Development Goals (SDGs). This means that sport can move forward quickly to focus on developing strategies for successfully implementing these SDGs within society through sport. Sustainable programs include, for example, policy development embedded with the tenets of S4SD; the leveraging of partnerships established for advancing the characteristics of S4SD for effectiveness across for-profit and non-for-profit governmental and non-governmental organizations and foundations. Another example includes programs that ensure the management of human and natural resources in a manner that improves performance and sets an example for other industries to follow to achieve sustainable development.

Additionally, our vision suggests that the leadership in sport follow previous research and collaboration between the United Nations Development Programme and United Nations Research Institute for Social Development (UNRISD). Scholars of sport and practitioners in the sport industry, including stakeholders of sport organizations, events, and teams, can examine the factors that make sport operations achieve sustainability outcomes. A study with these groups can identify the processes within sport that act as barriers toward achieving program success and can then break down such barriers. Notably, such work is embedded with the following foundational framework:

- That sport accepts that the task of transitioning to sustainable development is complex and agree to avoid working in silos. The goal of joint efforts is the sharing of data and plans as commonplace to guide all of sport to transition. This is necessary as sport organizations should not transition to sustainable practices alone for all six perspectives, that is, personal, social, economic, ecological, technological, and political. Sharing, supporting, and cooperating within particular sports and between sports offers synergies that can lead to efficient and effective progress

- That reaching our capacity in S4SD involves embedding the concept of sustainability into all aspects of sport. This includes embedding S4SD into all levels from the amateur to professional and elite levels of sport, all infra-structure development, competitions/events throughout the youth to the senior ranks, and programming, including human resource development (such as game officials/referees and volunteers). Capacity means all aspects of sport are saturated with the characteristics of S4SD

Overall, our vision encourages an agenda for S&SD to be built by designing achievable goals with measurable objectives for instituting the UN 17 SDGs.

Concluding remarks

1. Applying the normative and analytical concepts to S4SD can stimulate ideas, debate, and determine how to solve modern-world societal issues using sport as the forum. The combined application of these two theoretical concepts can give rise to sport contributing to a well-functioning global society
2. S4SD can be used to create positive changes in our modern world, such as a more prosperous future for global citizens, communities, and the natural environment
3. Sport leaders can influence and inspire advancements in governments and decision-makers across various societal issues, such as:

   a. Social justice, including decreasing inequalities based on gender, race, and sexuality
   b. The global climate crisis, where the advancement of technologies and behavioral changes can generate positive environmental sustainability outcomes

4. An application of the analytical concept to S4SD explains the potential of establishing global sustainability through sport from personal, social, eco-nomic, ecological, technological, and political perspectives
5. The normative concept supports the analytical approach that sport is a powerful platform for sustainable development
6. A conceptualization of S4SD can assist scholars and practitioners to bridge theory with practice to solve common problems impacting humanity and the natural environment

Future directions

1. One way to expand S4SD is to replicate successful programs. An example is to expand the Hockey Canada "Good Deeds Cup" (https://www.hockeycanada.ca/en-ca/corporate/partnerships/programs/good-deeds-cup) to other sports and additional countries. In this program, youth hockey teams (e.g., groups ages under 11, 13, and 15 years old) determine a good deed that they can accomplish in their community. They videotape the activity, submit a 30–60 second video to Hockey Canada, and add a statement about why their "good deed" was good for their community. All submissions are in the running for a financial reward that can make a difference in their community. The sponsored program declares three finalists that the public then votes on to select the winner. The winning team gets $100,000 to spend to assist a charity within their community. Such winnings have been used to pay for a horseback riding therapy program, tornado disaster relief, and a Valentine's Day celebration for residents in care homes. Other ways to spend it include contributing to a hospital foundation, the humane society to aid animals in the community, and so forth. Significantly, each team determines where the gaps are in the community, and then they set out to make a difference by working to solve them
2. Research should be conducted in all the growing cities worldwide to examine how the sport is solving problems on a larger scale of the societies
3. Research should be conducted to identify the most powerful tools of sport and therefore use those tools for making positive changes in the world
4. Academic endeavors should be created that focus on sustainable development across a variety of industrial sectors.

Review questions

1. In your own words, define S4SD
2. Do you agree with the approach of using sport as an agent of change for society? Or should leaders in sport only focus on the development of sport itself? Why?
3. Do you agree that the analytical concept presented can be applied to each of the six perspectives? Please explain why or why not
4. Do a critical review of the concept of S3SD and provide three opportunities and three challenges (or issues) found within S4SD. Outline how the challenges can be overcome
5. Have you seen the concept of S4SD be applied in practice within your local community? If so, how?
6. Please write what you would consider to be a foundational vision/mission statement for one of the S4SD programs mentioned in this chapter. Explain why you chose the elements in the vision statement

Discussion questions

1. How do the analytical and normative concepts of S4SD aid in understanding sustainability?
2. Why does sport have the power to influence people's perceptions toward sustainability?
3. How does media use sport to influence people's perceptions toward sustainability practices?
4. In your opinion, what is the most influential sport that could influence the most people to adopt sustainability practices? Please explain why?
5. How can sport influence people and communities in developing countries? And how in developed countries? Are there any differences in the way sport can influence people's perceptions and behaviors toward sustainability? What are the key differences?

Learning activities

1. Outline the values and objectives you consider important in a highly functioning society. Then, work in a small group to develop a consensus on a universal vision of what could be with respect to our complex world. Next, determine what is essential in society for you personally – and how sport can illustrate such concepts
2. Consider a sport of your choice and the conditions in which an athlete must compete. Then outline how you can apply the analytical concept to increase your community's understanding of the conditions athletes must face based on the personal, social, economic, ecological, technical, and political conditions
3. Sport has exhibited many ways to improve our global society. Review a website for a professional sport team of your choice and determine what programs they have implemented to improve society
4. Complete an online search to find a successful S4SD program that you could consider implementing in your community. Develop an overview of what the program could do for sport as well as the local community. Further, design a strategy for such an implementation
5. If you had the power to develop any S4SD program, record what it would be. Include a long-term goal and at least three objectives to meet the goal. The objectives should be S.M.A.R.T. – Specific, Measurable, Attainable, Relevant, and Time-bound

Further reading

1. Loland, S. (2006). Olympic sport and the idea of sustainable development. *Journal of the Philosophy of Sport, 33*(2), 144–156. https://doi.org/10.1080/00948705.2006.9714698

2. Lawson, H.A. (2005). Empowering people, facilitating community development, and contributing to sustainable development: The social work of sport, exercise, and physical education programs. *Sport, Education, and Society, 10*(1), 135–160. https://doi.org/10.1080/1357332052000308800

3. Lindsey, I., & Chapman, T. (2017). *Enhancing the contribution of sport to sustainable development goals.* Commonwealth Secretariat. Retrieved from https://www.sportanddev.org/sites/default/files/downloads/enhancing_the_contribution_of_sport_to_the_sustainable_development_goals_.pdf

4. Trail, G. T., & McCullough, B. P. (2020). Marketing sustainability through sport: Testing the sport sustainability campaign evaluation model. *European Sport Management Quarterly, 20*(2), 109–129. https://doi.org/10.1080/16184742.2019.1580301

5. Giulianotti, R., Darnell, S., Collison, H., & Howe, P.D. (2018). Sport for development and peace and the environment: The case for policy, practice, and research. *Sustainability, 10*(7), 2241. Retrieved from https://www.mdpi.com/2071-1050/10/7/2241/html

6. Schulenkorf, N. (2012, February). Sustainable community development through sport and events: A conceptual framework for sport-for-development projects. Sport Management Review, *15*(1), 1–12. http://doi.org/10.1016/k/s,r/2011.06001

7. Bu, T. (2009). Harmonious sports: The ideal pattern of sustainable development for competitive sports. *Journal of Sustainable Development, 2*(1), 29–35. https://doi.org/10.5539/jsd.v2n1p29

Relevant online resources

1. Sport and Development: https://www.sportanddev.org/en/learn-more/sport-and-sustainable-development-goals/measuring-contribution-sport-sustainable

2. We Are Guarding Earth Through Sport (We Are GETS): https://www.wearegets.org

3. International Olympic Committee (IOC): https://stillmed.olympic.org/Documents/Commissions_PDFfiles/SportAndEnvironment/Sustainability_Through_Sport.pdf

4. IOC: https://www.olympic.org/olympism-in-action/sustainability-through-sport

5. Sport and Development: https://www.sportanddev.org/en/article/news/bridging-gap-environmental-sustainability-through-sport

6. BBC News: https://www.bbc.com/news/world-us-canada-53273381

7. SportsPro Media: https://www.sportspromedia.com/from-the-magazine/social-justice-racial-gender-equality-black-lives-matter-diversity-sport

References

Bas, D., Martin, M., Pollack, C., & Venne, R. (2020). *The impact of COVID-19 on sport, physical activity, and well-being and its effects on social development*. United Nations Department of Economic & Social Affairs, Policy Brief, No. 73. Retrieved from https://www.un.org/development/desa/dspd/wp-content/uploads/sites/22/2020/06/PB_73.pdf

Beutler, I. (2008). Sport serving development and peace: Achieving the goals of the United Nations through sport. *Sport in Society, 11*(4), 359–369. 10.1080/17430430802019227

Broder-Nemeth, A., & Parshley, G. (2020, September 15). *IOC and Dow announce phase two of the Olympic Movement Carbon Initiative award*. Retrieved from https://corporate.dow.com/en-us/news/press-releases/ioc-and-dow-announce-phase-two-of-olympic-movement-carbon-initiative-award.htm

Broman, G.I., & Robèrt, K.H. (2017). A framework for sustainable strategic development. *Journal of Cleaner Production, 140*, 17–31. 10.1016/j.jclepro.2015.10.121

Brundtland Commission. (2001). *Climate change 2001: Impacts, adaptation, and vulnerability*. In J.J. McCarthy, O.F. Canziani, N.A. Leary, D.J. Dokken and K.S. White (Eds.), *Contributions of working group II to the third assessment report of the intergovernmental panel on climate change*. Cambridge: Cambridge University Press. Retrieved from https://www.ipcc.ch/report/ar3/wg2/

Chard, C., & Mallen, C. (2013). Renewable energy initiatives at Canadian sport stadiums: A content analysis of web-site communications. *Sustainability, 5*(12), 5119–5134. 10.3390/su5125119

Crouse, K. (2009, July 24). Swimming bans high-tech suits, ending an era. New York City, New York, US: The New York Times. Retrieved from https://www.nytimes.com/2009/07/25/sports/25swim.html

Dingle, G.W., & Stewart, B. (2018). Playing the climate game: Climate change impacts, resilience, and adaptation in the climate-dependent sport sector. *Managing Sport and Leisure, 23*(4–6), 293–314. 10.1080/23750472.2018.1527715

Filo, K., Lock, D., & Karg, A. (2015). Sport and social media research: A review. *Sport Management Review, 18*(2), 166–181. 10.1016/j.smr.2014.11.001

Funk, D., Jordan, J., Ridinger, L., & Kaplanidou, K. (2011). The capacity of mass participant sport events for the development of activity commitment and future exercise intention. *Leisure Sciences, 33*(3), 250–268. 10.1080/01490400.2011.564926

Giulianotti, R., Darnell, S., Collison, H., & Howe, P.D. (2018). Sport for development and peace and the environment: The case for policy, practice, and research. *Sustainability, 10*(7), 2241. 10.3390/su10072241

International Olympic Committee (IOC) Press Release. (2009, October 19). *IOC granted UN observer status*. Retrieved from https://www.olympic.org/news/ioc-granted-un-observer-status

Macovei, S., Tufan, A.A., & Vulpe, B.I. (2014). Theoretical approaches to building a healthy lifestyle through the practice of physical activities. *Procedia-Social and Behavioral Sciences, 117*, 86–91. 10.1016/j.sbspro.2014.02.183

McCullough, B.P. (2012). Identifying the influences on sport spectator recycling behaviors using the theory of planned behavior. *International Journal of Sport Management and Marketing, 14*(1-4), 146–168. 10.1504/IJSMM.2013.060631

Millington, R., Giles, A.R., van Luijk, N., & Hayhurst, L.M. (2021). Sport for sustainability? The extractives industry, sport, and sustainable development. *Journal of Sport and Social Issues*. 10.1177/0193723521991413

Sachs, J.D. (2015). *The age of sustainable development.* New York City, US: Columbia University Press. Retrieved from http://cup.columbia.edu/book/the-age-of-sustainable-development/9780231173155

Schulenkorf, N. (2012). Sustainable community development through sport and events: A conceptual framework for sport-for-development projects. *Sport Management Review, 15*(1), 1–12. 10.1016/j.smr.2011.06.001

Schulenkorf, N., Sherry, E., & Rowe, K. (2016). Sport for development: An integrated literature review. *Journal of Sport Management, 30*(1), 22–39. 10.1123/jsm.2014-0263

Sharma-Brymer, V., Brymer, E., Gray, T., & Davids, K. (2018). Affordances guiding Forest School practice: The application of the ecological dynamics approach. *Journal of Outdoor and Environmental Education, 21*(1), 103–115. 10.1007/s42322-017-0004-3

Smith, A.C., & Westerbeek, H.M. (2007). Sport as a vehicle for deploying corporate social responsibility. *Journal of Corporate Citizenship,* 25, 43–54. 10.9774/GLEAF.4700.2 007.SP.00007

Szathmári, A., & Kocsis, T. (2020). Who cares about gladiators? An elite-sport-based concept of sustainable sport. *Sport in Society,* 1–19. 10.1080/17430437.2020.1832470

Terrill, M. (2020, October 1). In photos: The sports world has been taking a stand. Atlanta, Georgia, US: CNN.com. Retrieved from https://www.cnn.com/2020/08/27/world/gallery/sports-protests/index.html

Triantafyllidis, S. & Darvin, L. (2021). Mass-participant sport events and sustainable development: gender, social bonding, and connectedness to nature as predictors of socially and environmentally responsible behavior intentions. *Sustainable Science, 16*(5), 239–253. 10.1 007/s11625-020-00867-x

Triantafyllidis, S., & Kaplanidou, K. (2019). Marathon runners: A fertile market for "Green" donations?*Journal of Global Sport Management,* 1–14. 10.1080/24704067.201 8.1561205

Tyler, F. (2019, August 1). New local youth sports equipment sharing program gets set to host first "shopping" event. Retrieved from https://canbyfirst.com/new-local-youth-sports-equipment-sharing-program-gets-set-to-host-first-shopping-event/

United Nations Office of Sport Development and Peace (UNOSDP). (n.d.). *Sport and the sustainable development goals.* Retrieved from https://www.un.org/sport/sites/www.un.org.sport/files/ckfiles/files/Sport_for_SDGs_finalversion9.pdf

University of California, Los Angeles (UCLA). (2021). *What is sustainability?* Retrieved from https://www.sustain.ucla.edu/what-is-sustainability/

Wicker, P. (2019). The carbon footprint of active sport participants. *Sport Management Review, 22*(4), 513–526. 10.1016/j.smr.2018.07.001

Wired (2021). *Social media helps Black Lives matter fight the power.* Retrieved from https://www.wired.com/2015/10/how-black-lives-matter-uses-social-media-to-fight-the-power/

4

SPORT AND THE UNITED NATIONS SUSTAINABLE DEVELOPMENT GOALS

Stavros Triantafyllidis and Marco Tortora

LEARNING OBJECTIVES

Upon completion of this chapter, learners should be able to successfully:

1. Determine the purpose of sport and sustainable development (S&SD)
2. Explain the links between S&SD and the United Nations (UN) 17 sustainable development goals (SDGs)
3. Distinguish how the UN 17 SDGs relate to S&SD across the two stages of sustainable development of sport (SDoS) and sport for sustainable development (S4SD)
4. Explain how S&SD can contribute to the global sustainable development goals (UN SDGs) to achieve sustainability
5. Outline the challenges and the opportunities of S&SD when aligning with the 17 UN SDGs
6. Distinguish whether sport is currently converging toward or diverging away from sustainability and what should be done to improve its role and the participation of all stakeholders
7. Design strategies for implementing S&SD ideas within your community

---

DOI: 10.4324/9781003128953-4

Overview

This chapter connects S&SD with the UN 17 SDGs. The UN is pushing for these goals to be implemented worldwide by 2030. Sport can be part of the implementation process through S&SD and its two stages, that is, stage I: SDoS and stage II: S4SD of society.

This chapter outlines the learning objectives and glossary of terms followed by a discussion that helps learners perceive the goals and S&SD. The chapter promotes that implementing the goals through sport can advance antifragility (or the capability to thrive despite change and stressors) (Taleb, 2012) within sport and throughout our societies worldwide.

Glossary

Antifragility

The pursuit of robust systems that help increase individuals' and organizations' capability to thrive despite stressors, shocks, volatility, noise, mistakes, faults, attacks, or failures (Taleb, 2012).

The 2030 Agenda for Sustainable Development

The 2030 Agenda is a plan of action to influence people, society, the economy, natural environment, technology, and politics. The purpose of the 2030 Agenda seeks to enhance universal peace and eradicate poverty in all its forms and dimensions. This Agenda includes 17 SDGs and 169 targets that intend to build on the Millennium development goals (MDGs) and complete what these did not achieve (United Nations, 2021).

United Nations Sustainable Development Goals (UN SDGs)

The UN SDGs include a set of 17 goals. Each SDG is to be applied with a targeted focus for a particular national circumstance (United Nations, 2021).

Sport

"Sport means all forms of physical activity which, through casual or organized participation, aim at expressing or improving physical fitness and well-being, forming social relationships or obtaining results in competition at all levels" (Szathmári & Kocsis, 2020, p. 4).

Sport and sustainable development (S&SD):

S&SD is a process that includes two stages: SDoS and S4SD that, together, enhance the development that meets the needs of current generations without compromising future generations' ability to meet their own needs at the personal, social, economic, ecological, technological, and political levels (Millington et al., 2021; Szathmari & Kocsis, 2020; Triantafyllidis & Darvin, 2021).

Sport for sustainable development (S4SD)

S4SD refers to the contribution of sport to our global societies' viability by encouraging sustainability across the six perspectives of personal, social, economic, ecological, technological, and political worldwide (Macovei et al., 2014; Millington et al., 2021; Schulenkorf, 2012).

Sustainability

The term refers to "the integration of environmental health, social equity, and economic vitality to create thriving, healthy, diverse and resilient communities for this generation and generations to come" (University of California Los Angeles, 2021, para. 2).

The term sustainable development encompasses the initiatives and progress in pursuit of sustainability. According to the Brundtland Commission (2001), sustainable development is defined as the "development that meets the needs of the present without compromising the ability of future generations to meet their own needs" (p. 82). This includes "the narrow notion of physical sustainability [that] implies a concern for social equity between generations, a concern that must logically be extended to equity within each generation" (p. 82).

Sustainable development of sport (SDoS)

SDoS refers to the sustainable practices taken by sport regarding the management of sport products, services, and sport consumer behaviors to achieve sustainability within the world of sport that encompasses six perspectives, including the personal, social, economic, ecological, technological, and political (McCullough et al., 2020; Szathmari & Kocsis, 2020; Triantafyllidis & Darvin, 2021).

Sustainable management

In this text, sustainable management is about managers and their approach to sustainability. It encompasses their vision of sustainability, including their way of thinking about the world and their capacity to face sustainability challenges within their organizations and the multiple aspects of work. Some competencies and skills have been noted as necessary (Shen et al., 2010). An example includes having an open mindset to explore different scientific sustainability-related theories and their applications to work. Such theories can offer ways of learning and thinking that expand knowledge. Examples include complexity and systems theories, design thinking, and innovation theories (Leal Filho et al., 2019).

Values

Values are defined as "all of the general moral beliefs that reflect common feelings, thoughts, goals, and interests by the majority to sustain the existence of society or social groups" (Balci & Erdeveciler, 2017, p. 197).

Linking S&SD with the UN SDGs

Suppose you were asked the question of when sustainability was officially linked to sport. You might answer that it was at a global sport event, such as the Winter Olympic Games in Vancouver (2010), London (2012), the FIFA World Cup of Soccer in Brazil (2014), or in Qatar (2022). Others may consider the FIA Formula E link, the electric version of the F1 Racing Championship. Extending our analysis to national and local events offers a broader range of potential answers. Despite the various choices, the critical solution involves the year 2015.

In fact, in April 2015, the UN secretary general Ban Ki-moon gave a speech about a high-level event entitled "United Action Towards Sustainable Development for All Through Sport" (Ki-moon, 2015). The UN secretary general indicated 2015 as the official year to encourage all sportsmen and women to throw their energy into advocating for the new sustainable development agenda of the UN. Specifically, the UN Office of Sport for Development and Peace (UNOSDP) delineated that the UN SDGs applied directly to sport; and further recognized that sport could impact members throughout the multiple levels within our global society. The impacts can emerge from sport disseminating universal and global messages concerning transformative and sustainable legacies for current and future generations. This ability was confirmed by the president of the International Olympic Committee, namely, Thomas Bach, when he indicated that sport had played a unique role in promoting the messages of a universal ethic with values such as fair play, respect for opponents, tolerance, and friendship (Burnett, 2015).

Therefore, sport was positioned as tool for achieving the UN sustainability goals. In September 2015, the UN members signed and launched the new Agenda of Development – replacing the renowned nine MDGs with the 17 SDGs and 169 targets in the 2030 Agenda for Sustainable Development.

Sport, was now to promote actions, engage communities, and impact individuals' lives within society (Yélamos et al., 2019). This included extending sport's influence, for example, to social inclusion, environmental sustainability, including tackling climate change risks to integrating sustainable products and services, along with promoting effective and resilient urban spaces management systems and practices (Yélamos et al., 2019). Therefore, sport organizations and bodies are positioned well to do their part by strategically reorienting their policies to promote and contribute effectively to sustainable development and encourage other groups to do the same. As stated by the UNOSDP, sport has a unique opportunity to inspire global action for sustainable development worldwide, thus confirming that sport can be a useful tool in promoting economic, social, and environmental development.

The year 2030 is approaching. Let's now examine the specific UN SDGs and their application to a sport that are to be fully implemented by the end of this decade.

As noted above, the UN officially recognized sport's role in sustainable development as an effective vehicle for translating targeted development objectives into reality and achieving tangible progress (United Nations Research Institute for Social Development, 2017; Yélamos et al., 2019). This means that the world of sport, from the grassroots to the professional levels, including the private and the public sector, can promote robust networks of partnerships and stakeholders that can share the commitment for S&SD. Further work, however, is needed to encourage those in sport to embrace and advance strategies that support sustainable development to meet the 2030 Agenda timeframe. The UN 17 SDGs offer a common framework, and sport now needs to act as a catalyst and an agent for initiating a culture for efficient and effective strategies to do their part to implement every goal. Is sport up to the task?

In the following paragraphs, the primary goals are introduced, and their application to sport is offered.

Sport and UN SDG 1: To help end poverty

The UN Research Institute for Social Development stated that it was necessary to "leave no one behind" (United Nations Research Institute for Social Development UNRISD, 2017, p. 12) and S&SD goal 1 focuses on moving people out of poverty through sport. An application of this goal involves the intentional use of sport to promote a fairer socio-economic system that respects everyone's rights to achieve a sustainable life. Sport currently has, for example, the established "Sport for Development and Peace" program that seeks to help individuals and communities reach their potential. The values taught through such programs include personal and social responsibility and team building that can aid developing economies (Martins et al., 2017; Paradia & Martin, 2012). The communication capability of sport, particularly the reach of online media (Hutchins, 2014), can also raise awareness of poverty and promote best economic growth practices (Vandermeerschen et al., 2016). Expanding and augmenting such sport programming is needed to reach the target.

Sport and UN SDG 2: To help end hunger and improve nutrition

S&SD goal 2 seeks to move people out of a state of hunger through the contribution of sport. Effective communication of sport can raise awareness on issues such as managing food resources well and where needed. Accordingly, sport venues and facilities have made an effort to reduce their waste, advocate for local and organic food consumption, and solicit food donations for local food banks (Brewer, 2021). Thus, sport can advance awareness of action to eliminate food issues in communities (Brewer, 2021). This work needs to be expanded by sport to tackle hunger, which is an issue in our local and distant communities.

Sport and UN SDG 3: To ensure active living and enhance well-being for all ages

S&SD goal 3 promotes good health and well-being throughout one's lifespan – no matter where one lives in the world. Sport has long been viewed as promoting health objectives (Edwards & Rowe, 2019; Malm et al., 2019). Further, public health efforts by sport have been considered "medicine by pinpointing how sport can be managed so that holistic health outcomes are likely achieved" (Warner, 2019, p. 38). These outcomes can encompass mental health issues, including prevention and early interventions for athletes and community members along with sexual health (Duffey et al., 2019; Liddle et al., 2017; Van Slingerland et al., 2019). Management of these issues is enhanced by creating partnerships with local health authorities and other industries and business leaders, such as fashion sport companies, pharmacological, food, and nutrition companies, to raise awareness. Successful sport-for-health partnerships have been noted as needing a "strong communication structure, building on capacity, visibility, and task management" (Hemens et al., 2019, p. 142). "Grassroots Soccer" (https://www.grassrootsoccer.org) is an example of a sport organization that uses sport (soccer or European football) to engage youth and to teach them what is necessary for a healthy and sustainable lifestyle. Expanding and augmenting active living and well-being sport programming can be utilized to reach the target.

Sport and UN SDG 4: To enhance quality education and promote life-long learning opportunities

It has been noted that "education is essential for developing human potential" (Stewart-Withers & Hapeta, 2020, para. 1), and S&SD goal 4 promotes educational learning opportunities through sport. To this end, top male and female athletes have offered powerful "stay in school" messages (Associated Press, 2016). Athletes are encouraged to do well in school as a requirement to retain eligibility to participate in sport (Dilley-Knoles et al., 2010), and in turn, many have encouraged others to do so as well. Sport also contributes to the critical learning development of leaders for today and our future (Ferkins et al., 2018). Quality education is an essential part of S&SD, as it supports one's growth at a socio-economic scale. For instance, it can eliminate poverty and teach ways to stop the adverse effects of climate change (Stewart-Withers & Hapeta, 2020). Also, S&SD can develop leaders and analytical, critical, and creative thinking to improve outcomes as we tackle our world's issues. To this end, McCullough and Orr (2020) have encouraged a subdivision within sport management education; that of sport ecology.

Sport and UN SDG 5: To achieve gender equality and empower all women and girls

S&SD goal 5 promotes equality for girls and women around the world and this can be accomplished within sport and through sport. S&SD can influence such equality with respect for – and illustrating the value of – girls and women by ensuring their opportunities and inclusion in sport (Harmon, 2020), including the transgender person. Further, sport-based programs developed by schools and universities or colleges in partnership with sport teams and organizations can empower girls relative to developing soft and hard skills and advance a network that can be applied and enhanced once in the workplace (Zeimers et al., 2019). This type of support provides lessons learned concerning gender equity transferable from sport into global societies and cultural norms (Triantafyllidis & Darvin, 2021). Sport can, thus, aid in illustrating life with equity.

Sport and UN SDG 6: To ensure availability and sustainable management of water and sanitation for all

Goal 6 deals with water as an essential limited resource with many geo–socio-economic implications. As with all organizations and industries, sport needs to do its part to manage water resources efficiently and effectively to safeguard them for today and into the future. Researchers have started to examine water quality in connection with athlete health (Eisenberg et al., 2016; Harder-Lauridsen et al., 2013) and water management in sport (Phillips & Turner, 2014). Further, sport facility managers have contributed to potential solutions to the water issue with actions such as low water volume toilets and low flow showers (Mallen & Chard, 2011) and using technology to irrigate grass fields efficiently (Mallen & Dingle, 2017). Significantly, sport and sport facilities can further contribute by ensuring all plastics used are biodegradable alternatives for food and beverage distribution, as plastics can end up in our world waterways (Watkin et al., 2021). Expanding and augmenting actions in sport to further safeguard water resources are needed to reach the target.

Sport and UN SDG 7: To ensure access to affordable, reliable, sustainable, and modern energy for all

Goal 7 focuses on renewable energy. An application of S&Sd to this goal involves a current trend whereby sport infrastructures promote new organizational models that adopt clean, renewable energy or the purchase of off-site renewable energy (Chard & Mallen, 2013). Further, examples can be found whereby sport shares renewable energy with their local community on dates when a sport event is not being held (Wentworth, 2018). The communication of these initiatives, and others by the sport facility promotes extending such renewable use in action within communities. More needs to be accomplished to reach the target goal.

Sport and UN SDG 8: To promote sustained, inclusive, and sustainable economic growth, full and productive employment, and decent work for all

Goal 8 promotes offering economic growth opportunities and decent employment to the many actors worldwide – including those in the sport industry. Sport needs to ensure decent work is provided by embedding appropriate sport policies in contracts, such as those for sourcing and suppliers. Significantly, sport can promote gender equity, the elimination of child labor, and align all warranties with fair labor standards. Sport tourism and events can create jobs and boost local cultures and product networks and the local workforce's engagement and training of volunteers, encouraging their participation in society, community engagement. Further advances that ensure decent work for all in the sport industry are needed to meet the target.

Sport and UN SDG 9: To build resilient infrastructure, to promote inclusive and sustainable industrialization, and to foster innovation

An applicaiton of S&SD and goal 9 pushes for an expansive array of employment opportunities, the modernization of infrastructures, nurturing innovations to fruition that advance the gross domestic product, along with an increase in supportive scientific research for newly developed endeavors. For instance, one infrastructure issue is that only 10% of the world population has access to a reliable and clean source of drinking water; another is that many do not have access to a reliable source of electricity (World Bank Data, 2020). A further issue involves communication capabilities. Notably, almost everyone in the world lives in an area with mobile phone coverage, and 96.5% has at least second-generation technology, but that still leaves many behind (UN SDG Compliance Progress Report, 2020). Resolving these and other infrastructure issues are essential for the sustainability of our societies (World Bank Data, 2020). S&SD can aid in improving these areas with the use of advanced technology within sport that advances innovation and jobs, such as in sporting footwear, clothing, equipment, and timing technology. Sport needs to ensure that the advancement of such elements of sustainability are embedded within its activities worldwide and assists world societies in also advancing their infrastructures.

Sport and UN SDG 10: Reduce inequity within and among countries

Goal 10 promotes reducing inequalities worldwide. Reducing inequalities is necessary because revoking one's rights has "had starkly inhumane consequences for minority groups and displaced peoples across the world" (Caudwell & McGee, 2018, p. 1). Such inequalities can be noted in the distribution of the pandemic vaccine and climate change impacts around the world (Brewer, 2021). Over time, sport has served to promote human rights (Caudwell & McGee, 2018; Donnelly, 2008), such as those examined by Kidd and Donnelly (2008), including such rights within sport, including athletes' rights, along with rights within communities such as efforts toward eradicating apartheid. Overall, S&SD can push for social change within sport and society (Frey & Eitzen, 1991).

Sport and UN SDG 11: Make cities and human settlements inclusive, safe, resilent, and sustainable

Goal 11 relates to safe and sustainable living, and S&SD can aid in this development. Examinations of sport can reveal inequities within society and then reduce such disparities within sport. This action can show communities how to eradicate inequities within cultures and society as a whole (Triantafyllidis & Darvin, 2021). Accordingly, sport can be a leader for ensuring fairness and equity for all, enacting a system for promoting safety in local communities and cities, promoting resilience during times of change, and acting sustainably. Further, sport is an excellent forum for protests concerning issues relating to inequality, such as diversity and inclusion. For example, sport can inspire the world to recognize diversity and enable local actors to improve institutional arrangements that allow them to follow suit. A recent example relates to protests for "Black Lives Matter" led by those in sport and conducted worldwide in 2020 (see https://www.cnn.com/2020/08/27/world/gallery/sports-protests/index.html). Such protests sought to bring awareness and an end to racism. Sport and its infrastructure must continue to promote sustainable healthy community settlements for all.

Sport and UN SDG 12: To ensure sustainable consumption and production patterns

Goal 12 encourages sustainable production and consumption and this can be achieved in sport and also through sport to become embedded within society. Sport has begun to raise awareness and influence stakeholders such as spectators

(Casper et al., 2020), sport event participants, sport tourists, local organizing bodies, committees, municipalities, and so forth to work together for sustainable consumption and production (Mallen & Chard, 2012). The advance of partnerships has been promoted to advance understandings of the issues and set strategies for encouraging sustainable practices (Watkin et al., 2021). Encouragement to adapt to sustainable consumption patterns has started to illuminate what exactly needs to be adjusted concerning our actions (Triantafyllidis & Darvin, 2021). However, more can be done to ensure that consistent product and sustainability standards are entrenched in all contracts and actions and sport must continue to act to generate continuous achievements in this area.

Sport and UN SDG 13: To take urgent action to combat climate change and its impacts

Goal 13 asks for action to mitigate and manage the impacts of climate change and this can be aided with the assistance of S&SD. Sport has made strides such as developing an understanding of the climatic impacts on sport (Dingle & Stewart, 2018; Dingle & Mallen, 2020) and efforts on reducing greenhouse gas emissions in sport equipment production and sport team traveling (Triantafyllidis, 2018). However, additional strides are needed to embed standards that encompass the advancement of green chemistry that provides environmental solutions or alternatives and life cycle thinking that considers production from the beginning to the end of life of every product (Iles, 2008). Further, standards for urgent action and established goals, targets, measurement strategies, reporting, monitoring, and accountability are needed. Therefore, sport must move quickly to stop the smattering of efforts to implement a comprehensive strategy that ensures working\ to combat climate change is fully realized.

Sport and UN SDG 14: To conserve and sustainably use the oceans, seas, and marine resources for sustainable development

Goal 14 involves our natural resources and McCullough and Orr (2020) have indicated that there is a "bidirectional" (p. 509) relationship between sport and these resources. This goal has direct linkages to goal 6 for safeguarding water resources and goal 13 to combat climate change. Goal 14 is aligned with S&SD as communication campaigns, and the introduction of technical solutions can promote safeguarding biodiversity in the oceans and marine protection. Sport can play a significant role in reducing impacts on these resources and can show the world the progress that can be made.

Sport and UN SDG 15: To protect, restore, and promote sustainable use of terrestrial ecosystems, sustainably manage forests, combat desertification, and halt and reverse land degradation and halt biodiversity loss

Goal 15 seeks to contribute by emphasizing a need for sustainable land and forest management, including biodiversity. The health of our ecology is foundational for sport and life into the future. Sports use of such resources needs to position our ecological future as a priority. Much work needs to be completed to ensure that the ecology is safeguarded through sport by being integrated within every policy and action. These safeguards are needed immediately as the destruction of our ecology is ongoing.

Sport and UN SDG 16: Promote peaceful and inclusive societies for sustainable development, provide access to justice for all, and build effective, accountable, and inclusive institutions at all levels

Goal 16 promotes justice within society, and S&SD has a role in promoting a framework for ensuring justice, including cooperation and peace throughout the world. For decades, examples of sport being used for advancing peace have been illustrated. There has been a rise in sport organizations promoting justice, such as, "Peace Players International" (https://www.peaceplayers.org/) that has a motto of "Play Together Live Together" and works to break down the barriers between communities by engaging youth to work toward peaceful living. Another organization, "Right to Play" (https://www.righttoplay.ca/en-ca/), focuses on children and their rights to play/participate in sport and the advance of inclusive, sustainable communities. Organizations such as these examples use sport to promote peace-building by advancing understanding between communities and nations, preventing conflict, and resolving issues in post-conflict situations. Bringing people together is critical for inclusive and just communities, and their institutions and sport need to continue to work to aid in this area.

Sport and UN SDG 17: To strengthen the means of implementation and revitalize the global partnership for sustainable development

Reaching goal 17 can be encouraged through S&SD that can aid in developing guidelines and frameworks to help policymakers, regulators, sport bodies and organizations, sport teams, and related industries work together to achieve the shared goals of sustainable development. In terms of targets and good practices, this goal requires sport to develop effective networks for partnerships and programs at the local, regional, national, and global levels. Much work is needed in sport to reach the capacity for this goal.

Concluding remarks

1. Sport has been recognized as a fundamental and strategic enabler for sustainable development at the UN level since 2015
2. Since introducing the 2030 Agenda, and the related 17 SDGs, governments, private organizations, and citizens are asked to immediately coordinate responsive action. Sport too must do their part to achieve these goals
3. An application of the main goals of the 2030 Agenda shows the influential role of sport as a catalyst agent and initiator of efficient and effective sustainability programs that can positively impact sectors, industries, territories, and even distant communities at multiple scales
4. This role of S&SD extends to a vast array of initiatives from impacting economic growth, social development with gender equity, and a reduction in inequities, sustainable infrastructure, safeguards for our natural resources, sustainable production and consumption, and so forth. It is a complex role for sport
5. Managers in sport organizations are essential in ensuring the transition toward sustainability of their organizations, fields, and sectors. Much work is needed to meet the UN goals through sport

Future directions

1. Recent trends in sport-related and supporting industries such as sport events, sport fashion, and food/nutrition show that future investments in responsible programs and projects will ask for a specific mindset and culture for supporting sustainable development
2. Innovative sport organizations are developing solutions based on a mix of new technologies with sustainable business models
3. Exciting trends to follow will include how sport will open new opportunities through innovative sport organizations that support the UN goals for sustainable development

Review questions

1. What is the primary purpose of S&SD?
2. How does S&SD link with the UN SDGs?
3. What is the difference between S&SD across the two stages of sustainable development: SDoS and S4SD?
4. Please explain how S&SD goals can contribute to global sustainability and provide specific examples of such contributions.
5. What are the challenges and the opportunities of S&SD in orienting sustainability outcomes and aligning with the 17 UN SDGs?
6. What do you think are the potential future performance and outcomes from S&SD?

7. Please write three strategies for implementing S&SD in your community and provide two tactics for implmenting each strategy.

Discussion questions

1. When did sport become globally recognized as a strategic sustainability driver for change?
2. What are the main SDGs that apply to the world of sport and why?
3. Is it possible to describe the role of sport for sustainability and sustainable development according to a priority list of the main SDGs?
4. What are the central SDGs in terms of the sustainable use of natural resources? What are the best practices in the world of sport to positively contribute toward these sustainability outcomes?
5. What is the contribution of sport in making the right investments to support human capital and human rights?
6. What are the main challenges and opportunities managers have in transitioning sport organizations for sustainability?

Learning activities

1. Imagine having the opportunity to interview the president of your National Olympic Committee: In small groups, prepare a list of 3–5 questions that relate to at least two SDGs that are relevant in your country or community
2. Draw a square for each of the 17 SDGs and fill in each box with a minimum of three positive actions/programs that sport has, or could develop at the national level to fulfil each goal, then discuss future opportunities, and the developmental challenges concerning implementation (In the alternative, change the scale of analysis to the community level)
3. After selecting a local sports team, develop a questionnaire to ask their supporters what they think about possible innovative ways this team can be engaged in the setting and implementing sustainability program that aids the community
4. Consider "what could be." Using augmented reality, build your scenario of what sport in your community would look like if the 17 SDGs were fully implemented. What changes would you see? What policy and actions are needed to reach such a scenario?
5. Consider the role of sport leadership in your community today. Should they be tasked with advancing the 17 SDGs within sport, or should another body be developed that works explicitly to help sport transition to the leading path for global sustainability? Additionally, who is responsible for measuring and monitoring progress and pushing to ensure full implementation?

Further reading

- European Circular Economy Stakeholder Platform. https://circulareconomy. europa.eu/platform/en/sector/culture-sports-and-leisure-activities
- World Economic Forum. (2019). *Four ways sport events are becoming more sustainable.* Available from https://www.weforum.org/agenda/2019/11/ sustainable-sport-olympics-showjumping-zero-waste-superbowl/
- Olympic Games. https://www.olympic.org/sustainability-essentials
- Green Sports Alliance. https://greensportsalliance.org/wp-content/uploads/2 019/02/Report-PlayingforOurPlanetFINAL-2018-05-02.pdf.

Relevant online resources

- The 17 SDGs: https://sdgs.un.org/goals
- The 2030 Agenda: https://sdgs.un.org/2030agenda
- Ellen MacArthur Foundation: Circular economy in sport https://www.facebook. com/watch/live/?v=692822911462926&ref=watch_permalink
- Startup Bootcamp: https://www.startupbootcamp.org/blog/2018/10/driving-innovation-3-0-advance-sustainable-development-goals/
- Cortina 2021 World Ski Championships: https://www.cortina2021.com/en/ short-supply-chains-circular-economy-and-big-data-a-more-crisis-resistant-mountain-sport-system-invests-in-innovation-and-sustainability/
- IFCPF: https://www.ifcpf.com/sustainability

References

Associated Press. (2016, October 29). *Abdul-Jabbar visits Harvard, tells players to stay in school.* USA Today. Retrieved from https://www.usatoday.com/story/sports/ncaab/2016/1 0/29/abdul-jabbar-visits-harvard-tells-players-to-stay-in-school/92964592

Bach, T. (2015). Remarks on the occasion of the adoption of the UN Sustainable Development Goals. UN Sustainable Development Summit. International Olympic Committee. Retrieved from https://www.olympic.org/

Balci, V., & Erdeveciler, O. (2017). Some sport managers' views about valued education through sport. *Journal of Education and Training Studies, 5*(5), 197–203. Retrieved from https://files.eric.ed.gov/fulltext/EJ1141384.pdf

Brewer, J. (2021, May). Using sport to end hunger and achieve food security. *United Nations Chronicle.* Retrieved from https://www.un.org/en/chronicle/article/using-sport-end-hunger-and-achieve-food-security

Brundtland Commission.(2001).Climate change 2001: Impacts, adaptation, and vulner-ability. In McCarthy, J.J., Canziani, O.F., Leary, N.A., Dokken, D.J. & White, K.S. (Eds.), Contributions of working group II to the third assessment report of the inter-governmental panel on climate change. Cambridge: Cambridge University Press. Weblink: https://www.ipcc.ch/report/ar3/wg2/

Burnett, D. (2015). The Olympic Movement, the United Nations and the pursuit of common ideals. Retrieved from https://www.un.org/en/chronicle/article/olympic-movement-united-nations-and-pursuit-common-ideals

Casper, J., McCullough, B., & Pfahl, M. (2020). Examining environmental fan engagement initiatives through values and norms with intercollegiate sports fans. *Sport Management Review*, *23*(2), 348–360. 10.1016/j.smr.2019.03.005

Caudwell, J., & McGee, D. (2018). From promotion to protection: Human rights and events, leisure and sport. *Leisure Studies*, *37*(1), 1–10. 10.1080/02614367.2017.1420814

Chard, C., & Mallen, C. (2013). Renewable energy initiatives at Canadian sport stadiums: A content analysis of web-site communications. *Sustainability*, *5*(12), 5119–5134. 10.33 90/su5125119

Dilley-Knoles, J., Burnett, J., & Peak, K. (2010, January). Making the grade: Academic success in today's athlete. *The Sport Journal*, *13*(1), 6. Retrieved from https://thesportjournal.org/article/making-the-grade/

Dingle, G., & Mallen, C. (2020). Community sports fields and atmospheric climatic impacts: Australian and Canadian perspectives. *Managing Sport and Leisure*,*26*(4), 301–325. 1 0.1080/23750472.2020.1766375

Dingle, G., & Stewart, B. (2018). Playing the climate game: Climate change impacts, resilience, and adaptation in the climate-dependent sport sector. *Managing Sport and Leisure*, *23*(406), 293–414. 10.1080/23750472.2018.1527715

Donnelly, P. (2008). Sport and human rights. *Sport in Society*, *11*(4), 381–394. 10.1080/1 7430430802019326

Duffey, K., Zulu, J., Asamoah, B., & Agardhi, A. (2019). A cross-sectional study of sexual health knowledge, attitudes, and reported behavior among Zambian adolescent girl participants in a football program. *Journal of Sport for Development*, *7*(12), 46–58. Retrieved from https://jsfd.org/

Edwards, M., & Rowe, K. (2019). Managing sport for health: An introduction to the special issue. *Sport Management Review*, *22*(10), 1–4. 10.1016/j.smr.2018.12.006

Eisenberg, J., Bartram, J., & Wade, T. (2016). The water quality in Rio highlights the global public health concern over untreated sewage. *Environmental Health Perspectives*, *124*(10), A180–A181. 10.1289/EHP662

Ellen MacArthur Foundation. (2016). *Intelligent Assets: Unlocking the circular economy potential*. Retrieved from https://www.ellenmacarthurfoundation.org/assets/downloads/publications/EllenMacArthurFoundation_Intelligent_Assets_030216.pdf

Ellen MacArthur Foundation. (2019). Completing the picture: How the circular economy tackles climate change. www.ellenmacarthurfoundation.org/publications

Ferkins, L., Skiller, J., & Swanson, S. (2018). Sport leadership: A new generation of thinking. *Journal of Sport Management*, *32*(2), 77–81. 10.1123/jsm.2018-0054

Frey, J., & Eitzen, D. (1991). Sport and society. *Annual Review of Sociology*, *17*(1), 503–522. 10.1146/annurev.so.17.080191.002443

Harder-Lauridsen, N., Kuhn, K., Erichsen, A., Mølbak, K., & Etheberg, S. (2013). Gastrointestinal illness among triathletes swimming in non-polluted versus polluted seawater affected by heavy rainfall, Denmark 2010-2011. *PLOS One*, 1–9. https://journals.plos.org/plosone/article?id=10.1371/journal.pone.0078371

Harmon, S. (2020). Gender inclusivity in sport? From value to values to actions to equality for Canadian athletes. *Journal of Sport Management*, *12*(2), 255–268. 10.1080/19406940.2 019.1680415

Hemens, N., Verkooijen, K., & Koelen, M. (2019). Associations between partnership characteristics and perceived success in Dutch sport-for-health partnerships. *Sport Management Review*, *22*(1), 142–152. 10.1016/j.smr.2018.06.008

Hutchins, B. (2014). Sport on the move: The unfolding impact of mobile communications on the media sport content economy. *Journal of Sport and Social Issues, 38*(6), 509–527. 10.1177/019323512458933

Iles, A. (2008). Shifting to green chemistry: The need for innovations in sustainability marketing. *Business Strategy and the Environment, 17*(8), 524–535. 10.1002/bse.547

International Olympic Committee (IOC). (n.d.). *Gender equity in sport.* Retrieved from https://www.olympic.org/gender-equality

Kidd, B., & Donnelly, P. Human rights in sport. *International Review for the Sociology of Sport, 35*(2), 131–148. 10.1177%2F101269000035002001

Ki-Moon, Ban. (2015, April 15). *Remarks at a high-level event entitled "United action toward sustainable development for all through sport."* Retrieved from https://www.un.org/sg/en/content/sg/speeches/2015-04-15/remarks-high-level-event-entitled-united-action-to-wards-sustainable

Leal Filho, W., Tripathi, S.K., Andrade Guerra, J.B.S.O.D., Giné-Garriga, R., Orlovic Lovren, V., & Willats, J. (2019). Using the sustainable development goals towards a better understanding of sustainability challenges. *International Journal of Sustainable Development & World Ecology, 26*(2), 179–190. 10.1080/13504509.2018.1505674

Lemke, W. (n.d.). The role of sport in achieving the sustainable development goals. *UN Chronicle.* Retrieved from https://www.un.org/en/chronicle/article/role-sport-achieving-sustainable-development-goals

Liddle, S., Deane, F., & Vella, S. (2017). Addressing mental health through sport: A review of sporting organizations websites. *Early Intervention in Psychiatry, 11*(2), 93–103. 10.1111/epi.12337

Macovei, S., Tufan, A., & Vulpe, B. (2014). Theoretical Approaches to Building a Healthy Lifestyle through the Practice of Physical Activities. *Procedia - Social and Behavioral Sciences, 117*(19), 86–91. https://doi .org/10.1016/j.sbspro.2014.02.183

Mallen, C., & Chard, C. (2011). A framework for debating the future of environmental sustainability in the Sport Academy. *Sport Management Review, 14*(4), 424–433. 10.101 6/j.smr.2011.10.001

Mallen, C., & Chard, C. (2012). "What could be" in Canadian sport facility environmental sustainability. *Sport Management Review, 15*(2), 230–243. 10.1016/j.smr.2011.10.001

Mallen, C., & Dingle, G. (2017). Climate change and community grass-based sport fields. *International Journal of Environmental Sustainability, 13*(2), 45–59. 10.18848/2325-1077/CGP/v13i02

Malm, C., Jakobsson, J., & Isaksson, H. (2019). Physical activity and sports – real health benefits: A review with insight into the public health of Sweden. *Sports (Basel), 7*(5), 127. 10.3390%2Fsports7050127

Martins, P. Rosado, A., Ferreira, V., & Biscaiá, R. (2017). Personal and social responsibility among athletes: The role of self-determination achievement goals and engagement. *Journal of Human Kinetics, 57*(1), 39–50. 10.1515%2Fhukin-2017-0045

McCullough, B.,Orr, M.& Kellison, T. (2020). Sport ecology: Conceptualizing an emerging subdiscipline within sport management. *Journal of Sport Management, 34*(6), 509–520. 10.1123/jsm.2019-0294

Millington, R., Giles, A.R., van Luijk, N., & Hayhurst, L.M. (2021). Sport for sustainability? The extractives industry, sport, and sustainable development. *Journal of Sport and Social Issues.* 10.1177%2F0193723521991413

O'Neal, S. (2013, January). *Shaq against age of one-and-done.* Retrieved from https://www.espn.com/mens-college-basketball/story/_/id/8851071/shaquille-oneal-says-players-stay-school-least-three-years

Paradia, K., & Martin, L. (2012). Team building in sport: Linking theory and research to practical application. *Journal of Sport Psychology in Action, 3*(3), 159–170. 10.1080/2152 0704.2011.653047

Phillips, P., & Turner, P. (2014). Water management in sport. *Sport Management Review, 17*(3), 376–389. 10.1016/j.smr.2013.08.002

Sachs, J.D. (2015). *The age of sustainable development.* New York City, New York, USA: Columbia University Press. Retrieved from http://cup.columbia.edu/book/the-age-of-sustainable-development/9780231173155

Schulenkorf, N. (2012). Sustainable community development through sport and events: A conceptual framework for Sport-for-Development projects. *Sport Management Review, 15*(1), 1–12. 10.1016/j.smr.2011.06.001.

Shen, L.Y., Tam, V.W., Tam, L., & Ji, Y.B. (2010). Project feasibility study: The key to the successful implementation of sustainable and socially responsible construction management practice. *Journal of cleaner production, 18*(3), 254–259. 10.1016/j.jclepro.2009.10.014

Stewart-Withers, R., & Hapeta, J. (2020). An examination of an Aotearoa/New Zealand plus-sport education partnership using livelihoods and capital analysis. *Journal of Sport for Development, 8*(15), 50–65. Retrieved from https://jsfd.org

Sustainable Development Goals Fund. (2018). *The Contribution of Sports to the achievement of the sustainable development goals: A toolkit for action.* Geneva: UN Sustainable Development Goals Fund.

Szathmári, A., & Kocsis, T. (2020). Who cares about gladiators? An elite-sport-based concept of Sustainable Sport. *Sport in Society,* 1–19. .10.1080/17430437.2020.1832470

Taleb, N. (2012). *Antifragile: Things that gain from disorder* (Vol. 3). Random House Incorporated.

Triantafyllidis, S. (2018). Carbon dioxide emissions research and sustainable transportation in the sports industry. *C—Journal of Carbon Research, 4*(4), 57. 10.3390/c4040057

Triantafyllidis, S., & Darvin, L. (2021). Mass-participant sport events and sustainable development: Gender, social bonding, and connectedness to nature as predictors of socially and environmentally responsible behavior intentions. *Sustainable Science, 16*(5), 239–253. 10.1007/s11625-020-00867-x

The World Bank Data. (2020) Accessto electricity(% of population). Retrieved from https://data.worldbank.org/indicator/EG.ELC.ACCS.ZS

United Nations (UN). (2020) The sustainable development goals report 2020. Retrieved from https://unstats.un.org/sdgs/report/2020/The-Sustainable-Development-Goals-Report-2020.pdf

United Nations. (2021, April). *Transforming our world: The 2030 Agenda for Sustainable Development.* Retrieved from https://sdgs.un.org/2030agenda

United Nations Global Compact (UNGC). (2020). Reporting on the SDGs. Action Platform. https://www.unglobalcompact.org/take-action/action-platforms/sdg-reporting

United Nations Office of Sport for Development and Peace (UNOSDP). (n.d.). Sport and the sustainable development goals: An overview outlining the contribution of sport to the SDGs. Retrieved from https://www.un.org/sport/sites/www.un.org.sport/files/ckfiles/files/Sport_for_SDGs_finalversion9.pdf

United Nations Research Institute for Social Development (UNRISD). (2017). Global trends: Challenges and opportunities in the implementation of the Sustainable Development Goals. Retrieved from https://www.undp.org/content/undp/en/home/librarypage/sustainable-development-goals/global-trends--challenges-and-opportunities-in-the-implementatio.html

University of California Los Angeles (UCLA). (2021). *What is sustainability?* Retrieved from https://www.sustain.ucla.edu/what-is-sustainability/

Vandermeerschen, H., Meganck, J., Seghers, J., & Vos, S. (2016). Sports, poverty and the role of the voluntary sector. Exploring and explaining nonprofit sports clubs' efforts to facilitate participation of socially disadvantaged people. *International Journal of Voluntary and Non-profit Organizations, 28*(1), 307–334. 10.1007/s11266-016-9799-8

Van Slingerland, K., Durant-Bush, N., Bradley, L., et al. (2019). Canadian Centre for Mental Health and Sport (CCMHS) position statement: Principles of mental health incompetitive and high-performance sport. *Clinical Journal of Sport Medicine, 29*(3), 173–180. Retrieved from https://journals.lww.com/cjsportsmed/Fulltext/2019/05000/Canadian_Centre_for_Mental_Health_and_Sport.1.aspx

Warner, S. (2019). Sport as medicine: How F3 is building healthier men and communities. *Sport Management Review, 22*(1), 38–52. 10.1016/j.smr.2018.06.006

Watkin, G., Mallen, C., & Hyatt, C. (2021). Management perspectives: Implications of plastics-free sport facilities' beverage service. *Journal of Management and Sustainability, 11*(1), 1–14. Retrieved from https://dr.library.brocku.ca/handle/10464/14984

Wentworth, A. (2018, July 2). *Amsterdam Arena installs central new battery storage.* Retrieved from https://www.climateaction.org/news/amsterdam-arena-installs-major-new-battery-storage

Yélamos, G., Carty, C., & Clardy, A. (2019). Sport: A driver of sustainable development, promoter of human rights, and vehicle for health and well-being for all. *Sport, Business and Management: An International Journal, 9*(4), 315–327. 10.1108/SBM-10-2018-0090

Zeimers, G., Anagnostopoulos, C., Zintz, T., & Willem, A. (2019). Examining Collaboration Among Nonprofit Organizations for Social Responsibility Programs. *Nonprofit and Voluntary Sector Quarterly, 48*(5), 953–974. https://doi.org/10.1177/0899764019837616

PART II

Sport and sustainable development perspectives

5

THE PERSONAL PERSPECTIVE OF SPORT AND SUSTAINABLE DEVELOPMENT

Stavros Triantafyllidis

LEARNING OBJECTIVES

Upon completion of this chapter, learners should be able to successfully:

1. Define the personal perspective of sport and sustainable development (S&SD)
2. Identify and describe the concepts of active/healthy living, sustainable living, and quality education
3. Examine the relationship between active/healthy, sustainable living, and quality education for cultivating a sustainable lifestyle through sport (SLTS)
4. Discuss the positive outcomes of an SLTS
5. Illustrate the similarities and differences of the two stages; sustainable development of sport (SDoS) and sport for sustainable development (S4SD), from the personal perspective of S&SD
6. Encourage learners to create a five-year SLTS plan for yourself

Overview

This chapter presents the personal perspective of S&SD, including the two stages – the SDoS and S4SD. According to self-determination theory (SDT), the development of the individual is enhanced through their psychological needs for performance and well-

DOI: 10.4324/9781003128953-5

being, and both can be achieved through sport. In the discussion below, SDoS relates to the assurance that sport is available over the long term as a forum for personal development. Meanwhile, S4SD involves developing the individual that, collectively, contributes to the long-term sustainability of our local and global societies. Macovei et al. (2014) indicated that "the development of a healthy lifestyle should be one of the priorities of the family, school, and society at large" (p. 86). Additionally, it is supported by the personal construct theory (whereby individuals need to learn about themselves, including their emotions and interconnections) that can also be developed through sport. Further, there is a link to a quality education that supports understanding one's needs and valuing one's health.

S&SD aims to cultivate an active/healthy, and sustainable lifestyle. Such a lifestyle includes developing habits that support one's welfare, including one's psychological development encompassing an individual's emotional and behavioral development and interconnections, along with their cognitive development. Importantly, this lifestyle includes a healthy local economy and natural environment contributing to personal and societal sustainability.

Glossary

Active/healthy living

This term refers to the person's behavioral outcomes from an active lifestyle, including physical activity and active sport participation linked with achieving better health levels, promoting well-being, and improving one's quality of life (Calogiuri & Chroni, 2014; Macovei et al., 2014).

Analytical concept

This concept reflects the thought process whereby a person can identify and define problems, collect information, and develop solutions for issues (Amer, 2005). An applicaiton of the analytical concept aims to test and verify the cause of the problem and develop solutions to resolve the issues identified (Amer, 2005).

Creative thinking

A person's ability to view ideas or concepts and discover new alternatives that solve problems (Mumford et al., 2013).

Critical thinking

A disciplined thought process includes active and skillful conceptualization, application, analysis, synthesis, and evaluation based on information provision (Fisher, 2011).

Normative concept

An application of the normative concept involves using sport as a platform "to view the world by defining the objectives of a well-functioning society that delivers well-being for its global citizens today and for future generations. The normative concept urges us to have a universal vision towards a good society" (Sachs, 2015, p. 11).

Quality education

An education that liberates the intellect, unlocks the imagination and is fundamental for self-respect (United Nations Sustainable Development Goal 4, 2021). Further, such education is noted as "purposeful, transformative, exceptional, and accountable" (Schindler et al., 2015, p. 7).

Self-education (autodidacticism)

One's education without the guidelines of a teacher or institution where a person chooses the subject one wants to study, the materials, along with the pace, space, and time for studying (Gadamer, 2001).

Sport

"Sport means all forms of physical activity which, through casual or organized participation, aim at expressing or improving physical fitness and well-being, forming social relationships or obtaining results in competition at all levels" (Szathmári & Kocsis, 2020, p. 4).

Sport and sustainable development (S&SD)

S&SD is the process that includes two stages: SDoS and S4SD that, together, enhance the development that meets the needs of current generations without compromising future generations' ability to meet their own needs at the personal, social, economic, ecological, technological, and political levels (Millington et al., 2021; Szathmári & Kocsis, 2020; Triantafyllidis & Darvin, 2021).

Sport for sustainable development (S4SD)

S4SD refers to the contribution of sport to our global societies' viability by encouraging sustainability across the six perspectives of personal, social, economic, ecological, technological, and political worldwide (Macovei et al., 2014; Millington et al., 2021; Schulenkorf, 2012).

Sustainable living

A person's lifestyle includes habits such as supporting one's own psychological needs, cognitive development, education, and the collective welfare generated with a healthy local economy, along with the protection of natural environmental resources that support healthy individuals, the economy, and society (Cubukcu, 2013).

Sustainability

The term refers to "the integration of environmental health, social equity, and economic vitality to create thriving, healthy, diverse and resilient communities for this generation and generations to come" (University of California Los Angeles, 2021, para. 2).

The term sustainable development (SD) encompasses the initiatives and progress in pursuit of sustainability. According to the Brundtland Commission (2001), sustainable development is defined as the "development that meets the needs of the present without compromising the ability of future generations to meet their own needs" (p. 82). This includes "the narrow notion of physical sustainability [that] implies a concern for social equity between generations, a concern that must logically be extended to equity within each generation" (p. 82).

Sustainable lifestyle through sport

This text defines a sustainable lifestyle through sport (STLS) as one's cognitive, emotional, and behavioral development being aided through sport participation. Values underscoring this type of lifestyle include self-enhancement (hedonism, achievement, and one's power), self-transcendence (benevolence and altruism, universalism and environmentalism), and an openness to change (self-direction and stimulation) that reflect respectively on its active and sustainable living levels (Cubukcu, 2013; Schwartz, 1992). These values can influence how one eats, periods of sleep, participates in active living, consumes, safeguards the natural environment, and overall, establishes personal lifestyle goals for oneself's healthy sustainability.

Sustainable development of sport (SDoS)

SDoS refers to the sustainable practices taken by sport regarding the management of sport products, services, and sport consumer behaviors to achieve sustainability within the world of sport that encompasses six perspectives, including the personal, social, economic, ecological, technological, and political (McCullough et al., 2020; Szathmári & Kocsis, 2020; Triantafyllidis & Darvin, 2021).

Defining and explaining the personal perspective of S&SD

Our world has been impacted by the coronavirus (Covid-19) pandemic (Chinazzi et al., 2020). According to the World Health Organization (WHO), the Covid-19 pandemic spread worldwide and hundreds of millions of cases have been confirmed with 3.5 million deaths to date (World Health Organization, 2021). The following link will present the current numbers for the updated cases and deaths as you click it (https://covid19.who.int). The WHO identified Covid-19 as a global pandemic and highlighted that the risk of spreading the virus could be significantly enhanced with social gatherings (World Health Organization, 2021). Therefore, local, national, and international authorities urged the development of new policies to control the virus's spread, such as social distancing and stay-at-home initiatives (World Health Organization, 2021). Government-mandated pandemic lockdown orders and social distancing restrictions have resulted in quarantine social isolation, which created a new challenge for every person on the planet concerning self-management and the self-regulation of their everyday habits. Given the new social norm experienced through the Covid-19 era, this chapter promotes the importance of an active/healthy and SLTS (including physical activity and exercise) for its physical and mental health benefits. To begin, we examine the theoretical frameworks that underscore such a lifestyle.

Theoretical frameworks

Two theories frame our discussion, the self-determination theory and personal construct theory. First, self-determination theory indicates that individuals have "innate psychological needs for competence, autonomy, and relatedness" (Deci & Ryan, 2000, p. 227) that they pursue "to satisfy their [psychological] basic needs [that] influences development, performance, and well-being" (Deci & Ryan, 2000, p. 263). Accordingly, sport offers a forum for the sustainable development of one's personal basic needs (Triantafyllidis & Kaplanidou, 2019). In addition, many personal attributes can be developed through sport, and these traits include, but are not restricted to, developing one's health and fitness (Macovei et al., 2014); building self-confidence (Gould & Carson, 2008); learning cognitive skills (Holt et al., 2020); advancing one's fortitude and resilience (Fletcher & Sarkar, 2016); resourcefulness; commitment (Scanlan et al., 1993); work ethic; dedication; the pursuit of personal excellence; self-respect; learning to set goals and to work toward them; developing a sense of pride and self-esteem; integrity; courage; perseverance (Triantafyllidis & Kaplanidou, 2019); and so forth. The S4SD stage for the personal perspective, therefore, empowers one to have an active lifestyle that is part of proactive self-care and preservation, self-growth and vitality, along with self-love.

Second, the personal construct theory purports that individuals piece together their perspectives concerning how the world works (Kelly, 1970). Notably, "people differ in their construing, despite also showing some commonalities" (Winter & Reed, 2020, para. 13). Applying this theory to sport reveals a microcosm of society (Frey & Eitzen, 1991). Sport, thus, plays a role that provides individuals with a forum for learning about themselves, their health, nutrition, and exercise, and how to be proactive on social and environmental issues within society (Kelly, 1970; Winter & Reed, 2020). An application of the personal construct theory at the personal perspective of S&SD is comprised of the intentional use of sport to learn to predict or anticipate outcomes, undergo a variety of emotions and connections, as well as to develop strategies to manage emotions and cope with situations (Winter & Reed, 2020). Also, the personal construct theory offers people the opportunity to optimize their openness to change, self-enhancement, and self-transcendence values and make a personal contribution to a group of people (Weiss, 1996). Personal construct theory links to the quality education concept because people share values, attain cultural awareness and morals, develop a sense of inclusion, build trust and loyalty, and respect themselves and others. Additionally, a quality education underscores an active/healthy and sustainable lifestyle. Such education is now outlined.

The value of education in the personal perspective of S&SD

At the personal level, in the pandemic-infused era in which we live, instructional guidance for learning and teaching online can optimize the perspective of self-education in combination with formal education. Achieving a quality education can be an effective solution for the challenges we face worldwide. There is an interconnection between such an education and active/healthy and sustainable living concepts. Quality education has such an essential part to play within the personal perspective of S&SD because it allows people to grow at the socio-economic scale (Lawson, 2005). This type of growth can, for example, help eliminate poverty, develop people's analytical and critical thinking skills, and make more productive choices related to our health, nutrition, family, friends, and the safeguarding of our natural environment, improving our networking, assist people in making more effective and responsible choices related to their health, nutrition, family/friends, community, and political views. Accordingly, education plays a vital role in allowing our global society to be governed ethically and live better. Education, including self-education and formal education, is, thus, valuable. And sport contributes to one's education.

Sport contributes to education by providing a forum for participants to develop an individual and their mental and physical health. In addition, this forum offers an opportunity for individuals to be in situations that aid in learning to manage one's emotions and behaviors. These elements can be examined using the analytical and normative concepts that are now presented.

The analytical and normative concepts and the personal perspective of S&SD

The personal perspective of S&SD incorporates the analytical and normative concepts to explain how we can evolve as individuals if we engage actively with sport. An application of the analytical concept involves using sport as a forum for individuals to learn to identify problems, collect information, develop solutions, including testing and verifying the solutions. An application of the normative concept involves using sport as a platform "to view the world by defining the objectives of a well-functioning society that delivers well-being for its global citizens today and for future generations. The normative concept urges us to have a universal vision toward a good society" (Sachs, 2015, p. 11). We then need to determine how to achieve such a vision. Thus, the analytical and normative concepts fundamentally underscore S&SD, including the two stages of SD*o*S and S*4*SD.

SD*o*S and the personal perspective

The SD*o*S ensures sport opportunities are available over the long term as a forum for one's development. The emphasis is on sport and ensuring that the personal perspective of S&SD aligns with the concept and values of sustainability. Further, these values are guided by the 17 United Nations' sustainable development goals (SDGs) (https://www.un.org/sustainabledevelopment/sustainable-development-goals/). These goals are promoted as needing to be fully implemented by 2030 and advocate for good health and well-being, equal and quality education, and so forth. If sport meets the SDGs, this enhances the chance of long-term sustainability of sport, which provides sustainable sporting opportunities that support individual development into the future. This personal development through sport includes the overall health outcomes for the individual (Macovei et al., 2014; Triantafyllidis & Kaplanidou, 2019).

S*4*SD and the personal perspective

S*4*SD emphasizes the use of sport for the sustainable development of the in-dividual. Sport is, therefore, a tool for active and healthy living interventions and promotions (Funk et al., 2011). Research in the sport management field suggests that a pillar of health and active living is an ultimate component to capture people's behavioral outcomes regarding their sustainability (Funk et al., 2011; Macovei et al., 2014; Sharma-Brymer et al., 2018; Triantafyllidis et al., 2018). Especially during the Covid-19 era, sport has had the privilege of offering a "safe house" where individuals involved with sport at any level (from recreational to elite and the professional levels) can build health.

The WHO defines a state of health as physical, mental, and social well-being (Macovei et al., 2014). In this chapter, health is extended to all elements that enhance our well-being, including nutrition and the natural environment. Further, understandings related to what supports well-being can be explained with psychological theories that explain human behavior with investigations of values, attitudes, perceptions, and behavioral intentions of people toward the given action (Pretty et al., 2017; Stets & Burke, 2000; Triantafyllidis & Kaplanidou, 2019; Wicker, 2019). A person's choices reflect personal–human values such as self-enhancement, self-transcendence, conservation, and openness to change (Schwartz, 1992).

Self-enhancement consists of hedonism (pleasure or sensual gratification for oneself), achievement (personal success through demonstrating competence to social standards), and power (social status and prestige, control or dominance over people and resources) (Hansel et al., 2020; Schwartz, 1992). Self-transcendence consists of the benevolence and altruism (preserving and enhancing the welfare of those with whom one is in frequent personal contact or in-group), universalism and environmentalism (interpretation and appreciation, tolerance and protection for the welfare of all people, and of nature including all the natural environment resources, living and non-living things). Conservation includes security (safety, harmony, and stability in oneself, in relationships in community and society), conformity (restraint of thoughts, emotions, and actions), and tradition (respect, commitment, and acceptance) (Hansel et al., 2020; Schwartz, 1992). And finally, an openness to change (including independent thoughts, feelings, and behaviors) (Hansel et al., 2020), along with self-direction and stimulation (Schwartz, 1992), reflects on one's active and sustainable living lifestyle.

Sport offers positive outcomes comprised of better health at the physical and mental, levels, in concert with improvements in one's well-being and quality of life (Macovei et al., 2014; Triantafyllidis & Kaplanidou, 2019). Sport, thus, makes a decisive and explicit contribution to advancing an active healthy lifestyle (Schulenkorf & Siefken, 2019) or active sustainable living.

This type of living includes personal development that can be extended to supporting other people's welfare, supporting the local economy, and protecting our global natural resources (Cubukcu, 2013).

The protection of our natural resources through sport includes a focus on individual consumption that has been introduced in the literature of sustainability, behavioral sciences, and consumer behavior (Black & Cherrier, 2010). Specifically, sustainable consumption encompasses "greener" products and services (Black & Cherrier, 2010) and the notion that continuous economic growth is based on the quality and the efficiency of the production in concert with the consumer's information about its compatibility with sustainability. This type of consumption supports the development of the individual and the collection of individuals that make up society. To better understand the relationship of sustainable behaviors of people involved with sport, we asked expert Michalis Triantafyllidis to outline this topic.

EXPERT'S VIEW - MICHALIS TRIANTAFYLLIDIS ON SUSTAINABLE LIVING OUTCOMES THROUGH BEACH VOLLEYBALL

Active involvement with a sport makes a person more disciplined and responsible. In the case of beach volleyball, that is a fact. If you are actively involved and committed to your favorite sport, you become responsible for yourself and others. My students are more responsible with their friends, family, and significant others. I have seen them make a lot more effort to preserve and improve their relationships, job performance and take care of themselves. I have evidence on how beach volleyball athletes behave after a few months on the court during pieces of training and games. They respect their teammates, and that respect reflects the cultivation of their self-respect through sport.

Now, in terms of environmental sustainability, I can tell you that their personal growth and self-development through sport participation cultivate their minds to be more concerned about bigger issues such as the natural environment and our society. This is a magical outcome that sport has to humanity.

I'd like to add further that sport is the best school. People learn a lot about life through sport. For example, active sport participation at all levels (amateur, professional) for all ages educates people on how to cultivate their sense of discipline, persevere and passion, learn about teamwork and leadership, and develop resilience for adversity problems, failure, and loss. Sport teaches you how to develop your self-esteem, your technical ability to memorize movement, you learn how to manage your stress levels, how to control your anger, and how to be fair and apply sportsmanship in your life.

At the amateur sport level, an active athlete spends on average three times per week for about two hours each time on his active participation with his favorite sport. The motivation for a person's frequent action and cultivation of skills and knowledge on his craft for better performance and quality interaction with his favorite sport offers them indirectly many health benefits. For example, an amateur athlete improves his physical health significantly by committing time and energy to train for his favorite sport. An athlete's active involvement with their sport improves their physical strength, stamina, speed, and overall athletic performance. At the beach volleyball context, we had athletes' cases that training on the sand prevents them from many injuries.

The social interaction with other people that train at the same favorite sport and spend together more than six to eight hours per week, it has proven that improves their mental health significantly. For instance, our members build long-term friendships, which in turn develops trust, teamwork, and better communication skills.

The social bonding among our athletes is becoming greater after time, and we have noticed that our members (amateur beach volleyball athletes) have positive moods inside and outside the courts. Overall, active participation with favorite sports produces endorphins due to the physical activity, which in turn improves people's psychological state and well-being (mental health) and enhances their immune systems (physical health).

Also, our members have shared with me that they feel more alive after a few months of training. They are passionate about living, going to work and interact with friends and family.

The previous input from the expert in the field leads our discussion to our propositions for S&SD.

Propositions for the personal perspective of S&SD

This section presents five propositions for three key concepts that constitute the SLTS. Accordingly, we suggest two propositions for active/healthy living, two for sustainable living, and one for quality education.

Active/healthy living

Proposition #1: Sustainable development involves active sport participation (and living)

Active sport involvement, including physical activity and exercise for wellness and pleasure, can have a crucial impact on people's habits. For example, active sport participation has been utilized by local governments as a platform that advocates for healthier, more active living, which, together with sustainable consumption and decisions, people can cultivate sustainable lifestyles in cities and communities worldwide. Thus, SDG 3 applied to active sport participation can provide an excellent opportunity for individuals to cultivate sustainable lifestyles in local communities.

Proposition #2: Sustainable development involves healthy choices (nutrition)

Active sport involvement, including physical activity and exercise for wellness and pleasure, can have a crucial impact on people's habits. For example, active sport participation has been utilized by local governments as a platform that advocates for healthier, more active living, which, together with sustainable consumption and decisions, people can cultivate sustainable lifestyles in cities and communities worldwide. Based on the United Nations developed goals, SDGs 3 and 12, active sport participation, together with active pro-environmental and pro-social consciousness, can provide an excellent opportunity for individuals to cultivate sustainable lifestyles. Both propositions #1 and #2 reflect on SDG 3 proposed by the UN:

SDG 3: *Ensure healthy lives and promote well-being for all of all ages*

Sustainable living propositions

Proposition #3: Pro-environmental engagement in sport and through S4SD

The pro-environmental engagement includes practices that reduce the levels of CO_2 emissions in the atmosphere. For example, pro-environmental methods can consist of consuming products and services that do not require energy and water and that their production does not have adverse effects on nature. For example, producing materials does not require a certain amount of energy and water (based on standards such as ISO) and has the least generation of CO_2 emissions. Also, individuals' practices such as recycling, eco-friendly products (local and organic), eco-friendly transportation, and voluntary carbon offsetting donations are considered the most significant at the personal level.

Proposition #4: Pro-social service and support in sport and through S4SD

The pro-social commitment and engagement of individuals can contribute significantly to tackle SDG 10. In collaboration with sport, pro-social service will be considerably enhanced.

Both propositions #3 and #4 reflect on SDGs 10, 12, and 13 proposed by the UN: (including in specific SDG for proposition #1):

> **SDG 10:** *Reduce inequality within and among countries*
>
> **SDG 12:** *Ensure sustainable consumption and production patterns*
>
> **SDG 13:** *Take urgent action to combat climate change and its impacts*

Quality education propositions

Proposition #5: Learning and teaching tools for online and self-education for sustainable development

The quality education movement aims to achieve SDG 4. Accordingly, at the personal level, in the Covid-19 era we live in, instructional guidance for learning and teaching online can optimize the perspective of self-education. Indeed, achieving quality self-education can become the most effective solution for the challenges we face worldwide. Therefore, proposition #5 reflects on SDG 4, developed by the UN:

> **SDG 4:** *Ensure inclusive and equitable education and promote lifelong learning opportunities*

Developing your SLTS plan

In this section, you will learn how to create your SLTS plan. The following principles will guide the strategic self-sustainable planning process. As a newly developed endeavor, S&SD can play a critical role in your lives and career mission and help you achieve your health, education, sustainability goals.

Before describing the planning process and highlighting some principles that every SLTS plan should have, visually illustrate the SLTS (Figure 5.1).

FIGURE 5.1   Sustainable lifestyle through sport

The sustainable lifestyle through sport (SLTS) process

In the planning for SLTS, an essential element is to define your values. To accomplish this task, you should identify and briefly describe your top five values. Please review the following example as presented by the authors and aim to help students evaluate your current values, better reorganize them, redefine them or add new values as they better apply to you in the current phase of your life.

Please review Figure 5.2. follow its order and form, and ready the following sections to detail each step.

Step 1 Personal values

Step 1 is the critical phase for the successful design of your SLTS plan. Specifically, your values should lead every other step (steps 2–6), and every further step should align with your core personal values.

Step 2 Your vision/mission

Step 2 is another crucial component of the planning process. Specifically, your vision/mission of your own life can be determined after you have a sense of purpose to understand, recall, recognize, and explain to yourself and others.

Step 3 Long-term goals

Step 3 includes your own goals that you should achieve in the long term and that these goals will play a crucial role in implementing your life's vision/mission.

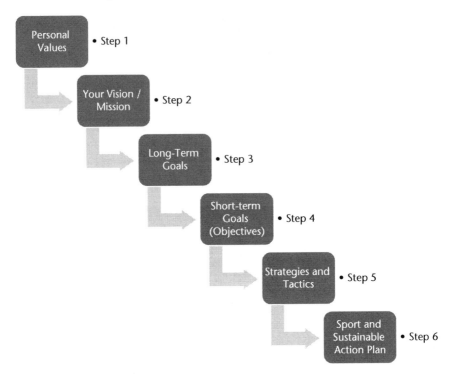

FIGURE 5.2 The planning stages of sustainable lifestyle through sport (SLTS)

Step 4 Short-term goals (objectives)

Step 4 is significant as objectives (short-term goals) are the elements that will assist you in achieving your long-term goals. Also, your objectives must be S.M.A.R.T., which stands for Specific, Measurable, Achievable, Relevant, and Time-based. See Figure 5.3.

Step 5 Strategies and tactics

Step 5 includes your strategies and tactics. Strategic design is the critical practice of experts in the fields of management and leadership.

Step 6 Action plan

Step 6 includes your personal action plan for cultivating an SLTS.

Concluding remarks

1. There are three concepts within SLTS, including active living, sustainable living, and a quality education

FIGURE 5.3 S.M.A.R.T. principles for building strategic objectives

2. A value system supported with an active SLTS includes self-enhancement, conservation, self-transcendence, and an openness to change
3. Education plays a critical role in cultivating an active and SLTS
4. The multiple similarities and differences of the two stages of S&SD, including SDoS and S4SD, are examined from the personal perspective of sport
5. There are five propositions for strategic planning with S&SD from the personal perspective

Future directions

1. Further investigation is needed concerning quality education through online learning and teaching practices – and – the role of cultivating self-education skills
2. Investigations and the application of theoretical approaches to encourage an active and SLTS are needed
3. Frameworks for the interconnections between health, well-being, active sport involvement, pro-social, pro-environmental actions, and sustainability need to continue to be advanced
4. Discuss the implications of the applied principles and outcomes of an active and SLTS
5. Work is needed to determine specific guidelines and principles on the aspects of the personal perspective and S&SD that are under the two stages, SDoS and S4SD
6. Explore how an active and SLTS can be applied to developing countries compared to developed countries – examine sport for development concepts

Review questions

1. Define the term "to an active and SLTS" by identifying and describing the key aspects of such a lifestyle
2. Explain how health, well-being, active sport participation, goodwill, charity, and environmentalism can be connected through one's personal–human value systems
3. What are some key outcomes of cultivating an active and SLTS worldwide?
4. Provide examples illustrating the similarities and differences between an active and SLTS and the personal perspective for SDoS and S4SD
5. Record your top three personal goals for adopting an active and SLTS within the next three years

Discussion questions

1. How would you explain the personal perspective of S&SD to another person (friend, family, colleague) that has not studied it?
2. At your personal level, how would you describe your active living and sustainable living approaches to your everyday life?
3. How could an active and SLTS improve each of the following?

- Your physical, mental, and spiritual health
- Your well-being
- Your quality of life
- Your life satisfaction
- The welfare of others
- The quality of our shared natural resources?

4. List three key challenges for applying an active and SLTS worldwide?
5. Which elements of this lifestyle would you consider to be under the SDoS stage and the S4SD stage?
6. Work with a peer and develop an active lifestyle through sport promotional plan aimed at members within your local community (school, gym, sport team, etc.)

Learning activities

First, read the analytical, critical, and creative thinking in the glossary section of this chapter. Second, read the following paragraph carefully and use it to reference this chapter's section of "Developing your SLTS plan."

> Globally, governments have adopted the SDGs by the UN, but it is still unknown if these goals can reflect on each community and each person the same. According to recent discussions, a new set of goals can help the world do what has not yet been done regarding sustainable development. Also, discussions refer to a further shift from dangerous business to paths that can bring true world sustainability. As sport is a vast business worldwide, we propose specific objectives/goals that sport in concert with sustainable development can have on a new path to worldwide sustainability.

Next, complete the following items:

1. Visit Figure 5.1 and use your analytical thinking to identify any issues related to the triangle relationship of active/healthy, sustainable living, and quality education. Next, define the problems and use your creative thinking to propose a solution and new ideas for cultivating an SLTS. Next, use your critical thinking to evaluate your propositions using the theoretical evidence for supporting your arguments and suggestions
2. Use the web to explore any potential athletes that have adopted an SLTS. Please provide the list of their names and descriptions for each athlete, determine how they practice a sustainable lifestyle in their everyday lives, and evaluate them using analytical, creative, and critical thinking

Developing your S&SD project

After the completion of this chapter, students should work on their S&SD project. Specifically, the S&SD project encourages students to think critically about how S&SD can move forward and contribute to global sustainability in the near future. Accordingly, for this chapter, students should use Figure 5.2 and complete the following items as part of their S&SD strategic planning process from the personal perspective of S&SD:

1. Write your top five personal values
2. Define your personal vision. Specifically, what do you envision a person to become? Vision should be a statement on how you envision yourself as part of the personal perspective of S&SD. For example, "Make the world a better place" is considered a vision. However, do not use this example for your vision. Instead, use the resources of this chapter and develop your vision statement
3. Next, write your top three long-term goals. What do you seek to achieve in the next 5–10 years?
4. Next, write nine short-term goals (which are S.M.A.R.T. and fall under each long-term goal). Accordingly, for each long-term goal, you should present three short-term goals
5. Next, please determine your strategies and tactics for each short-term goal (objective)
6. Finally, you should present an action plan to implement your vision in the next 5–10 years

Further reading

1. McCambridge, T. M., Bernhardt, D.T., Brenner, J.S., Congeni, J.A., Gomez, J.E., Gregory, A.J., ... & Li, S. (2006). Active, healthy living: Prevention of childhood obesity through increased physical activity. *Pediatrics*, *117*(5), 1834–1842. https://doi.org/10.1542/peds.2006-0472
2. Zaidi, A., Gasior, K., Zolyomi, E., Schmidt, A., Rodrigues, R., & Marin, B. (2017). Measuring active and healthy aging in Europe. *Journal of European Social Policy*, *27*(2), 138–157. https://doi.org/10.1177%2F0958928716676550
3. Denegri-Knott, J., Nixon, E., & Abraham, K. (2018). Politicizing the study of sustainable living practices. *Consumption Markets & Culture*, *21*(6), 554–573. https://doi.org/10.1080/10253866.2017.1414048
4. Isenhour, C. (2011). How the grass became greener in the city: On urban imaginings and sustainable living practices in Sweden. *City & Society*, *23*(2), 117–134. https://doi.org/10.1111/j.1548-744X.2011.01058.x
5. Black, I.R., & Cherrier, H. (2010). Anti-consumption as part of living a sustainable lifestyle: Daily practices, contextual motivations, and subjective

values. *Journal of Consumer Behaviour, 9*(6), 437–453. https://doi.org/10.1002/cb.337

6. Nussbaum, M.C. (2006). Education and democratic citizenship: Capabilities and quality education. *Journal of Human Development, 7*(3), 385–395. https://doi.org/10.1080/14649880600815974

7. Scheunpflug, A., & Asbrand, B. (2006). Global education and education for sustainability. *Environmental Education Research, 12*(1), 33–46. https://doi.org/10.1080/13504620500526446

Relevant online resources

1. Healthline: https://www.healthline.com/health/womens-health-active-lifestyle
2. AAFP: https://www.aafp.org/fpm/2011/0300/p16.html
3. Tips for sustainable Lifestyle: https://theminimalistvegan.com/live-a-more-sustainable-lifestyle/
4. UNICEF: https://www.unicefusa.org/stories/guide-sustainable-living/35821
5. Sustainable Development Goal 3: https://sdgs.un.org/goals/goal3
6. Sustainable Development Goal 4: https://sdgs.un.org/goals/goal4
7. Sustainable Development Goal 10: https://sdgs.un.org/goals/goal10
8. Sustainable Development Goal 12: https://sdgs.un.org/goals/goal12
9. Sustainable Development Goal 13: https://sdgs.un.org/goals/goal13
10. HuffPost: https://www.huffpost.com/entry/what-do-we-mean-by-a-qual_b_9284130
11. UNESCO: https://en.unesco.org/themes/education-sustainable-development

References

Amer, A. (2005). *Analytical thinking.* Cairo, Egypt: Pathways to Higher Education.

Black, I.R., & Cherrier, H. (2010). Anti-consumption as part of living a sustainable lifestyle: Daily practices, contextual motivations, and subjective values. *Journal of Consumer Behaviour, 9*(6), 437–453. 10.1002/cb.337

Calogiuri, G., & Chroni, S. (2014). The impact of the natural environment on the promotion of active living: An integrative systematic review. *BMC Public Health, 14*(1), 873. 10.1186/1471-2458-14-873

Chinazzi, M., Davis, J.T., Ajelli, M., Gioannini, C., Litvinova, M., Merler, S., Pionti, P., Mu, K., Rossi, L., Suan, K., Viboud, C., Xiong, X., Yu, H., Halloran, M.E., Longini Jr., I.M., & Vasignani, A. (2020). The effect of travel restrictions on the spread of the 2019 novel coronavirus (COVID-19) outbreak. *Science, 368*(6489), 395–400. Retrieved from https://science.sciencemag.org/CONTENT/368/6489/395.abstract

Cubukcu, E. (2013). Walking for sustainable living. *Procedia-Social and Behavioral Sciences, 85*, 33–42. 10.1016/j.sbspro.2013.08.335

Deci, E., & Ryan, R. (2000). The "what" and "why" of goal pursuits: Human needs and the self-determination of behavior. *Psychological Inquiry, 11*(4), 227–268. 10.1207/S15327965PLI1104_01

Fisher, A. (2011). *Critical thinking: An introduction.* Cambridge, England: Cambridge university press.

Fletcher, D., & Sarkar, M. (2016). Mental fortitude training: An evidence-based approach to developing psychological resilience for sustained success. *Journal of Sport Psychology in Action, 7*(3), 135–157. 10.1080/21520704.2016.1255496

Frey, J., & Eitzen, D.S. (1991). Sport and society. *Annual Review of Sociology, 17*(1), 503–522. Retrieved from https://www.annualreviews.org/doi/abs/10.1146/annurev.so.17.080191 .002443

Funk, D., Jordan, J., Ridinger, L., & Kaplanidou, K. (2011). Capacity of mass participant sport events for the development of activity commitment and future exercise intention. *Leisure Sciences.* 33(3), 250–268.

Gadamer, H.G. (2001). Education is self-education. *Journal of Philosophy of Education, 35*(4), 529–538. 10.1111/1467-9752.00243

Gould, D., & Carson, S. (2008). Life skills development through sport: Current status and future directions. *International Review of Sport and Exercise Psychology, 1*(1), 58–78. 10.1 080/17509840701834573

Holt, N.L., Deal, C.J., & Pankow, K. (2020). Positive youth development through sport. *Handbook of Sport Psychology,* New Jersey, US: John Wiley & Sons, 429–446. 10.1002/ 9781119568124.ch20

Kelly, G.A. (1970). A brief introduction to personal construct theory. *Perspectives in Personal Construct Theory, 1,* 29. Retrieved from https://www.aippc.it/wp-content/uploads/201 9/04/2017.01.003.025.pdf

Lawson, H.A. (2005). Empowering people, facilitating community development, and contributing to sustainable development: The social work of sport, exercise, and physical education programs. *Sport, Education, and Society, 10*(1), 135–160. 10.1080/135 7332052000308800

Macovei, S., Tufan, A.A., & Vulpe, B.I. (2014). Theoretical approaches to building a healthy lifestyle through the practice of physical activities. *Procedia-Social and Behavioral Sciences, 117,* 86–91. 10.1016/j.sbspro.2014.02.183

McCullough, B.P., Orr, M., & Kellison, T. (2020). Sport ecology: Conceptualizing an emerging subdiscipline within sport management. *Journal of Sport Management, 34*(6), 509–520. 10.1123/jsm.2019-0294

Millington, R., Giles, A.R., van Luijk, N., & Hayhurst, L.M. (2021). Sport for Sustainability? The Extractives Industry, Sport, and Sustainable Development. *Journal of Sport and Social Issues.* 10.1177%2F0193723521991413

Mumford, M.D., Giorgini, V., Gibson, C., & Mecca, J. (2013). Creative thinking: Processes, strategies, and knowledge. In *Handbook of research on creativity.* Massachusetts, US: Edward Elgar Publishing.

Pretty, J., Rogerson, M., & Barton, J. (2017). Green mind theory: How brain-body-behavior links into natural and social environments for healthy habits. *International Journal of Environmental Research and Public Health, 14*(7), 706. 10.3390/ijerph14070706

Sachs, J.D. (2015). *The age of sustainable development.* Massachusetts, US: Columbia University Press. Retrieved from http://cup.columbia.edu/book/the-age-of-sustainable-development/ 9780231173155

Scanlan, T.K., Carpenter, P.J., Simons, J.P., Schmidt, G.W., & Keeler, B. (1993). An introduction to the sport commitment model. *Journal of Sport and Exercise Psychology, 15*(1), 1–15. 10.1123/jsep.15.1.16

Schindler, L., Puls-Elvidge, S., Welzant, H., & Crawford, L. (2015). Definitions of quality in higher education: A synthesis of the literature. *Higher Learning Research Communications, 5*(3), 4–13. Retrieved from https://scholarworks.waldenu.edu/hlrc/ vol5/iss3/2/

Schulenkorf, N. (2012). Sustainable community development through sport and events: A conceptual framework for sport-for-development projects. *Sport management review*, *15*(1), 1–12. 10.1016/j.smr.2011.06.001

Schulenkorf, N., & Siefken, K. (2019). Managing sport-for-development and healthy lifestyles: The sport-for-health model. *Sport Management Review*, *22*(1), 96–107. 10.101 6/j.smr.2018.09.003

Schwartz, S.H. (1992). Universals in the content and structure of values: Theoretical advances and empirical tests in 20 countries. *Advances in Experimental Social Psychology*, *25*(1), 1–65. 10.1016/S0065-2601(08)60281-6

Sharma-Brymer, V., Brymer, E., Gray, T., & Davids, K. (2018). Affordances guiding Forest School practice: the application of the ecological dynamics approach. *Journal of Outdoor and Environmental Education*, *21*(1), 103–115.

Stets, J.E., & Burke, P.J. (2000). Identity theory and social identity theory. *Social Psychology Quarterly*, *63*(3), 224–237. 10.2307/2695870

Szathmári, A., & Kocsis, T. (2020). Who cares about gladiators? An elite-sport-based concept of Sustainable Sport. *Sport in Society*, 1–19. 10.1080/17430437.2020.1832470

Triantafyllidis, S., & Darvin, L. (2021). Mass-participant sport events and sustainable development: gender, social bonding, and connectedness to nature as predictors of socially and environmentally responsible behavior intentions. *Sustainable Science*, *16*(5), 239–253. 10.1007/s11625-020-00867-x

Triantafyllidis, S., & Kaplanidou, K. (2019). Marathon runners: A fertile market for "Green" donations? *Journal of Global Sport Management*, 1–14. 10.1080/24704067.201 8.1561205

Triantafyllidis, S., Ries, R. J., & Kaplanidou, K. K. (2018). Carbon Dioxide Emissions of Spectators' Transportation in Collegiate Sporting Events: Comparing On-Campus and Off-Campus Stadium Locations. *Sustainability*, *10*(1), 241. https://doi.org/10.3390/su1 0010241

United Nations(2021, April). Transforming our world: The 2030 Agenda for Sustainable Development. Retrieved from https://sdgs.un.org/2030agenda

University of California Los Angeles (UCLA). (2021). *What is sustainability?*, May 21, 2021, Retrieved from https://www.sustain.ucla.edu/what-is-sustainability/

Weiss, J. (1996). Organizational behaviour and change: Managing diversity, cross-culture dynamics, and ethics. Eagen, Minnesota, US: West Publishing Company.

Wicker, P. (2019). The carbon footprint of active sport participants. *Sport Management Review*, *22*(4), 513–526. 10.1016/j.smr.2018.07.001

Winter, D., & Reed, N. (2020). Unprecedented times for many but not for all: Personal construct perspectives on the Covid-19 pandemic. *Journal of Constructivist Psychology*, *34*(2), 1–10. 10.1080/10720537.2020.1791291

World Health Organization. (2021, February). COVID-19 weekly epidemiological update, *Situation Report*, March 12, 2021, Retrieved from https://www.who.int/publications/ m/item/weekly-epidemiological-update---2-february-2021

6

THE SOCIAL PERSPECTIVE OF SPORT AND SUSTAINABLE DEVELOPMENT

Lindsey Darvin and Curtis Fogel

LEARNING OBJECTIVES

Upon completion of this chapter, learners should be able to successfully:

1. Define and identify the social perspective of sport and sustainable development (S&SD)
2. Recognize the theories and determine the key factors that influence the social perspective of S&SD at the stages of sustainable development of sport (SDoS) and sport for sustainable development (S4SD)
3. Discuss the sociodemographic differences in SDoS
4. Explain how social justice can be achieved through sport (S4SD)
5. Develop strategic planning and programs from the social perspective of S&SD

Overview

This chapter presents the power of sport as a platform to influence positive social change. This change is encouraged as sport undertakes strategies that advance the sustainable development of societies and their people. The discussion begins with a contribution by Lindsey Darvin on the sustainable development of sport (SDoS) with sport as an influencer for social change. This discussion is supported with social identity theory, and then this theory's tenets are used to discuss sociodemographic

DOI: 10.4324/9781003128953-6

factors within SD*o*S that help drive change. Next, Curtis Fogel focuses on social justice, including the social issues of inequality and discrimination, such as racism, sexism, and homophobia, that can be found in society and reflected within sport. The discussion identifies how sport can promote social justice, remove access barriers, engender equality, and create systemic change for marginalized groups. Overall, this chapter is framed with sport and sustainable development (S&SD) by discussing social changes within sport (or the SD*o*S) and sport for positive changes in the broader social world (or sport for sustainable development – S4SD). Despite the advances, there is a continued need for social activism for gender equality, diversity, and inclusion both within and outside of the context of sport.

Glossary

Endosustainablility

Refers to acting in a manner that supports current and future needs (social, financial, and environmental) to continue over time without interruption (Abaza, 2017; Dictionary, 2021). Essentially, for this chapter, an application of endosustainable involves members within sport (internally) acting in a manner that supports the production and consumption of sport products and services today that does not impede the provision of the same opportunities into the future.

Ethnocentrism

Bizumic and Duckitt (2012) refer to ethnocentrism as people's attitude toward one's ethnic group, along with self-centeredness and self-importance. It has been noted that ethnocentrism captures two intragroup and four intergroup aspects (Bizumic & Duckitt, 2012). The intragroup elements encompass both group cohesion and devotion centered upon the beliefs concerning the person's ethnic group. The intergroup aspects include preference, superiority, purity, and exploitativeness, also centered upon the opinions concerning the value of the ethnic to the individual (Bizumic & Duckitt, 2012).

Gender socialization

Refers to a process by which males and females learn how to adapt and develop masculine and feminine values and orientations (Xiao & McCright, 2015).

Social change theory

This theory refers to the socio–psychological aspects that explain social behavior when interacting between two or more people (Cropanzano et al., 2017). The theory suggests that the interaction among people can reflect various relationship types such as promotions, friends, family, social gatherings, and community (Cropanzano et al., 2017).

Social identity theory

Scheepers and Ellemers (2019) recognized both the positive and opposing perspectives of social identity. In their study, the perspectives that explained social identity included solidarity, satisfaction, centrality, people's self-stereotypes, and in-group homogeneity (Scheepers & Ellemers, 2019). Accordingly, an individual's social identity reflects the latter concepts' level to determine their identity toward the groups they associate with (Scheepers & Ellemers, 2019).

Sociodemographic factors

The term refers to the demographic variables such as age, gender, race, ethnicity, etc., that help define individuals and their experiences and circumstances. Additionally, content variables take this notion further and include individual content variables (i.e., socio-demographic variables) and situational content variables such as job, organization, team affiliation, region, and external environment (McDevitt et al., 2007).

Social justice

The term refers to the view that people deserve equal social, economic, and political opportunities and functions. These virtues guide institutions (within sport and society) to lead human interactions based on values of equality, diversity, and inclusion within the community (Miller, 1999).

Sport

"Sport means all forms of physical activity which, through casual or organized participation, aim at expressing or improving physical fitness and well-being, forming social relationships or obtaining results in competition at all levels" (Szathmári & Kocsis, 2020, p. 4).

Sport and sustainable development (S&SD)

S&SD is the process that includes two stages: sustainable development of sport (SDoS) and sport for sustainable development (S4SD) that, together, enhance the development that meets the needs of current generations without compromising future generations' ability to meet their own needs at the personal, social, economic, ecological, technological, and political levels (Millington et al., 2021; Szathmári & Kocsis, 2020; Triantafyllidis & Darvin, 2021).

Sport for sustainable development (S4SD)

S4SD refers to the contribution of sport to our global societies' viability by encouraging sustainability across the six perspectives of personal, social, economic, ecological, technological, and political worldwide (Macovei et al., 2014; Millington et al., 2021; Schulenkorf, 2012).

Sustainability

The term refers to "the integration of environmental health, social equity, and economic vitality to create thriving, healthy, diverse and resilient communities for this generation and generations to come" (University of California, Los Angeles, 2021, para. 2).

The term sustainable development (SD) encompasses the initiatives and progress in pursuit of sustainability. According to Brundtland Commission (2001), sustainable development is defined as the "development that meets the needs of the present without compromising the ability of future generations to meet their own needs" (p. 82). This includes "the narrow notion of physical sustainability [that] implies a concern for social equity between generations, a concern that must logically be extended to equity within each generation" (p. 82).

Sustainable development of sport (SDoS)

SDoS refers to the sustainable practices taken by sport regarding the management of sport products, services, and sport consumer behaviors to achieve sustainability within the world of sport that encompasses six perspectives including the personal, social, economic, ecological, technological, and political (McCullough et al., 2020; Szathmári & Kocsis, 2020; Triantafyllidis & Darvin, 2021).

Lindsey Darvin Lind

DEFINING AND EXPLAINING THE SOCIAL PERSPECTIVE OF S&SD

The sport industry has long-held power to drive social change for years and perhaps decades before substantial shifts are seen throughout society. Given the intense emotional connection many have toward sport, any mode of activism shown by those throughout the industry is highly impactful. In most cases, these social changes are often the result of decades of behind-the-scenes work completed by numerous activists who see sport as agents of social change. These individuals understand the power of sport, the important role of sport throughout society, and use this forum to promote social change. At times, the social changes have been overt, while others are not as obvious. Examples of this power to shift public perception, and in many cases, public advocacy, has been found in sport within topics such as fights for gender equity, racial justice, and mental health awareness (Darvin & Demara, 2020).

Social issues in sport: SDoS

The power of the sport industry to shift public perception has been displayed in the fight for gender equity throughout the United States, as the sport industry continues to represent one of the most highly male-dominated segments of society (Darvin & Lubke, 2020; Walker et al., 2017). Specifically, before the passage of Title IX in 1972, a US federal policy that prohibits discrimination based on sex in educationally sponsored programs that receive federal aid, women and girls had been fighting tirelessly to gain athletic opportunities in primary, secondary, and higher educational settings. The push for change came from several governing bodies, individual teams, and the powerful Association for Intercollegiate Athletics for Women. Before Title IX, gender equity had stalled in many areas of society at large. Following Title IX's passage, however, huge strides have been made in gaining access to sport opportunities, forever shifting women and girls' status throughout the United States (Darvin & Demara, 2020).

Due to this success, the sport industry's role may be critically important in driving social change in the future. As a result, many scholars and practitioners have tagged the sport industry as an impactful influencer in areas such as sustainable actions and lifestyle changes (McCullough et al., 2016; Orr & Inoue, 2019; Triantafyllidis & Darvin, 2021). It has been noted, however, that the sport industry has only recently begun to scratch the surface of how diverse decision-makers may influence the sustainable actions of athletes, teams, programs, organizations, governing bodies, and beyond (McCullough et al., 2016; Orr, 2020; Triantafyllidis & Darvin, 2021).

Research has indicated that certain social aspects, demographics, qualities, and variables may each play a critical role in the sustainable actions conducted by individuals (Panzone et al., 2016; Sovacool et al., 2018). For example, previous research has indicated that, in addition to the strong emotional connection many individuals have toward sport, demographic factors such as education level, gender, and socio-economic status all play a role in an individual's sustainable behaviors (Panzone et al., 2016). To further understand this concept, several distinct theoretical frameworks and conceptual considerations have been applied to investigations of sport and sustainable behaviors, including social identity theory, sociodemographic factors, content variables, and gender socialization. These frameworks and their application to S&SD will be elaborated on as this critical change agent, the sport industry, is at the forefront of social change.

Social identity theory and SDoS

The social identity theory (SIT) has been applied to developing sustainable behaviors within and outside the sport industry setting. This theory maintains that specific groups (i.e., social class, family, football team, etc.) and the individuals they align with are an essential source of pride and self-esteem (Tajfel, 1982). These groups provide individuals with a sense of social identity or a sense of belongingness within their social world. In general, social identity also consists of specific group categories that can be based on demographic classifications (e.g., sex, race) or organizational membership (e.g., religious, educational, social institutions) (Fink et al., 2009). In connection to sport and the industry's potential to drive sustainable behavior, individuals are likely to become identified with an organization (or in this case, a sports team) if that organization or team represents similar attributes that they assign to their own self-concepts (Fink et al., 2009).

To that end, it is critically important to understand just how influential team identification, a subset of social identity, can be toward perceptions of efforts in social activism. If an individual is positively identified with a particular sport organization, team, and athlete, the likelihood of reacting positively toward that group or individual advocating for or working toward a segment of social awareness/justice is much greater (Scheepers & Ellemers, 2019). As a result, it can be argued that if a team, sport organization, or individual athlete is positioned as an ally for a specific social need, their positively identified fans will follow suit. For example, the Seattle Storm, a Women's National Basketball Association team, and the Seattle Kraken, a National Hockey League team located in Seattle, Washington, United States, will move to play all home games in Climate Pledge Arena (Palmer, 2020). This will be the first net zero carbon certified arena globally; the arena will generate zero waste from operations and events and be powered with 100% renewable electricity (Palmer, 2020). The arena will also use reclaimed rainwater in the ice system to create the NHL's greenest ice (Palmer, 2020). As a result of these initiatives, and through an application of social identity theory, one could argue that the fans of those two sport organizations, the Seattle Storm and Seattle Kraken, will likely support sustainable initiatives and actions based on their team identification.

Sociodemographic factors and sustainable development of sport (SDoS)

When discussing social change, a key aspect to consider is the demographic factors that may or may not influence individuals' behaviors and decisions. Building from the tenets of social identity theory, sociodemographic factors drive individual preferences, reactions, and either acceptance or denial of circumstances, displays of activism, as well as social change. This follows the notion that preferences and opinions do not develop in isolation (Darvin & Sagas, 2017). Both demographic influencers and content variables help shape and drive individual thought processes (Darvin & Sagas, 2017). Sociodemographic factors refer to demographic variables such as age, gender, race, ethnicity, etc., that help define individuals, experiences, and circumstances. Content variables take this notion further and include individual content variables (i.e., demographic variables) and situational content variables such as job, organization, team affiliation, region, and external environment (McDevitt et al., 2007). These sociodemographic factors and content variables have been applied in various settings to determine how they may influence decision-making, and applications to the sport industry and sustainable behaviors have also been employed. An essential part of understanding the impact involves working to self-reflect on their sociodemographic factors and content variables to navigate the sustainable behavior decision-making process.

While it has been found that sociodemographic factors play an essential role in the sustainability behaviors of individuals, previous research has been relatively inconsistent regarding the types of sociodemographic factors that predict pro-environmental behaviors (Triantafyllidis & Darvin, 2021). For example, based on the sociodemographic factors that individuals maintain, previous research has determined that factors such as annual household income, educational background, marital status, age, and race may play a role in predicting pro-environmental behavioral intentions, while other scholars have not found these to be as an influence in different or particular contexts (Dolnicar et al., 2008; Triantafyllidis & Kaplanidou, 2019). Some specific findings that incorporate sociodemographic factors include that people who maintain a higher annual income, have acquired a higher education level, and come from a higher social class are more willing to engage in pro-environmental behaviors.

Gender socialization and SDoS

While previous applications of these sociodemographic factors and content variables are relatively comprehensive in the sustainability literature, gender has typically been absent as a key indicator of sustainability behaviors. Recent research has indicated that gender is a critical sociodemographic factor that positively explains environmental concerns and environmentally responsible behavioral intentions (Triantafyllidis & Darvin, 2021; Triantafyllidis & Kaplanidou, 2019). These previous findings have relied on the tenets of gender socialization to further expand on the role this distinct sociodemographic variable may play on pro-environmental behaviors. Previous research regarding the gender differences in pro-environmental behavioral intentions suggests that males and females may reflect differently toward the natural environment. More specifically, research has determined that women express more significant pro-environmental responses early in the lifecycle than their male counterparts (Schultz et al., 2005).

Outside of the sport industry, research concerned with gender and pro-environmental behaviors has determined that females tend to show higher environmental concern levels than their male counterparts (Schultz et al.,

2005; Xiao & McCright, 2015). Moreover, females often convey higher rates of assessed scientific knowledge of environmental issues than do males. They frequently score higher on all three factors of ecological concern, including (1) egoistic, or environmental concern focused on the self, (2) social–altruistic, or environmental concern focused on other humans such as children, and (3) biospheric, or ecological interest focused on the biosphere such as plants and animals (Schultz et al., 2005).

As a result of those above pro-environmental behavioral differences based on gender, gender socialization similarly plays a critical role in this outcome. Gender socialization refers to a process by which males and females learn how to adapt and develop masculine and feminine values and orientations (Xiao & McCright, 2015). Specifically, females often socialize toward a feminine identity due to feelings of attachment, empathy, and care, while males often socialize toward a masculine identity stressing detachment, control, and mastery (Xiao & McCright, 2015).

Beyond that, females are often more socially concerned than males as they are commonly socialized to adapt to a caregiving social role (Xiao & McCright, 2015). As a result, recent research concerned with the socio-demographic variable of gender and pro-environmental behaviors within the sport context has determined that female sport participants do maintain a higher connectedness to nature and are more likely to engage in pro-environmental behaviors than their male sport participant counterparts (Triantafyllidis & Darvin, 2021).

This finding is highly significant once one considers the role of situational content variables in sport such as team affiliations, organizational affiliations, leadership, and industry stakeholders. More specifically, given that females in sport maintain higher rates of positive associations and intentions to favor the environment if additional females are hired within sport leadership, sport organizations may find themselves serving as change agents within this space. To that end, those fans and those with high rates of team identification may follow suit, be more accepting of these pro-environmental actions, and become activists of climate change in their ways. In essence, further diversifying sport industry employee and leadership proportions in the years to come may have a far-reaching influence over society's sustainable behaviors at large.

As indicated above, SD*o*S involves the development of the sport world sustainably. Accordingly, once sport implements its sustainable development efforts, it would be time to act as an effective platform for sustainable development interventions. Therefore, using the power of sport to shift perceptions and encourage positive social changes reflects the second stage, S*4*SD.

The range of focus is multi-directional. A critical element of this type of development within sport, however, involves social justice. This topic will now be discussed.

Curtis Fogel

S&SD: SOCIAL JUSTICE

Social justice refers to the promotion of equality, diversity, and inclusion within society. Social justice is closely connected to the concept of human rights, which are fundamental rights granted to all people regardless of age, ability, race, gender, or creed. More significant social issues of inequality and discrimination, such as racism, sexism, and homophobia, can be found in society and are often reflected within sport organizations. Such reflections within sport can thus serve to reinforce and perpetuate broader social inequalities and injustices in society. Sport, however, also has transformative potential to promote social justice, remove access barriers, engender equality, and create systemic change for marginalized groups both within sport and in the broader social world that sport is situated within.

Social justice in sport: SDoS

Efforts to address equality issues in sport have commonly focused on formal equality, which refers to being treated similarly. Equal treatment can, however, lead to inequalities. For example, many boxing organizations worldwide have a rule that athletes must be cleanly shaven to compete. When that rule is applied equally to all, many male Sikh and Muslim athletes might not compete if they grow and maintain a beard for religious reasons. Though the rule applies equally to all, it creates an inequality in an outcome that disadvantages specific groups. For this reason, it is vital for social justice efforts to focus on substantive equality, which involves the promotion of equal opportunities and outcomes for all groups.

There is a long history of social justice activism in sport. At the 1936 Olympics, many athletes worldwide boycotted worldwide attention to virulent anti-Semitism in Germany (Menkis & Troper, 2015). In 1947, the Brooklyn Dodgers broke the color barrier in professional baseball when a Black athlete, Jackie Robinson, joined the team. Though Robinson faced intense discrimination, his presence and courage have been credited for breaking down some more considerable racial barriers in the United States (Kahn, 2006). In 1967, a woman named Katherine Switzer entered the Boston Marathon under the name K.V. Switzer. She used her initials because, at the time, women were prohibited from competing in the race. Though race officials attempted to remove her once the race had begun, she resisted and competed in the race, which challenged dominant ideas that women could not compete in long-distance runs (Switzer, 2017).

After Tommie Smith won gold at the 1968 Olympics in Mexico City and John Carlos won silver in the men's 200 m, both stepped onto the podium shoeless, in black socks and gloves, raising their fists above their bowed heads to silently protest racial discrimination. The image has become iconic in the fight for racial justice (Carlos & Zirin, 2011). In the 1970s and 1980s, many athletes boycotted sporting events hosted in South Africa. International sport federations banned South African teams from competing in their events in protest of the Apartheid regime, which eventually contributed to its downfall (Darnell et al., 2019). Most recently, in 2020, teams in the National Basketball League (NBA) boycotted playoff games in protest of police shootings of unarmed Black people in the United States and other racial injustices as part of the more extensive Black Lives Matter movement, which cast worldwide attention onto the issue (Stein, 2020).

These are just a few of countless examples of social justice activism in sport, all of which aimed to generate systemic changes within sport to provide equal opportunities of access and treatment and more extensive societal changes to rectify systemic injustices. These courageous acts are not without consequences. For example, after Tommie Smith's and John Carlos's iconic Black power salute on the Olympic podium in 1968, they were subsequently expelled from the Olympic Village and banned from the games' remainder (Carlos & Zirin, 2011). After Colin Kaepernick refused to stand for the singing of the national anthem in the National Football League (NFL) in protest of racial injustices in the United States, teams across the league colluded to not sign him to a new contract (Braun, 2019). The NFL also instituted a rule that requires all players to stand during the singing of the national anthem, with disciplinary consequences if they refused to comply (Haislop, 2020). With social justice progress, there is often backlash and resistance.

Despite resistance to systemic changes that promote equality, diversity, and inclusion within sport and broader society, social justice activism in sport appears to be at an all-time high. Athletes at all levels of sport and in countries worldwide are engaged in acts of peaceful protest and activism to fight for their rights within sport and others' rights more broadly. Offensive and discriminatory sport team names and logos are being challenged and replaced. There are moves toward ensuring pay equity and equal media coverage of male and female athletes. Links between social justice and environmental justice are beginning to be identified and examined. And athletes with physical and cognitive disabilities are fighting for more opportunities to participate and compete in sport, as are intersex and transgender athletes. Though much progress has been made, there is still much more progress to be made.

Sport for social justice and activism: S4SD

Two main factors have bolstered the rise of athlete social justice activism. An example involves the continued growth of social media. Athletes can reach and engage with a large international audience through social media activism. This positions these athletes as influencers. For example, when NBA player Lebron James posted a short message on Twitter criticizing former US President Donald Trump, over 1.5 million people liked his tweet (Chavez, 2017). Primary shoe and athletic apparel companies, such as Nike and Under Armor, also endorse athletes who fight for social justice causes but are now actively promoting their reasons in their advertising. For example, Nike stood behind South African runner Caster Semenya as she has fought against sex, gender, and intersex discrimination in athletics (Chutel, 2018). Nike has aired a series of advertisements promoting Semenya's athletic accomplishments while subtly criticizing those who seek to ban or limit her from competing.

The rapid rise of S4SD initiatives worldwide has also promoted social justice within and through sport. The primary goals of S4SD are typically to alter existing systems and structures of inequality, safeguard athletes from abuse and discrimination, increase inclusion, and promote positive social change. These goals align with social justice aims. S4SD has resulted in greater access to sport for increasingly diverse people by providing them with sustainable opportunities to participate in organized sport. However, as with sport organizations, S4SD initiatives can sometimes work against social justice aims, relying on top-down approaches from the global north that reinforce social inequalities and injustices, reify cultural stereotypes, and further entrench global hierarchies' race-ethnicity and social class. S4SD initiatives need to integrate transformative visions for positive social change. All participants are given equal opportunities to participate, individually and collectively, to pursue social justice and systemic change.

Much work is still to be done while much progress has been made toward greater equality, inclusion, and diversity within and through sport. Gender gaps in pay, resources, media coverage, and leadership positions persist in sport and society. Likewise, while disability rights continue to develop and evolve, sport programming often falls short in providing inclusive, barrier-free access. Systemic racism and ethnocentrism persist at all levels and positions in sport. The rights of transgender and intersex athletes continue to be routinely violated in sport policies, procedures, and practices, such as the World Athletics (International Amateur Athletic Federation or IAAF) rules on athletes with differences of sexual development (available online at worldathletics.org). A history of social justice progress has also been met with a history of backlash and resistance. For this reason, there will be a continued need for social justice activism in sport to work toward increased equality, diversity, and inclusion both within and outside of the context of sport.

In the next section, feedback from an expert in the field, Joshua Opolot, is offered.

Expert's view: Joshua Opolot examine aspects of S&SD throught the perspective of Youth Sport Uganda

The Youth Sport Uganda (YSU) was established in 2006 to offer educational, health, and life skills opportunities to vulnerable youth among the refugees, internal displaced people, and the community in Uganda by harnessing sport's power. The YSU works with the Ministry of Education and Sports, Ministry of Health, Ministry of Gender, Labor and Social Development, and local governments to deliver programs and has reached over 100,000 youth across the county of Uganda. Mr. Opolot is the executive director of the management of YSU.

During this interview, the common aspects of YSU with the social perspective of S&SD were explored. Specifically, social inclusion and justice, gender differences, social sustainability, and partnerships were discussed. Mr Opolot revealed that in his organization, social inclusion requires the accomplishment of social participation and social integration in communities whereby participants, both male and female, might achieve power over their present and their future primarily through sport. However, female access to safe spaces becomes increasingly restrictive, enclosed, and domestic as girls in various communities reach adolescence. The YSU sport programs show that sport activities can help women and girls access opportunities and participate safely. Through this access, they may exercise control and ownership and freely express themselves. Although women's and girls' participation in sport continues to remain imbalanced compared to the involvement among men and boys, YSU believes that the continued and consistent participation of women and girls in sport has had a significant impact on achieving gender equality in various communities. The YSU uses sport as a gateway to ongoing personal development and address such issues as child marriages and teenage pregnancies. Also, the sport program is used to encourage the youth to engage in its counseling sessions. YSU has established quality engagement indicators of success for its management of personal development issues. Additionally, partnerships with other sport organizations aids in developing realistic, measurable, timely, and achievable objectives for sustainable development. The partnerships include working closely with the different local leaders in the various communities because they understand the social and environmental issues within their specific communities.

Concluding remarks

1. Sport has the power to influence members within society in many ways, including shifting perspectives on issues
2. Sport can use this power of influence to aid in the sustainability of both sport and society

3. Sport and the concept of sustainable development can be used as a framework to examine the characteristics expressed within sport concerning social sustainability such as sustainable sporting communities, their relationships, and social bonding efforts
4. Outline how theory can also be used to examine and explain behavior found within sport
5. Sociodemographic factors, including age, race, gender, ethnicity, individual experiences, and so forth impact behavior and are vital when examining sport's social sustainability
6. Social justice (the promotion of equality, diversity, and inclusion) is a critical aspect of sustainability concerning the sport's future

Future directions

1. Much work needs to be completed in the pursuit of sustainable social sport
2. Activism will continue for social justice in sport – and to have such advances impact society as a whole. This includes influencing change in various areas, such as the gender pay gap in sport, media coverage, and leadership positions open to both genders and fighting for racial equality
3. Disability rights continue to need to be advanced in sport and society
4. Solutions and accompanying policies, procedures, and attitudes need to be advanced concerning integrating transgender and intersex athletes in sport
5. Overall, sport will push for greater access by all sustainable initiatives and opportunities within sport into the future
6. Directions taken within sport for social justice, disability rights, transgender, and intersex athletes will influence society's general perspectives

Review questions

1. In your own words, define the social perspective of S&SD
2. List the fundamental theories discussed in chapter 5 that concern the social perspective of S&SD. Outline the characteristics of each theory
3. What are the critical factors that influence the social perspective of S&SD?
4. How would you explain the state of social justice in sport? And how would you describe social justice in society through sport?
5. What is the role of social media in social justice activism in sport?
6. What are your suggestions for the future of the social perspective of S&SD?

Discussion questions

1. What examples have you noticed within your community whereby sport has influenced positive social change?
2. Discuss social injustice in society and how it is reflected within sport

3. What are barriers hindering fulfilling the elimination of discrimination, racism, sexism, and homophobia?
4. Is there any other societal influencer in society (beyond sport) that can cause social change?
5. A conclusion in this chapter is that social activism needs to progress. Accordingly, what strategies could be implemented to remove barriers to advancing the social sustainability of sport and society?

Learning activities

1. Reflect on a sport program with which you have participated or are familiar, and review the social perspective of S&SD across the two stages (SDoS and S4SD). Record the social issues or challenges that emerge in practice. Outline how these issues can be accurately communicated in the media to aid in resolving them
2. In small groups of students, collaborate to generate transformative visions for positive social change through sport by selecting an inequity in society, determining how such inequity is represented within sport, and how sport can influence social change (examples include gender gaps in pay or racism – but there are many more revealed in the discussion above). What are the arising issues in finding a consensus concerning the vision?
3. Divide the class into three groups: (1) complainants, (2) World Athletics (IAAF) representatives, and (3) arbitrators. Each group should review the new World Athletics (IAAF) eligibility regulations for the female classification concerning athletes with differences of sex development (see: https://www.worldathletics.org/news/press-release/eligibility-regulations-for-female-classification). Complainants argue that the rules are discriminatory and identify how they marginalize and oppress particular groups. The IAAF representatives present responses on why they think the rules are justifiable. The arbitrators decide on whether to remove, amend, or maintain the existing rules
4. Write a personal overview of how S&SD can contribute to global efforts for sustainability. Record two steps that can be taken today to work toward this contribution

Further reading

1. Harvard Review (2021). *Sport and social justice*. Retrieved from https://hbr.org/2021/01/sports-and-social-justice
2. Lee, W., & Cunningham, G. (2019, March). Moving towards understanding social justice in sport organizations: A study of engagement in social justice advocacy in sport organizations. *Journal of Sport and Social Issues, 43*(3), 245–263. https://doi.org/10.1177%2F0193723519832469

3. Schweiger, G. (2014). Social justice and professional sports. *International Journal of Applied Philosophy, 28*(2), 373–389. https://doi.org/10.5840/ijap2 01412834

4. Forde, S., & Wilson, B. (2009). Radical sports journalism?: Reflections on "alternative" approaches to covering sport-related social issues. *Sociology of Sport Journal, 35*(1), 66–76. https://doi.org/10.1123/ssj.2017-0162

5. Jackson, D., Trevisan, F., Pyullen, E., & Silk, M. (2020). Towards a social justice disposition in communication and sport scholarship. *Sport Communication and Social Justice, 8*(4–5), 435–451. https://doi.org/10.1177%2F216747952 0932929

6. Cavaiani, A. (2020). Rhetoric, materiality, and the disruption of meaning: The stadium as a place of protest. *Sport Communication and Social Justice, 8*(4–5), 473–488. https://doi.org/10.1177%2F2167479519900161

7. Harrison, V., & Boehma, J. (2020). Sport for development and peace: Framing the global conversation. *Sport Communication and Social Justice, 8*(3), 291–316. https://doi.org/10.1177%2F2167479519831317

Relevant online resources

1. The Day Sports Stood Still (HBO Sports): https://www.hbo.com/documentaries/the-day-sports-stood-still
2. Black Lives Matters (BLM): https://blacklivesmatter.com
3. Social Change Fund: https://www.thesocialchangefund.org
4. Sport and Social Justice: https://sportandsocialjustice.org
5. Changing lives through the power of sport: http://www.sportandsocialjustice.org
6. Peace and Sport: http://www.peace-sport.org

References

Abaza, W. (2017). Comparing internal and external impacts of sustainable innovation: An exploratory study. *Journal of Global Entrepreneurship Research, 7*, 3. 10.1186/s40497-017-0061-7

Bizumic, B., & Duckitt, J. (2012). What is and is not ethnocentrism? A conceptual analysis and political implications. *Political Psychology, 33*(6), 887–909. 10.1111/j.1467-9221 .2012.00907.x

Braun, E. (2019). *Colin Kaepernick: From free agent to change agent.* Minneapolis: Lerner.

Brundtland Commission. (2001). Climate change 2001: Impacts, adaptation, and vulnerability. In J.J. McCarthy, O.F. Canziani, N.A. Leary, D.J. Dokken and K.S. White (Eds.), *Contributions of working group II to the third assessment report of the intergovernmental panel on climate change.* Cambridge: Cambridge University Press. Retrieved from https://www.ipcc.ch/report/ar3/wg2/

Carlos, J., & Zirin, D. (2011). *The John Carlos Story: The sports moment that changed the world.* Chicago: Haymarket Books.

Chavez, C. (2017). LeBron James 'U Bum' tweet to Donald Trump is the most retweeted athlete post of 2017. *Sports Illustrated.* Retrieved from https://www.si.com/nba/201 7/12/05/lebron-james-donald-trump-tweet-most-retweeted-2017

Chutel, L. (2018). Nike's latest advertisement features yet another athlete taking a stand. *Quartz Africa*. Retrieved from https://qz.com/africa/1385843/after-colin-kaepernick-nike-backs-south-africas-caster-semenya/

Cropanzano, R., Anthony, E.L., Daniels, S.R., & Hall, A.V. (2017). Social exchange theory: A critical review with theoretical remedies. *Academy of Management Annals*, *11*(1), 479–516. 10.5465/annals.2015.0099

Darnell, S., Field, R., & Kidd, B. (2019). *The history and politics of sport-for-development: Activists, idealogues & reformers*. London: Palgrave.

Darvin, L., & Demara, E.H. (2020). The emergence, experiences, and empowerment of women administrators, coaches, and athletes. In *Critical reflections and politics on advancing women in the academy* (pp. 87–104). Hershey, Pennsylvania, US: IGI Global.

Darvin, L., & Lubke, L. (2020). Assistant coach hiring trends: An updated investigation of homologous reproduction in intercollegiate women's sport. *Sports Coaching Review*, *10*(1), 1–23. 10.1080/21640629.2020.1760001

Darvin, L., & Sagas, M. (2017). Objectification in sport media: Influences on a future women's sporting event. *International Journal of Sport Communication*, *10*(2), 178–195. 10.1123/IJSC.2017-0022

Dictionary (2021, April). *Endo*. Retrieved from https://www.dictionary.com/browse/endo-

Dolnicar, S., Crouch, G.I., & Long, P. (2008). Environment-friendly tourists: What do we really know about them? *Journal of Sustainable Tourism*, *16*(2), 197–210. 10.2167/jost738.0

Fink, J.S., Parker, H.M., Brett, M., & Higgins, J. (2009). Off-field behavior of athletes and team identification: Using social identity theory and balance theory to explain fan reactions. *Journal of Sport Management*, *23*(2), 142–155. 10.1123/jsm.23.2.142

Geissdoefer, M., Savaget, P., Bocken, N., & Van Hultink, E. (2017). The circular economy – A new sustainability paradigm? *Journal of Cleaner Production*, *143*, 757–768. 10.1016/j.jclepvo.2016.12.048

Haislop, T. (2020). *What is the NFL's national anthem protest policy? Here are the rules for kneeling in 2020*. Charlotte, North Carolina, US: Sporting News. Retrieved from https://www.sportingnews.com/ca/nfl/news/nfl-national-anthem-policy-2020-kneeling-protests/174qdao8q34l51n1mpm9ukuwuk

Heere, B. (2018). Embracing the sportification of society: Defining e-sports through a polymorphic view on sport. *Sport Management Review*, *21*(1), 21–24. 10.1016/j.smr.2017.07.002

Kahn, R. (2006). *The boys of summer*. New York: HarperPerennial.

Macovei, S., Tufan, A.A., & Vulpe, B.I. (2014). Theoretical approaches to building a healthy lifestyle through the practice of physical activities. *Procedia-Social and Behavioral Sciences*, *117*, 86–91. 10.1016/j.sbspro.2014.02.183

McCullough, B.P., Orr, M., & Kellison, T. (2020). Sport ecology: Conceptualizing an emerging subdiscipline within sport management. *Journal of Sport Management*, *34*(6), 509–520. 10.1123/jsm.2019-0294

McCullough, B.P., Pfahl, M.E., & Nguyen, S.N. (2016). The green waves of environmental sustainability in sport. *Sport in Society*, *19*(7), 1040–1065. 10.1080/17430437.2015.1096251

McDevitt, R., Giapponi, C., & Tromley, C. (2007). A model of ethical decision making: The integration of process and content. *Journal of Business Ethics*, *73*(2), 219–229. 10.1007/s10551-006-9202-6

Menkis, R., & Troper, H. (2015). *More than just games: Canada and the 1936 Olympics*. Toronto: University of Toronto Press.

Miller, D. (1999). *Principles of social justice.* Cambridge, Massachusetts, USA: Harvard University Press.

Millington, R., Giles, A.R., van Luijk, N., & Hayhurst, L.M. (2021). Sport for sustainability? The extractives industry, sport, and sustainable development. *Journal of Sport and Social Issues.* 10.1177%2F0193723521991413

Orr, M. (2020). On the potential impacts of climate change on baseball and cross-country skiing. *Managing Sport and Leisure, 25*(4), 307–320. 10.1080/23750472.2020.1723436

Orr, M., & Inoue, Y. (2019). Sport versus climate: Introducing the climate vulnerability of sport organizations framework. *Sport Management Review, 22*(4), 452–463. 10.1016/j.smr.2018.09.007

Palmer, A. (2020). *Amazon wins naming rights to the new Seattle stadium and will call it the Climate Pledge Arena.* Retrieved from https://www.cnbc.com/2020/06/25/amazon-wins-naming-rights-to-new-seattle-stadium-climate-pledge-arena.html

Panzone, L., Hilton, D., Sale, L., & Cohen, D. (2016). Socio-demographics, implicit attitudes, explicit attitudes, and sustainable consumption in supermarket shopping. *Journal of Economic Psychology, 55*, 77–95. 10.1016/j.joep.2016.02.004

Sachs, J.D. (2015). *The age of sustainable development.* New York City, New York, US: Columbia University Press. Retrieved from http://cup.columbia.edu/book/the-age-of-sustainable-development/9780231173155

Scheepers, D., & Ellemers, N. (2019). Social identity theory. In *Social psychology in action* (pp. 129–143). Cham: Springer. Retrieved from https://scholarlypublications.universiteitleiden.nl/handle/1887/81763

Schulenkorf, N. (2012). Sustainable community development through sport and events: A conceptual framework for sport-for-development projects. *Sport Management Review, 15*(1), 1–12. 10.1016/j.smr.2011.06.001

Schultz, P.W., Gouveia, V.V., Cameron, L.D., Tankha, G., Schmuck, P., & Franěk, M. (2005). Values and their relationship to environmental concern and conservation behavior. *Journal of Cross-Cultural Psychology, 36*(4), 457–475. 10.1177%2F0022022105275962

Sovacool, B.K., Kester, J., Noel, L., & de Rubens, G.Z. (2018). The demographics of decarbonizing transport: The influence of gender, education, occupation, age, and household size on electric mobility preferences in the Nordic region. *Global Environmental Change, 52*, 86–100. 10.1016/j.gloenvcha.2018.06.008

Stein, M. (2020). *Led by NBA, boycotts disrupt pro sports in the wake of Blake shooting.* New York City, New York, US: New York Times. Retrieved from https://www.nytimes.com/2020/08/26/sports/basketball/nba-boycott-bucks-magic-blake-shooting.html

Switzer, K. (2017). *Marathon woman: Running the race to revolutionize women's sport.* Cambridge, MA: Da Capo Press. Retrieved from https://www.dacapopress.com/titles/kathrine-switzer/marathon-woman/9780306825668/

Szathmári, A., & Kocsis, T. (2020). Who cares about gladiators? An elite-sport-based concept of sustainable sport. *Sport in Society*, 1–19. 10.1080/17430437.2020.1832470

Tajfel, H. (1982). The social psychology of intergroup relations. *Annual Review of Psychology, 33*(1), 1–39. Retrieved from https://www.annualreviews.org/doi/abs/10.1146/annurev.ps.33.020182.000245

Triantafyllidis, S. & Darvin, L. (2021). Mass-participant sport events and sustainable development: gender, social bonding, and connectedness to nature as predictors of socially and environmentally responsible behavior intentions. *Sustainable Science, 16*(5), 239–253. 10.1007/s11625-020-00867-x

Triantafyllidis, S., & Kaplanidou, K. (2019). Marathon Runners: A Fertile Market for "Green" Donations? *Journal of Global Sport Management*, 1–14. 10.1080/24704067.2018.1561205

University of California, Los Angeles (UCLA). (2021). *What is sustainability?* Retrieved from https://www.sustain.ucla.edu/what-is-sustainability/

Walker, N.A., Schaeperkoetter, C., & Darvin, L. (2017). Institutionalized practices in sport leadership. In *Women in sport leadership: Research and practice for change* (pp. 33–46). The Routledge Publication.

World Athletics. (2018, April). *IAAF introduces new eligibility regulations for female classification.* Monaco: World Athletics, Press Release. Retrieved from https://www.worldathletics.org/news/press-release/eligibility-regulations-for-female-classifica

Xiao, C., & McCright, A.M. (2015). Gender differences in environmental concern: Revisiting the institutional trust hypothesis in the USA. *Environment and Behavior, 47*(1), 17–37. 10.1177%2F0013916513491571

7

THE ECONOMIC PERSPECTIVE OF SPORT AND SUSTAINABLE DEVELOPMENT

Marco Tortora

LEARNING OBJECTIVES

Upon completion of this chapter, learners should be able to successfully:

1. Define the economic perspective of sport and sustainable development (S&SD)
2. Identify the elements of the economic S&SD that reflect sustainable development of sport (SDoS) and sport for sustainable development (S4SD)
3. Discuss the difference between sustainable finance and investments
4. Outline the opportunities and challenges of developing effectiveness for the promotion of sustainability projects
5. Interpret from real cases the complexity of designing innovative projects and investments oriented toward sustainability
6. Design strategic plans and programs for the economic perspective of S&SD

Overview

The economic perspective of sport and sustainable development (S&SD) can be achieved through the two stages, the sustainable development of sport (SDoS) and sport for sustainable development (S4SD) within society. For SDoS, the discussion encompasses sustainable investing in sport, fiscal transparency,

DOI: 10.4324/9781003128953-7

integrity, good governance for sport organizations, and responsible management of strategic assets in sport, such as sustainable sport facility management (Tortora, 2020). For S4SD, we present examples where sport is used to raise funds for charitable causes and generate innovative business approaches. In addition, the chapter discussion includes examples from the strategic choices sport organizations and managers have to make in their daily routine, especially regarding sustainable financing and sourcing. Finally, the role of sustainable finance and economics is discussed to explain how sustainable financial plans and strategies can be applied in sport and further developed and executed by sport organizations. The chapter ends with an expert's perspective on the economic perspective of S&SD.

Glossary

Artificial intelligence

Artificial intelligence (AI) are software systems designed by humans to perceive an "environment of data acquisition, interpreting collected structured and unstructured data, reasoning knowledge, and processing information" (High-Level Expert Group on Artificial Intelligence, 2019, p. 6).

Balanced scorecard

Kaplan and Norton (1992) outlined a strategy on analyzing "measures that drive performance" (p. 71), based on four perspectives: The financial, customer, internal business, and innovative and learning perspectives.

Blockchain

Blockchain is a public ledger consisting of all transactions across a peer-to-peer network (European Union Agency for Cyber Security, 2021).

Circular economy

An economic paradigm with three main principles including: (1) Design out waste and pollution; (2) keep products and materials in use; and (3) regenerate natural systems. Applying these principles to businesses and economic systems means, operationally, developing a systemic approach to economic development designed to benefit businesses, society, and the environment (Ellen MacArthur Foundation, 2016, 2019). This type of economy is possible in sport as noted in a manifesto supported by The Federation of the European Goods Industry (Euratex.eu, 2019).

Financial integrity

"Being sound, whole, reliable and sustainable, fair and principled, responsible and morally upright in economic structures, transactions, and relationships" (Andrews & Harrington, 2016, p. 5).

Fiscal responsibility

The meeting of one's obligations such as ensuring taxes and social payments (SIGA Universal Standards and Implementation Guidelines, 2020).

Sport

"Sport means all forms of physical activity which, through casual or organized participation, aim at expressing or improving physical fitness and well-being, forming social relationships or obtaining results in competition at all levels" (Szathmári & Kocsis, 2020, p. 4).

Sport and sustainable development

Sport and sustainable development (S&SD) is the process that includes two stages: SDoS and S4SD that, together, enhance the development that meets the needs of current generations without compromising future generations' ability to meet their own needs at the personal, social, economic, ecological, technological, and political levels (Millington et al., 2021; Szathmári & Kocsis, 2020; Triantafyllidis & Darvin, 2021).

Sport for sustainable development (S4SD)

Sport for sustainable development (S4SD) refers to the contribution of sport to our global societies' viability by encouraging sustainability across the six perspectives of personal, social, economic, ecological, technological, and political worldwide (Macovei et al., 2014; Millington et al., 2021; Schulenkorf, 2012).

Stakeholder theory

This theory offers a framework to assist in understanding the decision-making process in an organization by focusing on both individuals and groups that affect action (Freeman, 1984; Mahon & Waddock, 1992). "The theory allows for the comprehensive and systematic identification of constituents, claims, and expectations of those involved in different issues, and recognizes those groups with which an organization must effectively interact to be successful" (Friedman et al., 2004, p. 174).

Sustainability

The term refers to "the integration of environmental health, social equity, and economic vitality to create thriving, healthy, diverse and resilient communities for this generation and generations to come" (University of California Los Angeles, 2021, para. 2).

The term sustainable development (SD) encompasses the initiatives and progress in pursuit of sustainability. According to the Brundtland Commission (2001), sustainable development is defined as the "development that meets the needs of the present without compromising the ability of future generations to meet their own needs" (p. 82). This includes "the narrow notion of physical sustainability [that] implies a concern for social equity between generations, a concern that must logically be extended to equity within each generation" (p. 82).

Sustainable development of sport (SDoS)

Sustainable development of sport (SDoS) refers to the sustainable practices taken by sport regarding the management of sport products, services, and sport consumer behaviors to achieve sustainability within the world of sport that encompasses six perspectives including the personal, social, economic, ecological, technological, and political (McCullough et al., 2020; Szathmári & Kocsis, 2020; Triantafyllidis & Darvin, 2021).

Sustainable finance

The focus is on: (1) improving "the contribution of finance to sustainable and inclusive growth by funding society's long-term needs" (European Commission, 2018, p. 6) and (2) strengthening "financial stability by incorporating environmental, social, and governance (ESG) factors into investment decision-making" (European Commission, 2018, p. 6).

Introducing the economic perspective of sport and sustainable development (S&SD)

The economic perspective of S&SD will be sub-divided into two parts. The first part will focus on SDoS, and the second part will focus on S4SD

Part 1: SDoS

The discussion on the SDoS is sub-divided into four sections. We begin with a discussion on financial sustainability and investments in sport. Next, sustainability investments in sport operations and then policy development for fiscal transparency in sport is presented. The final section discusses spectators as donors in sport.

Financial sustainability and investments in sport: SDoS

An innovative approach is required to achieve financial sustainability for fiscal management that will guide sport organizations and businesses to invest and develop to respond to the complexity of economic, environmental, and social risks. Solutions to such risks must be designed, developed, applied, monitored, and corrected over time to improve performances. Accordingly, an innovative approach is to plan for a sustainable financial ecosystem. A sustainable financial ecosystem is "a movement that addresses a perceived inadequacy of the given economic model by requiring actors to acknowledge the importance of factors and outcomes, other than the pursuit of profit in their business models" (Oranefo, 2019, para. 2). It leads to "having the finances to generate value over time through sound management" (SIGA Universal Standards and Implementation Guidelines, 2020, p. 27). Such a system requires many resources including, for example, human competencies and roles concerning information, knowledge, data, and finance, and a re-design of the organization and its corporate governance structure. There are guides available, such as Sport England and United Kingdom (n.d.), that outline a sport governance code (see https://www.sportengland.org/campaigns-and-our-work/code-sports-governance). A sustainable finance ecosystem should be continuously evolving to meet the market's primary trends. The market trends primarily include the newly developed environmental, social, and governance (ESG) portfolio that optimizes solutions and enhances traditional corporate strategies on risk management choices (PWC, 2020). Sport organizations must learn to develop their culture for financial sustainability (Glassdoor, 2019), including ESG.

An investment in ESG data analytics can contribute to the advanced multi-layer quality control systems. The ESG system has to ensure full access to and the reliability of data, total transparency, and the capacity to report the data according to the market's highest standards. Not all organizations can, however, complete such an analysis. For example, all sport businesses, sport leagues, international and national sport associations, federations, and sport governmental bodies may not complete such examinations.

However, sport is a platform for positive contributions. Global sport entities should take the leading role and set the example on investments toward sustainable ESG standards and metrics. To this end, the markets of capital are in the process of transitioning and investing in sustainability as ESG issues are now considered to be "a pillar of performance" (Calvert, 2020, para. 1). Markets have currently invested so much that they are already impacting and changing the behaviors of their clients in the business-to-business sector as well as in the private/families and firm's markets (e.g., bonds, loans) (BlackRock, 2018; Schrank, 2014; UNPRI – UN Principles of Responsible Investments, 2020).

An investment in ESG standards and metrics supports sport organizations and their financial manager's strategic decisions concerning risk based on data-driven and fully transparent vital parameters. The ESG approach enables the sport organizations to set and organize their data to benefit most of their needs regarding access to capital, quantitative and qualitative terms (i.e., higher funds, lower interest rates). Another advantage of the ESG is that the sustainability performances will be monitored, measured, and compared to those of the industry's leading players and the industry at large. Among the key performance indicators that sport managers could use in the comparisons are the performances in terms of the director roles and advances, in corporate environmental and social performance.

Efficient use of data can lead managers to search for and adopt more effective standards. These standards can be set for each sport operation and generate suitable certification schemes for processes, products, or services. Also, organizations that follow such standards can set an example on the international, national, regional, or local related industry sectors worldwide. Finally, sport organizations can become the building blocks for a seminal sustainability report (Adidas, 2020; Ferrari.com, 2019; UN Global Compact, 2018a, 2018b). An example of this type of sport report is the Korea Sports Promotion Foundation (2019).

Sustainable investments in sport operations: SDoS

Every endeavor or project should be financially sustainable, including from the grassroots up to the professional levels in sport. Accordingly,

> A project is financially sustainable when services and activities are secured by short-term and long-term financing like taxes, local fees, and funds. Also, organizations should not depend solely on temporary foreign [or national to local] grants to provide their services and activities. Instead, they should have sufficient structural and local financial resources to not only maintain and operationalize existing services and activities but also to improve them. (ISA, 2015, p. 2)

Financial resources are essential to acquire the other resources that organizations need to operate and develop their projects and programs sustainably. In these terms, the sourcing process is a crucial element to consider. The goods and services sport organizations decide to buy, rent, or license for their activities, as well as the spending decisions on how much of the planned budget to spend on every single action, will have an impact in terms of control and influence, such as direct and indirect impacts on people, communities, and the environment as well as the industry. This happens because sustainable sourcing covers a wide range of aspects. These should be reduced to a group of five fundamental questions managers should try to resolve before making any decisions, including

1. **Products needed:** In managerial terms, sustainability requires increasing efficiency levels in managing operations and processes. It means to do more with the same number of resources – or getting the same result with fewer resources (and of better quality). Thus, this aspect covers how an organization

could impact society and the environment and what can be done to reduce it according to our organization's strategic goals and vision

2. **Sourcing materials:** Like other industries, such as the food and fashion industries, the sport industry is a global, complex network of inter-relations with cumulative effects at multiple scales. The sport industry acts as a worldwide ecosystem whose impacts and consequences are unevenly distributed in different territories and communities, particularly international events such as the Olympic Games or World Cups. The materials that enter the global ecosystem's organizational flows should be considered based on their negative and positive product or service delivery effects. For example, organizing committees or event managers can set social and environmental guidelines or standards to select suitable suppliers according to their main principles and values. That is the case of suppliers providing people (i.e., ensuring gender diversity, equal access, wages conditions), food (local production, no toxic chemicals), etc.

3. **The composition of the materials used within products** can be widely accepted based on certification schemes that testify to the minimal negative or positive impact on human health and the environment. In terms of the environment, sport bodies should pay special attention to the quantity and quality of the elements embedded in the product in terms of material (recycled, upcycled, refurbished, toxic, or polluting substances), energy (renewables, nonrenewable), and other natural resources (water, air, biodiversity).

4. **Packaging and logistics are connected and are a significant issue in terms of waste management and resource use.** Sport bodies and organizations should select their partners based on a clear policy and operations certified by a third partner whenever possible. A guide or sport policy toolkit and checklist are offered by The Commonwealth Secretariat (2018). Also, partner selection should be based on sustainable packaging and green logistics or reverse logistics (taking back and reusing or recycling the packaging material).

5. **End of life of products:** This involves considering what will happen to the product and its main components after use. For example, what happens to a sport event regarding its end life. Here the focus should be on the responsible disposal of goods and materials after their use. This area requires a specific and detailed program based on an initial assessment of all the product use implications (such as the regulatory, legal, ecological, financial, technical implication), including unexpected costs and risks to the operation. Decisions on handling the after-use of the products should be determined before their use (i.e., before a sport tournament begins).

These five areas are relevant since they introduce the foundations for innovative business models that organizations should pursue. This pursuit can create a better and more significant impact on our society and the planet through a different and innovative model focusing on the circular economy. In addition, guidance can be acquired from certification organizations. Examples include the Leadership in Energy and Environmental Design (LEED) program for sports venues (Cameron, 2017; United States Green Building Council, 2020), the International Standards Organization (ISO) 20121:2012 Event Sustainability Management Systems (ISO, 2020); the European Union Eco-Management and Audit Scheme (EMAS) certification (EMAS, n.d.), and the Environmental Protection Agency (2020) Green Building program.

Policy development for fiscal transparency in sport: SDoS

There is a lack of transparency and robust governance regarding funding at all sports levels, as recent scandals indicate. Sport has the ability, however, to contribute to sustainability (European Commission, 2011), and this opportunity should not be squandered. Thus, reformations and innovations are in demand, mainly to ensure that they align with policies for the promotion and integrity of sport (The Commonwealth Secretariat, 2018) and its sustainability. Essentially, sport must invest in innovating its governance to uphold financial management's very highest governance standards. These standards support sport organizations operating more efficiently and successfully while being accountable for their actions (including social and environmental impacts) and transparency. It is important to create the organization's capacity to launch innovative and responsible financial guidelines for projects that align with the expected outcomes. It is also important to note that the role of governments at different levels is crucial either as a guide for policy setting, codes of conduct, or frameworks (e.g., the UK, 2017, Code for Sports Governance) a partner or principal founder.

Spectators as sustainability donors in sport: SDoS

Donors include those who provide financial aid to their favorite team, often at a grassroots or collegiate level. These donations help the organization develop, launch, or maintain specific programs. The donors, thus, are critical strategic financial stakeholders for many sport organizations. An effective strategy for keeping donors over the long term should consider the stakeholders' needs and expectations – and donors are part of this group. These donors should be engaged from the beginning to the end of a program, including ensuring they understand the financial goals for program sustainability as established by the organizations (PWC, 2020).

An application of stakeholder theory indicates that donors' engagement aids in supporting the greening of stadiums, arenas, and alike that directly benefit financial savings, attract sponsors, attract tenants and entertainment clients, enhance the spectators' experience, and build local economic growth. The role of donors acquires importance and strategic weight also from another perspective: The Balanced Scorecard. This tool offers a fundamental strategy for all the non–profit associations, organizations, cooperatives that invest daily in change for sustainability. The Balanced Scorecard is a strategic performance management tool, and it measures organizations' performances.

We now transition to discuss the other stage in S&SD – involving S4SD.

Part II: S4SD)

The discussion on the economic perspective of S4SD is sub-divided into two sections. These include sport for fundraising and sport for sustainable business development. Each section will now be outlined.

Sport for fundraising: S4SD

Sport can be a powerful catalyst for making a difference by collecting funds, directing these funds to specific societal problems, and reaching the determined goals. Sport fundraising programs can empower spectators, supporters, tourists, and everyone involved in sport to achieve a better future for all of humanity. Fundraising activities by those in sport are also crucial in supporting the education of specific societal issues such as climate change, poverty, and hazardous chemical use. Sport can educate those in society through fundraising activities by organizing and strategically designing marketing and communications campaigns developed to raise awareness and change people's behavior.

Fundraising should be managed professionally. Essentially, the sport sector needs to fully invest in training its workforce to advance the necessary competencies and skills for fundraising. Increasingly, this training needs to include utilizing the technological world of big data, cloud computing, social media, and AI. In addition, all fundraising activities should be managed with the highest standards and quality possible in project management.

Sport for sustainable business development: S4SD

The recent trends in the business development model for sport-related industries, such as sport fashion and food/nutrition shows, involve design thinking and system thinking with lean startups that meld strategic management and innovations. This approach is not oriented toward a re-adjustment of linear or as-usual business models toward sustainability goals. Instead, it requires a complete and profound change in vision, mentality, perspective, and sustainability expectations. Global sporting brands, such as Adidas and Nike, mix sustainability and new technologies such as blockchain and big data or AI to design new experiences, services, and products. This is completed according to the principles of the circular economy and models exploiting new resources coming from innovative types of collaborations between big brands, startups, innovative small and medium enterprises, venture capitalist, public funds, and many more actors in unprecedented ways (Connolly, 2019; Ellen MacArthur Foundation, 2016, 2019; McKinsey

Company, 2016; Pero, 2019). Sport is an integral component in the advancement of trends in business model development.

An expert from the industry now offers their perspective regarding practical approaches to strategic financial planning of S&SD.

Expert's view: Stefano Gobbi, Project Management, Sport e Salute Spa, Rome, Italy

Sport is a strategic asset for sustainable economic development, including increased job opportunities and financial growth. Even in its moments of maximum diffusion, if sport is only a parallel segment of people and communities' lives, then the sport will be considered only an ancillary activity: An activity to access during one's free time despite the high benefits for health and social life. Instead, sport must be in the important times of a person's daily life and not in interstitial spaces. The result of this political view – sport as an ancillary component of people's lives – was a model that dealt only with organizations' sports management and not with the service (the value), much less with the end users' needs. Suppose culturally, it falls within the whole span of life, in everyday life. In that case, it becomes a critical time that positively impacts people's well-being and communities and economic terms. Despite the strategy to date, the economic impact is still high. Indeed, the market seems saturated even though it is not. On the contrary, there are enormous development opportunities for the sporting sector, related industries, possible partnerships (IT, Augmented Reality, Virtual Reality, AI, Green Mobility and Logistics, wearables, technical clothing, Global Positioning System technology, health, and wellness, etc.). From this perspective, Italy is unique at an international level if we consider the widespread diffusion of sports organizations throughout the territory – 77,000! –which become strategic garrisons of the territory. As the most pervasive connectivity places in the territory, sports venues can impact multipliers for relationships and economic opportunities in all Italian municipalities. The impact of sport venues on local municipalities will happen if there is a change in the State and the institutions' vision: from a merely organizational vision to impact, value, and service.

Therefore, to achieve these results, various strategies can be developed. The first is the investment in the culture of sport from primary school. In Italy today, sport is not practiced among younger children. If this was done, the multiplier effect over time would be enormous from a psychophysical point of view with all the related benefits of social, cultural, and economic impacts. Indeed, the positive effects could be measured, for example, in terms of more traditional job opportunities in sport and associated services and the creation of new jobs.

The second strategy concerns investments in sports venues. In this case, we can distinguish between investments in facilities, such as redevelopment or new green facilities, and new sports venues. In the first case, for example, the theme is that of green buildings. In the second case, the theme is linked to the sports tourism sector. In Italy, the value of tourism is €5 billion. The natural environment – for example, the mountains – becomes a new opportunity to make a new life and professional choices (e.g., micro-enterprises established to deliver health, wellness, and sports tourism services).

Each strategy is intricately linked to the economic perspective of sport. Financial planning is necessary to support implementing these strategies and their monitoring, management, and evaluation. Sport organizations need to evaluate their distribution of funds to ensure actions today support sport sustainability into the future.

Concluding remarks

1.   The sport sector should increase its investments to advance a culture of efficiency in financial, innovative, and managerial terms
2.   Sustainability is a complex issue that consists of strategies, projects, and programs that need investments in supportive programming for human knowledge and skills
3.   To reach sustainability within sport, there is a need for a satisfactory level of investments in financial, managerial, and innovation that generates the necessary culture and knowledge
4.   There are challenges in transitioning from being just as usual to designing new sustainable or circular business models
5.   Recent trends and emerging drivers of the global economy show that organizations worldwide should find better solutions to satisfy the main stakeholders and society's sustainability expectations. The challenge conveys the inner complexity of our contemporary time and global community
6.   Many shortcomings need to be resolved in sport from the economic perspective including transparency and accountability and the evolution toward the highest levels of quality and standards in responsible management and technological innovation for the sustainability of sport and society

Future directions

1.   The circular economy and innovation to develop disruptive business models to change the paradigm and vision of the industry will continue to advance
2.   Social inclusiveness and fairness will rise in importance as essential sustainability pillars in sport and society – with a global impact
3.   New job creation will continue thanks to new niche markets in society through sport
4.   Innovative integrated business models developed by startups and creative firms in the sport industry and beyond will continue to grow
5.   There will be increased stakeholder engagement and industrial partnerships for designing innovative solutions or reengineering existing processes, activities, and services

6. There will continue to be an increasing innovative role for technology that has the potential to change the management of sport and non-sport organizations. Such technology offer solution options for being economically viable into the future

Review questions

1. What are the economic benefits for the sport industry that should emerge from investments in sustainability?
2. What are the critical economic actions necessary for the sustainable development of the sport?
3. To align sport organizations toward sustainability, what is the role of sustainable finance, and why is it different from conventional investments?
4. Sustainability and technological innovation are drivers of change in sport and society. What are the main challenges and barriers to the development of innovative and sustainable projects?

Discussion questions

1. Consider a local sport organization and discuss their financial business models in terms of how they align toward achieving sustainability?
2. What role can sustainable investments have in promoting the social inclusiveness of sport organizations?
3. What kind of indicators would you adopt to measure strategic stakeholders' engagement levels, such as donors and spectators?

Learning activities

1. In small groups whereby each is a member of the board of directors of an existing sports team, propose and discuss a new sustainability programming and the (potentially) primary sources of sustainability financing
2. In small groups, select a sport organization and download its financial and economic report. Indicate how the report could be changed to introduce sustainability investments that you would like to propose. Is this report an effective tool for reporting the impact of sustainable financing and investments?
3. Search for sport organizations that publish a sustainability report. What is the structure of this document? What are the key areas they report? What is the role of the economic position in supporting their social and environmental sustainability?
4. In small groups, design a post for a social media communication campaign to raise money for a sport organization. What will be the sustainability key terms and messages that you think to use to engage your spectators?
5. Develop an S&SD project that encourages students to think critically about how S&SD can contribute to global sustainability. Students should complete

the following items as the initiation of their S&SD strategic planning process for the economic perspective:

- Envision and record your perspective of what the economic perspective of S&SD can contribute to the global efforts for sustainability
- Establish a goal statement on how you envision S&SD. For example, "Make the world a better place" is considered a vision. However, do not use this example for your vision
- Next, write two objectives to meet the goal. These objectives are your short-term goals that fall under each of your long-term goals
- Finally, write the strategies and tactics you would use to reach each objective for the economic S&SD

Further reading

1. Amer Sports. (2020). *Circular economy principle*. Amersports.com. Retrieved from https://www.amersports.com/responsibility/environment/circular-economy-principles/
2. Capgemini (2020). *Emerging technologies in sports. Reimagining the fan experience*. Retrieved from https://www.capgemini.com/pt-en/research/emerging-technologies-in-sports/
3. Deloitte. (2021). *2021 outlook for the US sports industry*. Retrieved from https://www2.deloitte.com/us/en/pages/technology-media-and-telecom-munications/articles/sports-business-trends-disruption.html
4. Associated Press. (2020). *Michael Garcia sends a World Cup report to FIFA*. USA Today Sports. Retrieved from https://eu.usatoday.com/story/sports/soccer/2014/09/05/michael-garcia-sends-world-cup-report-to-fifa/15119773/
5. Amorim Sports. (2020). *Circular economy principles and Innovation Culture*. Amorim-sports.com. Retrieved from https://amorim-sports.com/en/innovation/innovation-culture/
6. Blaustein, L. (2015, July). *How Adidas is pioneering open-source sustainability for sports*. GreenBiz. Retrieved from https://www.greenbiz.com/article/how-adidas-pioneering-open-source-sustainability-sports

Relevant online resources

1. Mugello Circuit: https://mugellocircuit.com/en/sistemi-di-gestione/kiss-mugello
2. Reynard, S. (2013): *"Fundraising in sport for development"* Series. SportandDev.org. Retrieved from https://www.sportanddev.org/en/news-and-views/article-series/fundraising-sport-development
3. Campelli Matthew. (2020, September): *Football's executive guide to sustainability strategy*. The Sustainability Report. Retrieved from https://sustainabilityreport.com/2020/09/03/the-football-executives-guide-to-sustainability-strategy/

4. CES 2021: Retrieved from https://www.ces.tech/Topics/Sports/Sports-Technology.aspx
5. Barca Innovation Hub: Retrieved from https://barcainnovationhub.com/

References

Adidas. (2020). *Sustainability Report.* Adidas.com. https://www.adidas-group.com/en/sustainability/reporting/sustainability-reports/

Andrews, M., & Harrington, P. (2016). Off Pitch: Football's financial integrity weaknesses, and how to strengthen them. CID Working Paper No. 311. Centre for International Development at Harvard University. Retrieved from http://sports.growthlab.cid.harvard.edu/publications/pitch-football%E2%80%99s-financial-integrity-weaknesses-and-how-strengthen-them

BlackRock. (2018, July). *ESG integration statement.* BlackRock.com. Retrieved from https://www.blackrock.com/ch/individual/en/literature/publication/blk-esg-investment-statement-web.pdf

Brundtland Commission. (2001). *Climate change 2001: Impacts, adaptation, and vulnerability.* In J.J. McCarthy, O.F. Canziani, N.A. Leary, D.J., Dokken and K.S. White (Eds.). *Contributions of Working Group II to the Third Assessment Report of the Intergovernmental Panel on Climate Change.* Cambridge: Cambridge University Press. https://www.ipcc.ch/report/ar3/wg2/

Brundtland, G.H., Khalid, M., Agnelli, S., Al-Athel, S., & Chidzero, B.J.N.Y. (1987). *Report of the World Commission on Environment and Development: Our common future.* Forty-second session, Item 83, Development and International Economic Co-operation: Environment, Committee on Development Planning. New York: United Nations. Retrieved from https://oliebana.files.wordpress.com/2012/09/1987-brundtland.pdf

Calvert, L.S. (2020, September). *The actual value of ESG data.* Retrieved from https://www.refinitiv.com/perspectives/future-of-investing-trading/the-true-value-of-esg-data/

Cameron, C. (2017, June). *New standards of environmental accountability in sports venues.* Athletic Business. Retrieved from https://www.athleticbusiness.com/stadium-arena/new-standards-of-environmental-accountability-in-sports-venues.html

Climate change. (2001). Impacts, adaptation, and vulnerability. In J.J. McCarthy, O.F. Canziani, N.A. Leary, D.J. Dokken and K.S. White (Eds.). Contributions of Working Group II to the Third Assessment Report of the Intergovernmental Panel on Climate Change. Cambridge: Cambridge University Press.

Connolly, E. (2019, December). *Round: Why the circular economy provides sport an opportunity to rethink everything.* Sports Pro Media. Retrieved from https://www.sportspromedia.com/from-the-magazine/circular-economy-climate-crisis-sports-sustainability-ellen-macarthur

Desmarais, C. (2017, November). *7 Reasons Athletes Make the Best Employees.* INC.com. Retrieved from https://www.inc.com/christina-desmarais/heres-why-kids-who-play-sports-do-better-in-life.html.

Eco-Management and Audit Scheme (EMAS). (n.d.) *What is EMAS?* Retrieved from https://ec.europa.eu/environment/emas/index_en.htm

Ellen MacArthur Foundation. (2016). *Intelligent Assets: Unlocking the Circular economy potential.* Retrieved from https://www.ellenmacarthurfoundation.org/assets/downloads/publications/EllenMacArthurFoundation_Intelligent_Assets_030216.pdf

Ellen MacArthur Foundation. (2019). *Completing the Picture: How the Circular Economy Tackles Climate Change.* Retrieved from https://www.ellenmacarthurfoundation.org/

assets/downloads/Completing_The_Picture_How_The_Circular_Economy-_Tackles_ Climate_Change_V3_26_September.pdf

Environmental Protection Agency (EPA). (2020).*Green Building. Components of Green Building.* Retrieved from https://archive.epa.gov/greenbuilding/web/html/components.html

European Commission. (2018). Final report 2018 by the high-level ex pert group on sustainable finance. Retrieved October 12, 2021 https://ec.europa.eu/info/sites/ default/files/180131-sustaina ble-finance-final-report_en.pdf

Eurate x.eu. (2019) A manifesto to deliver a circular economy in textiles. Retrieved October 12, 2020 from http://euratex.eu/wp-c ontent/uploads/Circular-Economy- Manifesto-Digital.pdf

European Commission (2011). *Communication from the Commission to the European Parliament, The Council, The European Economic and Social Committee, and The Committee of the Regions: Developing the European Dimension in Sport.* Retrieved from https://eur-lex.europa.eu/ legal-content/EN/TXT/HTML/?uri=CELEX:52011DC0012&from=MT

European Commission. (2016a). *High-Level Group on Grassroots Sport. Report to Commissioner Tibor Navracsics 'Grassroots Sport - Shaping Europe'.* Retrieved from https://ec.europa.eu/ assets/eac/sport/library/policy_documents/hlg-grassroots-final_en.pdf

European Commission. (2016b, June). *Report to Commissioner Tibor Navracsics 'Grassroots Sport - Shaping Europe'.* European Commission. Retrieved from https://ec.europa.eu/ assets/eac/sport/policy/cooperation/documents/290616-hlg-gs-final-report_en.pdf

European Commission. (2020a). *EMAS Global. EC.Europa. EU. Environment Section.* Retrieved from https://ec.europa.eu/environment/emas/join_emas/emas_global_en.htm

European Commission. (2020b). *Sport and Integrity. Commission policies for integrity in Sport.* EC.Europa. EU. Sport Section. Retrieved from https://ec.europa.eu/sport/policy/ integrity_en

European Council. (2020c, December). *Report by The Expert Group on Sustainable Financing of Sport (XG FIN) (2012). Strengthening financial solidarity mechanisms within the sport.* Retrieved from https://ec.europa.eu/assets/eac/sport/library/documents/xg-fin-2 01211-deliverable.pdf

European Commission. (2020d). *EC Europa. EU. Sport Section. About funding opportunities.* Retrieved from https://ec.europa.eu/sport/funding_en

European Union Agency for Cyber Security. (2021, April). What is *blockchain?* Retrieved from https://www.enisa.europa.eu/topics/csirts-in-europe/glossary/blockchain

Federation of the European Sporting Goods Industry (FESI). (2020, March). *FESI supports The Policy Hub's Statement on the Circular Economy Action Plan Publication.* Retrieved from https://fesi-sport.org/fesi-supports-the-policy-hubs-statement-on-the-circular-economy- action-plan-publication/?utm_source=rss&utm_medium=rss&utm_campaign=fesi-sup- ports-the-policy-hubs-statement-on-the-circular-economy-action-plan-publication

Ferrari.com.(2019). 2019 sustainability report. Retrieved October 12, 2020 from https:// corporate.ferrari.com/en/2019-sustainability-report

Freeman, R. (1984). *Strategic management: A stakeholder approach.* Boston, MA: Pitman.

Friedman, M., Parent, M., & Mason, D. (2004). Building a framework for issues man- agement in sport through stakeholder theory. *European Sport Management Quarterly, 4*(3), 170–190. 10.1080/16184740408737475

Glassdoor. (2019, July). *New Survey: Company Mission & Culture Matter More Than Compensation.* Glassdoor Inc. Retrieved from https://www.glassdoor.com/employers/ blog/mission-culture-survey/

Heere, B. (2018). Embracing the sportification of society: Defining e-sports through a polymorphic view on sport. *Sport Management Review, 21*(1), 21–24. 10.1016/j.smr.201 7.07.002

High-Level Expert Group on Artificial Intelligence. (2019, April). *A definition of AI: Main capabilities and scientific disciplines*, 8 April 2019, Brussels: European Commission. Retrieved from https://digital-strategy.ec.europa.eu/en/library/definition-artificial-intelligence-main-capabilities-and-scientific-disciplines

ISA. (2015). *Towards Sustainable Sport for Development Organizations. Sport & Society, International Sports Alliance & Utrecht University*. August 2015. Retrieved from https://www.uu.nl/en/news/new-publication-towards-sustainable-sport-for-development-organisations

ISO. (2020). *Sustainable Events with ISO 20121*. Geneva, Switzerland: ISO. https://www.iso.org/iso-20121-sustainable-events.html

Kaplan R., & Norton D. (1992, January-February). The Balanced Scorecard - Measures That Drive Performance. *Harvard Business Review, 70*(10), 71–79.

Korea Sports Promotion Foundation (KSPO). (2019, November). *2018 KSPO Sustainability Report: Communication on engagement*. Retrieved from https://www.unglobalcompact.org/participation/report/cop/create-and-submit/detail/434874

Macovei, S., Tufan, A.A., & Vulpe, B.I. (2014). Theoretical approaches to building a healthy lifestyle through the practice of physical activities. *Procedia-Social and Behavioral Sciences, 117*, 86–91. 10.1016/j.sbspro.2014.02.183

Mahon, J., & Waddock, S. (1992). Strategic issues management: An integration of issue life cycle perspectives. *Business and Society, 31*, 19–32. 10.1177%2F000765039203100103

McCullough, B.P., Orr, M., & Kellison, T. (2020). Sport ecology: Conceptualizing an emerging subdiscipline within sport management. *Journal of Sport Management, 34*(6), 509–520. 10.1123/jsm.2019-0294

McKinsey Company. (2016). *The Circular Economy: Moving from theory to practice*. Retrieved from https://www.mckinsey.com/business-functions/sustainability/our-insights/the-circular-economy-moving-from-theory-to-practice

Millington, R., Giles, A.R., van Luijk, N., & Hayhurst, L.M. (2021). Sport for Sustainability? The Extractives Industry, Sport, and Sustainable Development. *Journal of Sport and Social Issues*. 10.1177%2F0193723521991413

Mugello Circuit. (2020). *Kiss Mugello Program*. Retrieved from http://www.kissmugello.com/en/

Oranefo, C. (2019, May). *Building a sustainable finance ecosystem*. CMS Law. Retrieved from https://cms.law/en/gbr/publication/building-a-sustainable-finance-ecosystem

Pero, J. (2019, November). *European regulatory context on the circularity for the textile sector. Federation of the European Sporting Goods Industry – FESI*. Presented at Textile Mission Conference Berlin. Retrieved from https://textilemission.bsi-sport.de/fileadmin/assets/bilder/Konferenz_7._November_2019/TextileMission_7.11.2019_Praesentation_Pero.pdf

PWC. (2020). *ESG: Understanding the issues, the perspectives, and the path forward*. Retrieved from https://www.pwc.com/us/en/services/governance-insights-center/library/esg-environmental-social-governance-reporting.html

Sachs, J.D. (2015). *The age of sustainable development*. Columbia University Press. Retrieved from http://cup.columbia.edu/book/the-age-of-sustainable-development/9780231173155

Schrank K. (2014, June). *Top sports, media, and entertainment brands: A focus on ESG metrics*. Cornerstone Capital Group. Retrieved from https://cornerstonecapinc.com/top-sports-media-entertainment-brands-a-focus-on-esg-metrics-2/

Schulenkorf, N. (2012). Sustainable community development through sport and events: A conceptual framework for sport-for-development projects. *Sport Management Review, 15*(1), 1–12. DOI: 10.1016/j.smr.2011.06.001

SIGA Universal Standards and Implementation Guidelines. (2020). *Good Governance in Sport, Financial Integrity in Sport, Sports Betting Integrity*. Belgium: Bruxelles. Retrieved from https://t9i.e65.myftpupload.com/wp-content/uploads/2020/04/SIGA-UNIVERSAL-STANDARDS-IMPLEMENTATION-GUIDELINES-2020-EDITION.pdf

Sport England & UK Sport. (2021, June). *A code for Sports Governance*. UK SportGov.com. Retrieved from https://www.uksport.gov.uk/resources/governance-code

Szathmári, A., & Kocsis, T. (2020). Who cares about gladiators? An elite-sport-based concept Sustainable Sport. *Sport in Society*, 1–19. 10.1080/17430437.2020.1832470

The Commonwealth Secretariat. (2018). *Strengthening Sport-Related Policy Coherence Commonwealth Toolkit and Self-Evaluation Checklist*. Retrieved from https://thecommonwealth.org/sites/default/files/inline/Strengthening%20Sport%20Related%20Policy%20Coherence.pdf

The Finnish Innovation Fund Sitra. (2020). *The Circular Economy in sport project 2017-2018*. Finland: Helsinki. Retrieved from https://www.sitra.fi/en/projects/circular-economy-sport/#what-was-it-about

Tortora, M. (2020). *Responsible Management for Innovative and Sustainable Firms in the Age of Complexity*. In: Leal Filho W., Azul A.M., Brandli L., Lange Salvia A., Wall T. (eds) Decent Work and Economic Growth. Encyclopedia of the UN Sustainable Development Goals. Cham: Springer.

Triantafyllidis, S. (2018). Carbon Dioxide Emissions Research and Sustainable Transportation in the Sports Industry. *C—Journal of Carbon Research*, 4(4), 57. DOI: 10.3390/c4040057

Triantafyllidis, S., & Darvin, L. (2021). Mass-participant sport events and sustainable development: gender, social bonding, and connectedness to nature as predictors of socially and environmentally responsible behavior intentions. *Sustainability Science*, 16(5), 239–253. 10.1007/s11625-020-00867-x

United Nations Global Compact (UNGC). (2018a). *Global Compact Integrating the SDGs into Corporate Reporting: a Practical Guide*. Retrieved from https://d306pr3pise04h.cloudfront.net/docs/publications%2FPractical_Guide_SDG_Reporting.pdf

United Nations Global Compact (UNGC). (2018b). *2018 KSPO Sustainability Report*. Retrieved from https://www.unglobalcompact.org/participation/report/cop/create-and-submit/detail/434874

United States Green Building Council. (2020). *LEED Rating System*. Retrieved from https://www.usgbc.org/leed

UNPRI – UN Principles of Responsible Investments. (2020). *A practical guide to ESG integration for equity investing*. Retrieved from https://www.unpri.org/listed-equity/a-practical-guide-to-esg-integration-for-equity-investing/10.article

University of California Los Angeles (UCLA). (2021). *What is sustainability?* Retrieved from https://www.sustain.ucla.edu/what-is-sustainability/

8

THE ECOLOGICAL PERSPECTIVE OF SPORT AND SUSTAINABLE DEVELOPMENT

Cheryl Mallen and Greg Dingle

LEARNING OBJECTIVES

Upon completion of this chapter, learners should be able to successfully:

1. Define the terms adaptations, adaptive capacity, appreciative theory, climate, climate change, and partnerships
2. Describe examples of partnerships developed by those within sport to advance climate action
3. Consider the advantages of sport generating partnerships for climate action and climate action of sport partnerships
4. Investigate the need for further climate action by those in sport and society
5. Contemplate sport in your local area and the types of partnerships that can be generated to aid climate action

---

Overview

This chapter examines a critical issue in our contemporary times – our climate – and the need for climate action. Sport is uniquely positioned to be part of the solution. This solution includes advancing the sustainable development of sport (SD*o*S) and using sport as a platform to advance sport for sustainable development (S*4*SD) of our world societies. The discussion opens with an overview of our

DOI: 10.4324/9781003128953-8

climate issues and then turns to discuss sport's partnerships in the process of mitigating and managing these issues. Sport has utilized diverse partnerships to promote an awareness of – and action on – safeguarding our climate, and multiple examples are outlined. Overall, the chapter supports understandings of current actions and promotes further partnerships for efficient and effective progress for our contemporary climate-related issues.

Glossary

Adaptations

"The process of adjustment to actual or expected climate and its effects, to moderate harm or exploit beneficial opportunities" (Intergovernmental Panel on Climate Change, 2012, p. 556). The modifications are made due to the vulnerability and risks of climate and climate change.

Adaptive capacity

"The combination of the strengths, attributes, and resources available to an individual, community, society, or organization that can be used to prepare for and undertake actions to reduce adverse impacts, moderate harm, or exploit beneficial opportunities" (Intergovernmental Panel on Climate Change, 2012, p. 556).

Appreciative theory

It promotes "a paradigm of thought and understanding that holds organizations to be affirmative systems created by humankind, as solutions to problems" (Watkins & Cooperrider, 2000, p. 6). An application of appreciative theory implies that actions within sport can act as part of climate action.

Behavioral-based theory

This theory indicates that concerns encompass "goals, expectations, and choice" (Bowen, 2007, p. 98). An application of this theory means that those within sport have an option to engage in climate action.

Carbon neutrality

"A means of production where the total output of carbon dioxide during production is neutral, i.e., equal to zero. Carbon neutrality does not imply that businesses will have zero carbon emissions, but that these emissions are offset, i.e., counterbalanced" (Becker et al., 2020, p. 274).

Circular economy

Its main three principles are: (1) Design out waste and pollution; (2) keep products and materials in use; and (3) regenerate natural systems. Applying these principles to businesses and economic systems means, operationally, developing a systemic approach to economic development designed to benefit businesses, society, and the environment (Ellen MacArthur Foundation, 2019).

The focus is to have a regenerative system "through long-lasting design, maintenance, repair, reuse, remanufacturing, refurbishing, and recycling" (Geissdoefer et al., 2017, p. 761).

Climate

Following the expertise of the Intergovernmental Panel on Climate Change, the climate is

> the average weather, or more rigorously, ... the mean and variability of relevant quantities over a time period ... [with] the classical period for averaging these variables are 30 years, [and] the relevant quantities are most often surface variables such as temperature, precipitation, and wind. (Solomon et al., 2007, p. 942)

Climate change

The "consequences of human activities on world climate" (Rahman, 2013, p. 2); whereby there is "a long-term change in the statistical distribution of weather patterns (e.g., temperature, precipitation, etc.) over ... time" (Rahman, 2013, p. 3). The change means that "the nonlinearity of the climate system may lead to abrupt climate change" (Intergovernmental Panel on Climate Change, 2012, p. 556).

Partnerships

In this chapter, partnerships are voluntary collaborations to deliver messages or services for climate action. Partnerships involve blocks of people/organizations that advance all parties' legitimacy and allow each party to "win" by offering complementary resources (Zeimers et al., 2019). The partnerships can be same-sector or cross-sector collaborations that offer synergies by co-operating for strategy or program development and delivery (Bailey, 2004) and increasing the chances of success compared to working independently (Wildridge et al., 2008).

Sport

"Sport means all forms of physical activity which, through casual or organized participation, aim at expressing or improving physical fitness and well-being, forming social relationships or obtaining results in competition at all levels" (Szathmári & Kocsis, 2020, p. 4).

Sport and sustainable development (S&SD)

Sport and sustainable development (S&SD) is the process that includes two stages: SDoS and S4SD that, together, enhance the development that meets the needs of current generations without compromising future generations' ability to meet their own needs at the personal, social, economic, ecological, technological, and political levels (Millington et al., 2021; Szathmari & Kocsis, 2020; Triantafyllidis & Darvin, 2021).

Sport for sustainable development (S4SD)

S4SD refers to the contribution of sport to our global societies' viability by encouraging sustainability across the six perspectives of personal, social, economic, ecological, technological, and political worldwide (Macovei et al., 2014; Millington et al., 2021; Schulenkorf, 2012).

Sustainability

The term refers to "the integration of environmental health, social equity, and economic vitality to create thriving, healthy, diverse and resilient communities for this generation and generations to come" (University of California Los Angeles 2021, para. 2).

The term sustainable development encompasses the initiatives and progress in pursuit of sustainability. According to Brundtland Commission (2001), sustainable development is defined as the "development that meets the needs of the present without compromising the ability of future generations to meet their own needs" (p, 82). This includes "the narrow notion of physical sustainability [that] implies a concern for social equity between generations, a concern that must logically be extended to equity within each generation" (p. 82).

Sustainable development of sport (SDoS)

SDoS refers to the sustainable practices taken by sport regarding the management of sport products, services, and sport consumer behaviors to achieve sustainability within the world of sport that encompasses six perspectives including the personal, social, economic, ecological, technological, and political (McCullough et al., 2020; Szathmari & Kocsis, 2020; Triantafyllidis & Darvin, 2021).

Introducing the ecological perspective of sport for sustainable development (S4SD)

Our discussion now outlines the global climate issue and then summarizes why climatic impacts are an issue for sport. Next, the focus turns to how sport has been working toward being part of the solution by mitigating and managing the climatic problems through partnerships. These partnerships are aiding sport to transition toward sustainability (SDoS) and assist society to also edge toward this transition (S4SD).

The climate issue: Beyond sport

Climate change can arise from the "consequences of human activities on the world" (Rahman, 2013, p. 2). It has been noted as "the greatest threat facing humankind" (Mpandeli et al., 2019, p. 1). This global issue has been exacerbated by human activities, such as the use of fossil fuels, which "are estimated to have caused approximately 1.0°C of global warming above pre-industrial levels" (Trenberth, 2018). A warming trend affects air and water temperatures. This warmer world causes multi-directional, detrimental climatic impacts (Trenberth, 2018). Examples include "land degradation ... increases in rainfall intensity, flooding, drought frequency, and severity, heat stress, dry spells, wind, sea-level rise and wave action, and permafrost thaw ... [that] has led to shifts of climate zones in many world regions" (Intergovernmental Panel on Climate Change, 2020, p. 10). The temperature increases can generate stress on our communities with risks that encompass "health, livelihoods, food security, water supply, human security, and economic growth" (Intergovernmental Panel on Climate Change, 2018, p. 11). Global warming's associated challenges are a contemporary real-life issue, and scientists worldwide predict the impacts will continue to advance throughout the upcoming decades (Herold et al., 2018).

It is essential to keep in mind that climatic impacts are *not* applied proportionally worldwide (Tol, 2018). Instead, the effects can be zone-specific and location-specific – making it a complex issue. This is because local and regional conditions, such as elevation levels, forests, and water bodies, can affect climate. This is illustrated as some world areas are getting drier, and more prolonged droughts occur (National Oceanic and Atmospheric Administration, 2019). Additionally, major forest fires are breaking out in places such as southeastern Australia (BBC News, 2020), parts of Greece (Reuters, 2020), and the west coast of the United States (Selva et al., 2020). Whereas other areas of the globe are concerned about rising sea levels, such as in the Gulf of Mexico (Lindsey, 2020) and in specific cities such as Osaka, Japan; Alexandria, Egypt; Rio de Janeiro, Brazil; and Shanghai, China (Holder et al., 2017). Consequently, all countries and their related industries are not affected in the same way by climate – local and regional variations in the climate impacts mean that responses need to be localized.

We will now examine the impacts of climate on sport and then delve into how sport organizations have responded.

Why climatic impacts are an issue for sport

The relationship between the natural environment and sport has been noted to be "bidirectional" (McCullough et al., 2020, p. 509). Safeguarding the natural environment for current and future generations of sporting participants, therefore, is essential. Yet, fossil fuels are used for travel to sport practices and competitions (Watanabe et al., 2019) and to heat sport facilities and, thus, contribute to global warming (Kellison & Orr, 2020). Additionally, plastic debris can be strewn across our land and blown by the wind into waterways (Jambeck et al., 2018) – including plastic waste from sport facility concessions (Watkin et al., 2021). There are associated environmental consequences based on this type of plastic waste management (Picazo, 2019), as plastics absorb heat from the sun resulting in the release of greenhouse gases (Picazo, 2019). Sport has, therefore, contributed to climate issues and is not immune to the impacts.

There are multiple climatic impacts on sport. Examples encompass the lack of snow for training and the hosting of competitions (Falk & Hagsten, 2017; Scott et al., 2018; Steiger et al., 2017); drought conditions that require sports fields to be given additional irrigation to remain viable; or extreme rain events that cause flooding and require excellent drainage systems to maintain their area playing use (Dingle & Mallen, 2020; Mallen & Dingle, 2017); as well as sport event cancellations due to forest fires (Taylor, 2019). The challenges have been particularly noted for outdoor sport events (Brocherie et al., 2015), where athletes have been exposed to thermal (heat) stress (Brocherie et al., 2015) and are impacted by fossil fuel induced air pollution (Donnelly et al., 2016; Lippi et al., 2008; Malchrowicz-Mośko et al., 2019). Notably, a recent study of sport venues indicates that climate change causes "organizational uncertainty, greater management complexity, cost risks associated with water and energy resources, and waste outputs" (Dingle & Stewart, 2018, p. 293). The various examples illustrate that climatic impacts have been felt at sport facilities, summer and winter sport events, and athletes.

Sport and climate action

Due to the impacts, many in sport have been working toward being part of the solution by mitigating and managing the climatic issues. To aid in developing a response, sport partnerships have endeavored to embed climate action. Each of these partnerships aids sport to be one step closer to reaching their adaptive capacity for climatic issues. Such partnerships are key elements that support climate action, and they will now be defined and examples are provided.

Partnerships and the ecological perspective of sport and sustainable development (S&SD)

Partnerships in this chapter refer to voluntary collaborations used to deliver messages or services for climate action. These same-sector or cross-sector collaborations advance all parties' legitimacy and allow each party to 'win' by offering complementary resources (Zeimers et al., 2019). The partnerships generate synergies by cooperating in strategy or program development and delivery (Bailey, 2004), establishing distributed problem solving (the power of the collective group), and increasing the chances of success compared to working independently (Wildridge et al., 2008).

Partnerships are needed as the climate issue is diverse and complex. Understanding the impacts of climate and climate change in each region and acting as part of the solution can be intricate – especially if it is not one's area of expertise. Partnerships offer linkages between the power of sport as a platform – with a particularly strong ability to communicate messages that can be used for promotion promoting climate action – and collectives that can pool their knowledge or with bodies that specialize in climate action.

This chapter purports that each partnership is founded within the tenets of the behavioral-based theory. This theory indicates that concerns encompass "goals, expectations, and choice" (Bowen, 2007, p. 98). Applying this theory means that those within sport choose to engage – or not engage – in climate action. A key challenge for sport organizations and events, however, is that when facing multiple priorities, they tend to concentrate on "day-to-day" objectives such as efficiency and effectiveness [of the current task], at the expense of the long-term gain (Ghobadian et al., 2001). Many in sport have utilized partnerships to make climate action happen despite the day-to-day pressures of managing sport.

Sport partnerships for climate action: Sport for sustainable development (S4SD)

Sport partnerships for climate action are diverse and continue to grow and develop. They each seek to utilize sport as a platform in an effort to safeguard the natural environment. Multiple examples will now be offered.

Athletes have formed a series of collective partnerships as they generate environmentally focused organizations and campaigns. Examples include "Players for the Planet" (http://playersfortheplanet.org) which is an organization founded by former Major League Baseball player Chris Dickerson that has connected over 75 professional athletes with a mission to "seek to unite to make sustainability and environmental responsibility foundational values of our sport" (Players for the Planet, n.d., para. 1). The focus is for the athletes to partake in – and to promote others to participate in – the "Save the Ocean Campaign" to clean beaches, recycle in their communities, along with reducing their use of plastics. Also, Nico Rosberg (www.nicorosberg.com), a retired world champion Formula One driver, launched the "GreenTech Festival" (https://greentechfestival.com) to promote green technologies and encourage living sustainably. Ellen McArthur, a world record holder in sailing (from Great Britain), set up her foundation (www.ellenmcarthurfoundation.org) that promotes the regeneration of products to generate a circular economy. This type of economy represents natural systems whereby products and material waste are mitigated. There are options to reuse the items at the end of the bottom of the product cycle. New Zealand pole vault Olympian, Eliza McCartney, partnered as a brand ambassador with *Trees That Count* (https://www.treesthatcount.co.nz) to encourage tree planting throughout the country to counteract air quality issues. In particular, McCartney has promoted native New Zealand Tōtaro trees that continue to grow for hundreds of years. Brett Sutter, a former professional baseball player, set up a #StrikeOutWaste campaign (Outrider Post, 2020).

Other examples involve organizations made up of those in sport that act to safeguard our natural resources. An example includes the "Sport Ecology Group" (http://www.sportecology.org). This group is a partnership of academics building a sport and ecological-based research database for other academics, students, and practitioners. The focus is on sharing the growing body of research and eliminating the academic–practitioner divide. Another example is "Sport4Climate" (https://connect4climate.org) with over 500 worldwide partners and seeks to bring athletes, sport organizations, fans, the media, and corporations together for climate action. The multiple international promotional events disseminate the message that "It takes everyone to make a difference" (Sport4Climate, n.d., para. 1). "Green Sport Alliance" (https://greensportsalliance.org/) pulls together stakeholders in sport, such as athletes and their fans. The focus within this organization is on program initiatives concerning our global communities' health and sustainability. And a final example includes "Sport and Sustainability International" (www.sportsustainability.org) whereby sports teams, leagues, and governing bodies work toward advancing sustainable supply chains. This organization promotes awareness of environmental issues and seeks to change attitudes to transition to climate action with a motto of "do more."

Climate action and sport partnerships: The sustainable development of sport (SDoS)

A number of international and national sport organizations have partnered to safeguard the natural environment by working to be carbon neutral. This means an effort to eliminate or offset their carbon impacts – generally from fossil fuel use and the greenhouse gas release. One begins by developing knowledge regarding their carbon impacts (or carbon footprint) and then continuously reducing carbon-emitting activities to bring down the level in one's carbon footprint. The International Olympic Committee partnered with the corporation Dow on a program that pushes over 200 National Olympic Committee's and 77 international sport federations to measure their carbon footprints and then develop and enact plans to mitigate their footprint (Broder-Nemeth & Parshley, 2020). Once an organization's carbon footprint is measured (using a carbon calculator that can be found online), there are multiple ways to reduce the footprint, such as diminishing deforestation in your community, advancing efficient energy use, and moving to renewable energy.

Sport facilities worldwide have used renewable solar energy – and there is a growing trend to use renewables to meet 100% of a sport facility's energy demand. For instance, in Sydney, Australia, Bankwest Stadium has a small solar installation and then partners with a local renewable source to purchase the rest of their energy requirements (Bankwest Stadium, 2019). Golden 1 Center in Sacramento, California, United States, utilizes 100% renewable energy for all of their sport facility operations with a rooftop array of solar photovoltaic (PV) panels and a partnership with a local solar farm (Golden 1 Center Credit Union - Newsletter, 2018). In Dublin, Ireland, Aviva Stadium purchases 100% of its power requirements from clean energy sources (Burke-Kennedy, 2016). New Lawn stadium in the United Kingdom has solar panels to develop clean energy and partners with Ecotricity to offer 100% clean energy (https://www.fgr.co.uk/another-way).

Interestingly, and recently, Climate Pledge Arena (https://climatepledgearena .com/) moved beyond just using renewable energy to reduce its carbon footprint – as it sought to make its total rebuilt facility carbon neutral. To do this, it partnered with the International Living Future Institute (ILFI) (https://living-future.org), an organization that acts as a third party to certify buildings that are energy efficient. This organization sets a high standard for certification and requires:

> One hundred percent of the operational energy use associated with the project must be offset by new – off-site renewable energy. One hundred percent of the embodied carbon emissions impacts associated with the construction and materials of the project must be disclosed and offset. (International Living Future Institute, n.d., para. 2)

Guided by the ILFI certification guidelines, the Seattle Hockey Partners collaborated with the naming rights partner, Amazon, to make Climate Pledge Arena the first sport facility in the world to acquire the "Living Future Institute Zero Carbon Certification." During the rebuilding of the Climate Pledge Arena, home of the National Hockey League Seattle Krakin, all items (such as mechanical or cooking systems) that use fossil fuel have been replaced with fossil-free options (Climate Pledge Arena, n.d.). Instead, the arena was outfitted with electrical outlets that were fed by 100% renewable energy, including solar panels on the roof and access to off-site renewable power generation (Climate Pledge Arena, n.d.). It has been noted that Amazon pushed to reconsider the rebuilding to ensure it was carbon neutral (Newcomb, 2020) and that the arena was not named after Amazon. Instead, the name of the arena promotes a pledge. This pledge stems from the American Business Act whereby 154 companies have signed on and pledged "to demonstrate their support for action on climate change and for the climate change agreement in Paris that takes a strong step forward toward a low-carbon sustainable future" (The White House Archives, n.d., para. 1). This multiple-party partnership represents a movement to ensure that the latest sports facilities are positioned for climate action.

Furthermore, some sport facilities have partnered with their local communities to feed renewable energy back into the grid to meet community power needs once their own facility needs have been met. For instance, Amsterdam Arena has a solar energy generating system and a battery storage system that provides power to the local community energy grid whenever needed to alleviate the pressure during extreme demand (Wentworth, 2018). This sport facility battery storage system utilizes second-hand/second-life Nissan "Leaf" batteries to advance their energy storage capacity (Pratt, n.d.; Wentworth, 2018).

Sport has also partnered to source power generation at sport facilities. For instance, in Philadelphia, United States, Wells Fargo Center is 100% reliant upon renewable energy. This facility has purchased wind power generated through a partnership with a community grid provider (Pratt, n.d.). Additionally, Tokyo Olympic Stadium in Tokyo, Japan, was built so that "every venue used at the Games will be powered by 100% renewable energy" (Golob, 2020, para. 6) with a combination of solar, biomass, and hydropower (Olympic News, 2019) along with a "geothermal heating/cooling system" (Tokyo 2020, 2019, para. 3). Further, a partnership with Toyota offers fuel cell electric cars (Tokyo 2020, 2019). Another example is Ashton Gate Stadium in Bristol, England, refurbished with 460 PV panels and a biofuel boiler (Bristol City Council Newsroom, 2016). Biofuel can be generated from various raw organic waste, such as plant-based molecules (dead leaves, corn), sugar, and starches (Nunez, 2014).

Furthermore, the National Collegiate Athletic Association in the United States has relied upon the National Weather Service's "Air Quality Forecast System" (www.ncaa.org/sport-science-institute/air-quality) for air quality reports. Also, sport has been utilizing ever-advancing technology to make it easier to measure indoor facility air quality, and government bodies have established indoor sport facility air quality recommendations. For instance, 12.5 ppm of CO is the maximum level recommended for ice skating arenas in the Province of New Brunswick in Canada (Government of New Brunswick, n.d.). This level is supported in the Province of Manitoba, Canada, where a further indoor recommendation for NO_2 is at a maximum of 0.25 ppm (Government of Manitoba, 2009). Government scientists are aiding sport to establish acceptable air quality levels for sport facilities.

And a final example involves waste management awareness programs. It is common to attend a sport event and to see messages concerning waste management recycling. Further, these messages can be guided by actions laid out by groups such as "Waste Management Sustainability Services" (https://www.wm.com) and their specific sustainable sports program.

Sport is impacted by a period of significant transition

The examples outlined above illustrate that a movement is underway in sport to engage in climate action. Sport and climate action include an awareness of contemporary climate issues and a partnering strategy to aid the movement's effectiveness toward safeguarding the natural environment. There is, however, an additional consideration due to our contemporary period of significant transition caused by the pandemic from Covid-19. Scott McRoberts will now discuss this issue as it relates to sport.

Experts view by Scott McRoberts, Director Athletics, University of Guelph and Associate Director, International Institute for Sport Business and Leadership and M.A. Student Andrew Masters

Due to the global impact of Covid-19, it is important to discuss the impact of such an occurrence on sport and environmental sustainability. The full extent of sport's recovery and adaptability as a result of the Covid-19 pandemic is still unknown; however, there continue to be opportunities and creative thinking that have laid the foundation for a transition to a more sustainable sport world. Certain sport events were forced to think of a new way of operating, simply for survival, but some were able to do so with an even greater sustainable method of operations.

Predictions that arise from the impacts of the pandemic on sport and sustainability include, for example, that in early December 2020, the world took note of events such as the Challenge Daytona (https://challenge-daytona.com/), a triathlon event that took place in the empty Daytona International Speedway (home of the Daytona 500). Dr. Norm O'Reilly, Professor and Director, International Institute for Sport Business and Leadership at the University of Guelph, said

> It took place in a venue that had many uses in the pandemic, from swimming events to orienteering championships. There were no fumes. There was no litter and no waste. The triathlon world loved it. From a sustainability standpoint, it was certainly an interesting view on what a world-class event could be.

The standard for a clean competition environment has been set for future events and looks to see how athletes fight for such conditions into the future. Also, consider that the lack of stadiums packed with spectators in future events may help advance sustainability. "With COVID's creation of a reluctance to travel, you could see less sport tourism in the years to come than in pre-pandemic times," says Tim Strobel, Professor Marketing and Sport Management at the University of Bayreuth in Germany. The management of this issue is already underway as "It will be easier to seamlessly integrate digital aspects into events … [as] People have become used to digital atmospheres at games," says Strobel. This trend will continue with further digital technological advances. Additionally, while the term "carbon neutral" may be a trending concern in many areas of the environment, it is one that some areas of sport may struggle to reach for some time. The reason is old facilities, says Steve Nyman, Director of Maintenance and Energy Services at the University of Guelph. He notes that, for example, to change some older athletic facilities' heat source to a grid, the electric power source may increase heating costs several times over. While new facilities may effectively implement these systems into their design, the outlay to alter old facilities may not be available in times of economic concern, when it can be tough to justify investing in green initiatives when staff is being furloughed. This means that actions toward economic sustainability in post-pandemic times will slow actions for environmental sustainability.

Notably, sport has the power to encourage a critical body of people around the globe to be aware of, and to act, to advance environmental sustainability. Sport for environmental sustainability is noted at the University of Guelph, like many other institutions, lists sustainability as a central focus in its operations. While specific "behind the scenes" changes can be made to a sport facility, such as adopting a more energy-efficient boiler, another factor involves optics. Nyman says. "The most important thing we do on campus, in terms of environmental sustainability, is not gathering up compost or any of those smaller measures. It's promoting the thinking behind our initiatives". Nyman noted that if 4500 students graduated per year, the power is actually in those graduates. Suppose the electric Zamboni at our arena (the ice cleaning machine) contributes a small tonnage of the carbon dioxide emissions, but the 2500 fans at a hockey game watching the Zamboni go around the ice is what is also important is that it should be a moving billboard saying, "We are sustainable at the University of Guelph." This means the Zamboni contributes a measurable reduction in air pollution towards sport sustainability, but the advertising effects become longer term impacts. As the students become aware of an environmental way of thinking sponsored by their alma mater and pass the mindset along to future generations, the effects of simple, low-cost efforts become much wider than their intended audience and have the potential for reimaging sport and the world and create a much greener world than the science in the machine can on its own.

Considering these points, write a statement that informs athletes of the environmental conditions they are to compete in (i.e., level of clean air, water). Outline how athletes can work to achieve these conditions for every sport competition. Next, discuss the impact on sport and our natural environment and financial sustainability of reduced sport travel and digital technology advances for broadcasting sport events worldwide. What advances can be expected in post-pandemic times if sport venues struggle financially while becoming carbon neutral? Consider the environmental awareness campaign proposed in the exposure of the Zamboni machine above. Design awareness campaigns for your sport/venues. What message would you promote?

Concluding remarks

1. To date, we have not resolved the climatic issues that impact sport and society
2. Much work remains to be done to reach our adaptive capacity
3. The authors of this chapter promote the groundwork (as illustrated in the examples above) to further climate action within all sports aspects
4. Partnerships are critical to effective solutions, and sport needs to continuously seek out the partners necessary to aid in effective and successful climate action
5. Sport is positioned well to show the world how to advance climate action and successfully safeguard the natural environment for sport and society
6. Let all of us contribute and do our part to achieve environmental sustainability!

Future directions

1. Sport is not exempt from the climate change issue – so let's be proactive. Be part of the solution. Consider how you can contribute to solving the real-world climate issues
2. Sport needs to find strategies to advance knowledge on location-specific climate impacts continuously
3. Sport must adapt to the vulnerabilities of climatic impacts by advancing the strategic options for mitigating and managing such impacts – and develop partnerships to aid in reaching adaptive sports capacity for climate action
4. Sport can continue to show the world how to successfully implement comprehensive climate action that becomes synonymous with sport to safeguard the natural environment for those in sport today, and into the future, along with our global societies

Review questions

1. In your own words, define adaptations, adaptive capacity, appreciative theory climate, climate change, and partnerships
2. How does the appreciative theory apply to sport climate action?
3. What is your understanding of how our contemporary climate change situation impacts sport?
4. What is your understanding of how sport impacts our natural environment?
5. How have partnerships aided sport in responding to climate impacts? Outline the advantages of these partnerships for sport
6. The chapter discussed sport's response to climate change, what has sport done to respond? Is it an adequate response?

Discussion questions

1. Should sport be used as a vehicle for climate action? Why or why not?
2. Is there an awareness of the climate issue impacting sport in your region? If not, how can this be advanced? If so, what is noted, and is it enough?

3. Is there an awareness of the climate issue impacting your local community? If so, how is it affecting the community?
4. What are athletes doing to safeguard the natural environment in your region? How can you get involved?
5. What are sport teams doing to safeguard the natural environment in your region? How can you get involved?

Learning activities

1. Envision and record your idea of what the ecological perspective of S&SD can contribute to the global efforts for sustainability
2. Generate a long-term goal and at least four objectives for your vision – ensure at least one objective applies to SDoS and one for S4SD for the ecological perspective of S&SD
3. Write strategies and tactics for achieving each objective for the ecological S&SD

Consider sport partnerships that can assist you in achieving your stated objectives. List five potential partnerships and outline the value these partnerships can provide for achieving climate action.

Further reading

1. McCullough, B.P., Orr, M., & Kellison, T. (2020). Sport ecology: Conceptualizing an emerging subdiscipline within sport management. *Journal of Sport Management, 34*(6), 509–520. https://doi.org/10.1123/jsm.2019-0294
2. McCullough, B.P., Orr, M., & Watanabe, N. (2019). Measuring externalities: The imperative next step to sustainability assessment in sport. *Journal of Sport Management, 34*(5), 393–402. https://doi.org/10.1123/jsm.2019-0254
3. Mallen, C., & Chard, C. (2012, May). "What could be" in Canadian sport facility environmental sustainability. *Sport Management Review, 15*, 230–243. https://doi.org/10.1016/j.smr.2011.10.001
4. Mallen, C., & Chard, C. (2011). A framework for debating the future of environmental sustainability in the Sport Academy. *Sport Management Review, 14*, 424–433. https://doi.org/10.1016/j.smr.2010.12.002
5. Sartore-Baldwin, M.L., & McCullough, B.P. (2018). Equity-based sustainability and ecocentric management: Creating more ecologically just sport organization practices. *Sport Management Review, 21*(4),391–402. https://doi.org/10.1016/j.smr.2017.08.009
6. Marlier, M., Constandt, B., Schyvinch, C., De Bock, T., Winand, M., & Willem, A. (2020). Bridge over troubled water: Linking capacities of sport and non-sport organizations. *Social Inclusion, 8*(3), 139–151.

Online relevant resources

1. 1 Green Sport Alliance (GAS): (https://greensportsalliance.org)
2. Sport Ecology Group (SEG): (https://www.sportecology.org)
3. Players for the Planet: (http://playersfortheplanet.org)
4. Sport Sustainability: (www.sportsustaibility.org)
5. International Living Future Institute: (http://living-future.org)
6. Connect for Climate: (https://connect4climate.org)
7. PlayGreen Project: (https://www.playgreenproject.eu)
8. Sport for Climate Action: (https://unfccc.int/sites/default/files/resource/Sports_for_Climate_Action_Declaration_and_Framework.pdf
9. Football 4 Climate: (https://www.football4climate.org/)

References

Bailey, N. (2004). Toward a research agenda for public-private partnerships in the 1990s. *Local Economy, 8*, 292–306. 10.1080/02690949408726205

Bankwest Stadium. (2019). Bankwest Stadkum sustainability case study. Retrieved from https://bankweststadium.com.au/wp-content/uploads/2019/09/BankwestStadiumSustainability1.pdf

Becker, S., Bouzdine-Chameeva, T., & Joegler, A. (2020, November). The carbon neutrality principle: A case study in the French spirits sector. *Journal of Cleaner Production, 274*, 1–10. https://doi.org/10.1016/j.jclepro.2020.122739

Bowen, F. (2007). Corporate social strategy: competing views from two theories of the firm. *Journal of Business Ethics, 75*(1), 97–113. 10.1007/s10551-006-9240-0

Burke-Kennedy, E. (2016, February). *Aviva goes green with a new clean energy deal.* The Irish Times. Retrieved from https://www.irishtimes.com/business/energy-and-resources/aviva-goes-green-with-new-clean-energy-deal-1.2518038

Bristol City Council Newsroom. (2016, July). *Ashton Gate Stadium latest to benefit from Bristol City Council's solar PV program.* Retrieved from https://news.bristol.gov.uk/news/ashton-gate-stadium-latest-to-benefit-from-bristol-city-council-s-solar-pv-programme

British Broadcasting Corporation News (BBC News). (2020, January). *Australia fires A visual guide to the bushfire crisis.* Retrieved from https://www.bbc.com/news/world-australia-50951043

Brocherie, F., Girard, O., & Millett, G. (2015). They are emerging environmental and weather challenges in outdoor sports. *Climate, 3*(3), 492–521. 10.3390/cli3030492

Broder-Nemeth, A., & Parshley, G. (2020, September). *IOC and Dow announce phase two of the Olympic Movement Carbon Initiative Award.* Retrieved from https://corporate.dow.com/en-us/news/press-releases/ioc-and-dow-announce-phase-two-of-olympic-movement-carbon-initiative-award.htm

Brundtland Commission (2001). Climate change 2001: Impacts, adaptation, and vulnerability. In McCarthy, J.J., Canziani, O.F., Leary, N.A., Dokke, D.J. & White, K.S. (Eds.), Contributions of Working Groupworking group II to the Third Assessment Reportthird assessment report of the Intergovernmental Panelintergovernmental panel on Climate Changeclimate change. Cambridge: Cambridge University Press. Weblink: https://www.ipcc.ch/report/ar3/wg2/

Climate Pledge Arena (CPA). (n.d.). *Sustainability.* Retrieved from https://climatepledgearena.com/sustainability

Dingle, G., & Mallen, C. (2020). Community sports fields and atmospheric climate impacts: Australian and Canadian perspectives. *Managing Sport and Leisure*, 26(4), 301–325. 10.1080/23750472.2020.1766375

Dingle, G., & Stewart, B. (2018). Playing the climate game: Climate change impacts, resilience, and adaptation in the climate-dependent sport sector. *Managing Sport and Leisure*, 23(4–6), 293–314. 10.1080/23750472.2018.1527715

Donnelly, A., MacIntyre, T., & O'Sullivan. (2016). Environmental influences on elite sport athletes' well-being: From gold, silver, and bronze to blue-green & gold. *Frontiers in Psychology*, 7, 1167. 10.3389/fpsyg.2016.01167

Ellen MacArthur Foundation. (2019). *Completing the picture: How the circular economy tackles climate change.* Retrieved from https://www.ellenmacarthurfoundation.org/assets/downloads/Completing_The_Picture_How_The_Circular_Economy-_Tackles_Climate_Change_V3_26_September.pdf

Falk, M., & Hagsten, E. (2017). Climate change threats to one of the world's most extensive cross-country skiing races. *Climatic Change*, 143(1–2), 59–71. https://link.springer.com/article/10.1007/s10584-017-1992-2

Geissdoefer, M., Savaget, P., Bocken, N., Van Hultink, E. (2017). The circular economy – A new sustainability paradigm? Journal of Cleaner Production, 143, 757–768. 10.1016/j.jclepvo.2016.12.048

Ghobadian, A., Viney, H., & Holt, D. (2001). Seeking unity in implementing corporate environmental strategy. *International Journal of Environmental Technology and Management*, 1(4), 384–401. ISSN: 1466-2132. Retrieved from http://www.inderscience.com/search/index.php?action=record&rec_id=771&prevQuery=&ps=10&m=or

Golden 1 Center Credit Union - Newsletter. (2018, April). *Golden 1 Center "solar days" builds on Sacramento Kings ambitious green performance and goals.* Retrieved from https://www.golden1center.com/news/detail/golden-1-center-solar-days

Golob, M., Flores, M., Al-Ashaab, A., Al-Ashaab, H., Herrera, M., & Maklin, D. (2020, June). Insights towards an agile enterprise. In the *2020 IEEE International Conference on Engineering, Technology and Innovation (ICE/ITMC)* (pp. 1–9). IEEE.

Government of Manitoba. (2009). *Arena air quality.* Retrieved from https://www.gov.mb.ca/health/publichealth/environmentalhealth/protection/docs/aaqg.pdf

Government of New Brunswick. (n.d.). *New Brunswick arenas indoor air quality recommended guidelines.* Retrieved from https://www2.gnb.ca/content/dam/gnb/Departments/h-s/pdf/en/HealthyEnvironments/Air/air-arenas_guidelines.pdf ISBN 978-1-4605-0752-010064-12-2014

Herold, N., Ekström, M., Kala, J., Goldie, J., & Evans, J.P. (2018). Australian climate extremes in the 21st century according to a regional climate model ensemble: Implications for health and agriculture. *Weather and Climate Extremes*, 20, 54–68. 10.1016/j.wace.2018.01.001

Holder, J., Kommenda, N., & Watts, J., (2017, November). *The tree-degree world: The cities that will be drowned by global warming.* The Guardian. Retrieved from https://www.theguardian.com/cities/ng-interactive/2017/nov/03/three-degree-world-cities-drowned-global-warming

Intergovernmental Panel on Climate Change (IPCC). (2012). Glossary of terms. In: *Managing the risks of extreme events and disasters to advance climate change adaptation.* Special Report of Working Groups I and II of the Intergovernmental Panel on Climate Change (IPCC). Cambridge, UK, and New York, NY, USA: Cambridge University Press, pp. 555–564.

Intergovernmental Panel on Climate Change (IPCC). (2018). *Special report: Global warming of 1.5⁰C – Summary for policymakers.* United Nations, IPCC. Retrieved from https://www.ipcc.ch/sr15/

Intergovernmental Panel on Climate Change (IPCC). (2020). *Climate change and land: An IPCC special report on climate change, desertification, land degradation, sustainable land management, food security, and greenhouse gas fluxes in terrestrial ecosystems – Summary for policymakers.* United Nations, IPCC. ISBN 978-92-9169-154-8

International Living Future Institute (ILFI). (n.d.) *Zero carbon certification: Overview.* Retrieved from https://living-future.org/zero-carbon-certification

Jambeck, J., Hardesty, B., Brooks, A. *et al.,* (2018). Challenges and emerging solutions to the land-based plastic waste issue in Africa. *Marine Policy,* 96, 256–263. https://doi.org/10.1016/j.marpol.2017.10.04 1

Kellison, T., & Orr, M. (2020). Climate vulnerability as a catalyst for early stadium replacement. *International Journal of Sports Marketing and Sponsorship,* 22(1), 126–141. 10.1108/IJSMS-04-2020-0076

Lindsey, R. (2020, August). *Climate change: Global sea level. Climate.gov.* Retrieved from https://www.climate.gov/news-features/understanding-climate/climate-change-global-sea-level

Lippi, G., Guidi, G.C., and Maffulli, N. (2008). Air pollution and sports performance in Beijing. *International Journal of Sports Medicine,* 29(8), 696–698. Retrieved from https://www.thieme-connect.de/products/ejournals/abstract/10.1055/s-2008-1038684

Macovei, S., Tufan, A.A., & Vulpe, B.I. (2014). Theoretical approaches to building a healthy lifestyle through the practice of physical activities. *Procedia-Social and Behavioral Sciences,* 117, 86–91. 10.1016/j.sbspro.2014.02.183

Malchrowicz-Mośko, E., Motiková, Z., & Poczta, J. (2019). "Because we don't want to run in smog": Problems with the sustainable management of sport event tourism in protected areas (A case study of National Parks in Poland and Slovakia). *Sustainability,* 11(2), 325. Retrieved from 10.3390/su11020325

Mallen, C., & Dingle, G.W. (2017). Climate change and Canadian communities' grass-based sport fields. *International Journal of Environmental Sustainability,* 13(2), 45–59. 10.18848/2325-1077/CGP/v13i02

McCullough, B.P., Orr, M., & Kellison, T. (2020). Sport ecology: Conceptualizing an emerging subdiscipline within sport management. *Journal of Sport Management,* 34(6), 509–520. 10.1123/jsm.2019-0294

Millington, R., Giles, A.R., van Luijk, N., & Hayhurst, L.M. (2021). Sport for sustainability? The extractives industry, sport, and sustainable development. *Journal of Sport and Social Issues.* 10.1177/0193723521991413

Mpandeli, S., Nhamo, L., Moeletsi, M., Masupha, T., Magidi, J. Nshikolomo, K., Liphadzi, S., Naidoo, D., & Mabhaudhi, T. (2019). Assessing climate change and adaptive capacity at local scale using observed and remotely sensed data. *Weather and Climate Extremes,* 26(10), 1013. Retrieved from https://hdl.handle.net/10568/106732

National Oceanic and Atmospheric Administration. (2019). *Climate change impacts.* Retrieved from https://www.noaa.gov/education/resource-collections/climate/climate-change-impacts

Newcomb, T. (2020, December). *Seattle Kraken's Climate Pledge Arena is going carbon neutral, an 'unbelievalby' challenge task.* Forbes. Retrieved from https://www.forbes.com/sites/timnewcomb/2020/12/09/climate-pledge-arena-going-carbon-neutral-an-unbelievably-challenging-task/?sh=492664e01a7d

Nunez, C. (2014). "Fantasy" of fuel from corn waste gets big U.S. test. *National Geographic.* Retrieved from https://www.nationalgeographic.com/news/energy/2014/09/140911-project-liberty-cellulosic-ethanol-us-test/

Olympic News, (2019, July). *Tokyo 2020: Sustainable Games for a sustainable society.* Retrieved from https://www.olympic.org/news/tokyo-2020-sustainable-games-for-a-sustainable-society

Outride post (2020, January). *Winning Over my Baseball Teammates to Strikeout Waste.* Retrieved from https://outrider.org/climate-change/articles/brent-suter-milwaukee-brewers-strikeout-waste/

Picazo, M. (2019, June). *How plastic pollution is contributing to climate change. The Weather Network.* Retrieved from https://www.theweathernetwork.com/ca/news/article/plastic-pollution-is-contributing-to-climate-change-greenhouse-gas

Players for the Planet. (n.d.). Our mission: Uniting athletes for global change. Retrieved from https://playersfortheplanet.org

Pratt, C. (n.d.). *Comcast Spectacor secures 100% renewable energy supply for Wells Fargo Centre.* Constellation News. Retrieved from https://www.edisonenergy.com/news/comcast-spectacor-secures-100-renewable-energy-supply-for-wells-fargo-center/

Rahman, M. (2013). Climate change: A theoretical review. *Interdisciplinary Description of Complex Systems, 11*(1), 1–13. 10.7906/indecs.11.1.1

Reuters. (2020, September). *Greek wildfire rages near Athens: Residential areas evacuated.* Retrieved from https://ca.reuters.com/article/idUSKBN2601ZR

Sachs, J.D. (2015). *The age of sustainable development.* Columbia University Press. Retrieved from http://cup.columbia.edu/book/the-age-of-sustainable-development/9780231173155

Schulenkorf, N. (2012). Sustainable community development through sport and events: A conceptual framework for sport-for-development projects. *Sport management review, 15*(1), 1–12. 10.1016/j.smr.2011.06.001

Scott, D., Steiger, R., Rutty, M., & Fang, Y. (2018). The changing geography of the Winter Olympics and Paralympics in a warmer world. *Current Issues in Tourism, 22*(11), 1301–1311. 10.1080/13683500.2018.1436161

Selva, J., Vercammen, P., Colbert, C., & Silverman, H. (2020, September). *Fast-moving fires in California send thousands of residents in wine country fleeing.* Cable News Network (CNN). Retrieved from https://www.cnn.com/2020/09/28/us/california-wildfires-zogg-fire-glass-fire-monday/index.html

Solomon, S., Qin, D., Manning, M., Chen, Z., Marquis, M., Averyt, K.B., Tingor, M., & Miller, H.L. (2007). *Climate Change 2007: The Physical Science Basis.* Cambridge: Cambridge University Press.

Sport4Climate. (n.d.). *Initiatives.* Retrieved from https://www.connect4climate.org/initiatives/sport4climate.

Steiger, R., Scott, D., Abegg, B., Pons, M., & Aall, C. (2017). A critical review of climate change risk for ski tourism. *Current Issues in Tourism,* 1–37. 10.1080/13683500.2017.1410110

Szathmári, A., & Kocsis, T. (2020, November). Who cares about gladiators? An elite-sport-based concept of Sustainable Sport. *Sport in Society,* 1–19. 10.1080/17430437.2020.1 832470

Taylor, L. (2019, August). *Canceled races, fainting players: How climate change is affecting the sport.* World Economic Forum. Retrieved from https://www.weforum.org/agenda/2 019/08/climate-change-turns-up-heat-on-sports/

The White House: President Barack Obama – Archives. (n.d.). *American Business Act on Climate Change.* Retrieved from https://obamawhitehouse.archives.gov/climate-change/pledge

Tokyo 2020. (2019). *Sustainability progress report.* Retrieved from https://gtimg.tokyo202 0.org/image/upload/production/dpmsi7vxksqzouhwdsdz.pdf

Tokyo 2020. (2020, April). *Tokyo 2020 unveils the pre-Games sustainability report.* Retrieved from https://www.paralympic.org/news/tokyo-2020-unveil-pre-games-sustainability-report

Tol, R. (2018). The economic impacts of climate change. *Review of Environmental Economics and Policy, 12*(1), 4–25. 10.1093/reep/rex027

Trenberth, K. (2018). Climate change caused by human activities is happening, and it already has major consequences. *Journal of Energy & Natural Resources Law, 36*(4), 463–481. 10.1080/02646811.2018.1450895

Triantafyllidis, S., & Darvin, L. (2021). Mass-participant sport events and sustainable development: Gender, social bonding, and connectedness to nature as predictors of socially and environmentally responsible behavior intentions. *Sustainability Science, 16*(5), 239–253. 10.1007/s11625-020-00867-x

University of California Los Angeles (UCLA). (2021). *What is sustainability?* Retrieved from https://www.sustain.ucla.edu/what-is-sustainability/

Waste Management Sustainability Services. (n.d.). *Waste management sustainable sports programs: Sustainable sports as a game-changer for business.* Retrieved from https://www.wm.com/sustainability-services/documents/solutions/Sustainable%20Sports%20Service%20Menu.pdf

Watanabe, N., Yan, G., Soebbing, P., & Fu, W. (2019). Air pollution and attendance in the Chinese Super League: Environmental economics and the demand for sport. *Journal of Sport Management, 33*(4), 289–302. 10.1123/jsm.2018-0214

Watkin, G., Mallen, C., & Hyatt, C. (2021). Management perspectives on plastics free sport facilities' beverage service. *Journal of Management and Sustainability, 11*(1), 1–15. 10.5539/jms.v11n1p1

Watkins, J., & Cooperride, D. (2000). Appreciative inquiry: A transformative paradigm. *Journal of Organization Development Network, 32,* 6–12.

Wentworth, A. (2018, July). *Amsterdam Arena installs central new battery storage.* Retrieved from https://www.climateaction.org/news/amsterdam-arena-installs-major-new-battery-storage

Wildridge, V., Childs, S., Cawthra, L., & Madge, B. (2008). How to create successful partnerships – A review of literature. *Health Information and Libraries Journal.* Retrieved from https://onlinelibrary.wiley.com/doi/full/10.111/j.1740-3324-2004.00497x

Zeimers, G., Anagnostopoulos, C., Zintz, T., et al. (2019). Examining collaboration among nonprofit organizations for social responsibility programs. *Nonprofit and Voluntary Sector Quarter, 48*(5), 953–974. 10.1177/0899764019837616

9

THE TECHNOLOGICAL PERSPECTIVE OF SPORT AND SUSTAINABLE DEVELOPMENT

Cheryl Mallen and Stavros Triantafyllidis

LEARNING OBJECTIVES

Upon completion of this chapter, learners should be able to successfully:

1. Define the technological perspective of sport and sustainable development (S&SD)
2. Outline how emerging technologies relate to the sustainable development of sport (SDoS) and sport for sustainable development (S4SD)
3. Review current technological sustainable trends in S&SD and beyond
4. Explain why sport requires a comprehensive strategy related to the management of emerging innovations
5. Propose ideas, programs, and strategic plans for managing effectively emerging technologies that are good for one's life but impact fair and equitable sporting competitions

---

Overview

Technological innovations are increasingly impacting sport (Ratten, 2020). New technologies have been utilized in various sports, such as athletes' experiences during their training and competition, sport facilities and events, spectatorship, media communications, and sport manufacturing. Applying determinist theory indicates that these technologies contribute to societal change with a series of

DOI: 10.4324/9781003128953-9

"revolutionary leaps forward" (Omoregie, 2016, p. 896). The impacts from these leaps make it "more important to understand how to develop a comprehensive strategy regarding the management of innovation" (Ratten, 2020, para. 1).

This chapter uses the example of emerging brain technology and its potential applications within sport to outline a framework for managing such issues. The aim is to encourage organizational preparation for the next generation of technologies to pursue sport and sustainable development (S&SD) that promotes meeting the needs of current sporting participants without negatively impacting future sporting generations. S&SD is comprised of the sustainable development of sport (SDoS) (that focuses on adaptions within sport) as well as sport for sustainable development (S4SD) (that focuses on how sport can be used as a vehicle to help society transition to achieve sustainability).

The learning objectives and glossary of terms will now be presented. In the following sections, further discussion is provided on the emerging technologies that have integrated sport and why we need to manage such innovations. Then we will discuss emerging brain technology.

Glossary

Determinist theoretical view of technology

The determinist theoretical view promotes a "belief that technology is an autonomous and revolutionary force" (Omoregie, 2016, p. 298) in our contemporary society. This theory positions technology as "neutral, or value-free, but it has become autonomous, or self-directed" (Omoregie, 2016, p. 298). Once a technology is integrated, in this case within sport, pressure is felt by other parties to utilize the technological innovations, and this sets up a continuous spiral forward for the integration of technology (Omoregie, 2016).

Somatosensory information

The somatosensory system is defined as the sensory system, and it builds upon sensory neurons and neural pathways that respond to changes at the surface or inside the body (Jenmalm & Johansson, 1997).

Sport

"Sport means all forms of physical activity which, through casual or organized participation, aim at expressing or improving physical fitness and well-being, forming social relationships or obtaining results in competition at all levels" (Szathmári & Kocsis, 2020, p. 4).

Sport and sustainable development (S&SD)

S&SD is the process that includes two stages: SDoS and S4SD that, together, enhance the development that meets the needs of current generations without compromising future generations' ability to meet their own needs at the personal, social, economic, ecological, technological, and political levels (Millington et al., 2021; Szathmári & Kocsis, 2020; Triantafyllidis & Darvin, 2021).

Sport for sustainable development

S4SD refers to the contribution of sport to our global societies' viability by encouraging sustainability across the six perspectives of personal, social, economic, ecological, technological, and political worldwide (Macovei et al., 2014; Millington et al., 2021; Schulenkorf, 2012).

Sustainable

Human actions "causing little or no damage to the environment and therefore able to continue for a long time" (Cambridge dictionary, n.d., para.1).

Sustainability

The term refers to "the integration of environmental health, social equity, and economic vitality to create thriving, healthy, diverse and resilient communities for this generation and generations to come" (University of California Los Angeles, 2021, para. 2).

The term sustainable development encompasses the initiatives and progress in pursuit of sustainability. According to Brundtland Commission (2001), sustainable development is defined as "development that meets the needs of the present without compromising the ability of future generations to meet their own needs" (p. 82). This includes "the narrow notion of physical sustainability [that] implies a concern for social equity between generations, a concern that must logically be extended to equity within each generation" (p. 82).

Sustainable development of sport (SDoS)

SDoS refers to the sustainable practices enacted by sport regarding the management of sport products, services, and sport consumer behaviors to achieve sustainability within the world of sport that encompasses six perspectives including the personal, social, economic, ecological, technological, and political (McCullough et al., 2020; Szathmári & Kocsis, 2020; Triantafyllidis & Darvin, 2021).

Technologies

In this chapter, technologies is defined as

> a technical means by which athletes attempt to improve their training and competitive surroundings to enhance their overall athletic performance. It is the knowledge and application of using specialized equipment and the latest modern technologies to perform tasks more efficiently. (Gulhane, 2014, p. 1)

The analytical concept and emerging technologies in sport

The analtyical concept refers to a theoretical approach that can be used for analyzing sport as a platform to understand the world as a complex interaction of personal, social, economic, ecological, technological, and political systems. Understandings of the individual parts can be combined to determine the SD*o*S applied as a microcosm of society (Millington et al., 2021; Szathmári & Kocsis, 2020; Triantafyllidis & Darvin, 2021).

The normative concept and emerging technologies in sport

The normative concept referes to a theoretical approach whereby examinations can be completed using sport as a platform to view the world by defining the objectives of a well-functioning society that delivers well-being for its global citizens today and for future generations. The normative concept urges us to have a universal vision toward a good society. These examinations lead to an understanding of where we are currently and the gaps that need to be addressed in the future based on the six perspectives outlined above (Millington et al., 2021; Szathmári & Kocsis, 2020; Triantafyllidis & Darvin, 2021).

Emerging technologies have integrated sport

An essential view using the determinists theory promotes a "belief that technology is an autonomous and revolutionary force" (Omoregie, 2016, p. 298). Interestingly, this theory positions technologies as "neutral, or value-free, but it has become autonomous, or self-directed" (Omoregie, 2016, p. 298). Further, once a technology is integrated within sport, pressure is felt by others also to utilize the technology (Omoregie, 2016), and it sets up a continuous upward spiral as emerging technologies are omnipresent (Omoregie, 2016).

Technologies have been used to advance sport safety, such as improving helmet technology to reduce head trauma in ice hockey, American football, skiing, and cycling (Hasler, 2018). Further, emerging technologies provide an advantage in sport by reducing the energy required by a participant to perform (Gulhane, 2014). Striving to acquire a technological edge has been occurring for decades, and such innovations have been noted as being "essential to the future well-being of sports" (Petrovic et al., 2015, p. 175). Examples abound, for instance, according to Muniz-Pardos et al. (2021),

> every women's and men's world records from 5 km to the marathon has been broken since the introduction of carbon fiber plate (CFP) shoes in 2016 [with an] … increase [in] the elastic properties of the shoe thereby reducing the energy cost of running. (p. 371)

Indeed, researchers have proposed that the improvements in running times are most likely due to the shoe technology and not the runners' physiological development (Muniz-Pardos et al., 2021). Sensor technology is also growing (Ryan et al., 2016) and has been used in robotics that aid athletes to train. One such robot was outfitted with sensors and programmed to measure the endurance and speed of techniques applied by athletes training for fencing. Interestingly, if the athlete exhibited cues concerning a particular attack, the sensors picked this up and the robot arm moves to avoid or "parry expected attacks" (Weichenberger et al., 2015, p. 95). Further, miniature sensors, or "micro–electromechanical systems" (Lutz et al., 2020, p. 59), and other monitoring technology have been integrated right into sport clothing (Scataglini et al., 2020). This wearable technology supports the collection of data during practices and games and "allows the analysis of physical as well as individual and team-tactical behavior" (Lutz et al., 2020, p. 60).

Technologies are impacting sport beyond the traditional competition and team. For instance, non-athletes have also gotten into the game by advancing their version of the technology. For example, Manchester City (a Premier League Club) has held events called a "hackathon." The aim is to have the competitors use available data to develop strategies for athletes to improve their games. The first winner generated a machine algorithm that assists players in enhancing their decision-making during games (Business Cloud, 2016). Also, technology has given rise to a new and growing sports phenomenon; e-sport competitions. There is evidence of an overlap between e-sports and traditional sport (ESPN.com, 2016). For example, the professional basketball team, the Philadelphia 76ers (National Basketball League), purchased e-sport franchises – Dignitas and Team Apex (ESPN.com, 2016), and Manchester City has two professional FIFA players representing the team in e-sport competitions (Bliss, 2021).

Moreover, sports betting opportunities have changed with technology (Bell, 2021). For example, St. Louis Blues (National Hockey League) asked fans questions before games and during the games, such as: "which team would be first to reach three shots on net, allowing fans to build up points for the chance to win prizes, including season's tickets" (Fast Company, 2020, para. 2). This strategy supports betting during sport events.

Interestingly, sport and technology linkages extend to communications technology. For example, AS Roma (Italian Football Club) started a "Football Cares" program with the International Centre for Mission and Exploited Children. They send out video information on missing children in Europe with their communications regarding newly signed players (AS Roma, 2020). Other teams share the information on missing children via Twitter. The program has helped find several missing children (Aljazeera.com, 2019). Overall, "technology has added to both economic and social impacts of sports events" (Petrovic et al., 2015, p. 176).

Not everyone is pleased with the development of technology within sport. For instance, it has been noted that:

> —the number-crunching data, the enhanced equipment, the push for precision superior to the human eye—is undeniably making athletes smarter and better. It has helped unlock new levels of team performance. But I wonder if sports are starting to get too smart for our good, to the point where the games we love are becoming less interesting. (Gay, 2020, para. 2)

Further, emerging technologies have been noted to be "without exception, tainted with frustration and ambivalence" (Omoregie, 2016, p. 896), along with uncertainty. Additional controversies arose from emerging technologies that "have serious ramifications for fairness, innovation and the integrity of sport as a whole" (Brown, 2020, p. 8).

Due to potentially arising issues concerning emerging technologies in sport, a call has been made "for more guidance on, and regulation of, novel sports equipment" (Brown, 2020, p. 8). In addition, it has been stated "that those managing, handling and using sport must be equipped to make wise choices on the type and use of sport technologies that would assist in the right performance" (Omoregie, 2016, p. 896). Importantly, there is a noted need to develop an overall "comprehensive strategy regarding innovation management" (Ratten, 2020, n.p.). In response to these statements, we now look at emerging technology and consider key elements in a response framework.

Computer-to-human brain and brain-to-brain technology: An emerging technology impacting sport soon?

The new frontier for emerging technology encompasses the brain. The brain technology being discussed includes computer-to-human brain and brain-to-brain technologies. First, this type of technology will be outlined and then applied to sport. Next, a framework for developing a strategy to mitigate and manage the impacts of the technology on sport is outlined.

Since the early 1970s, computer-to-human brain technologies have been heading toward reality (Vidal, 1973) "with the hope for restorative and even enhanced human capacities" (Trimper et al., 2014, para. 2). Intriguingly, this technology means that scientists can record neuron activity in the brain and can translate this activity to a computer (O'Doherty et al., 2011). But, things have advanced even further, and by the early 2010s, scientists could generate a linkage between one brain directly to another brain – or "brain-to-brain interfacing

(BTBI)" (Pais-Vieira et al., 2013; Trimper et al., 2014, para. 2). Accordingly, this has been accomplished between two rats, and it was found that somatosensory information could be transferred and provide enhancements between the brains (Pais-Vieira et al., 2013). Thus, it is only a matter of time before the technology is advanced for human use.

Brain technology and sport scenario

Our scenario places computer-to-brain technology in sport and is used by athletes to enhance cognitive processes. Essentially, the computer will assist athletes with rational thoughts, advanced perceptions, detection, identification, and judgments that lead to better problem-solving and decisions. For training sessions, this may shorten the time it takes to train an elite athlete, and the technology will impact athletes' ability to succeed in sport.

Additionally, the brain-to-brain technology will link the coach's brain to the athlete's brain. The athletes will not have a coach in their ear through these linkages – but right in their brain. The coach can send their thoughts directly to the athlete for real-time instruction and feedback on other athletes that an athlete in the competition simply does not have the means to access. The brain-to-brain technology can be applied to multiple athletes, and they can be linked to share data during a team event – as a means to talk directly to each other. Or, the personnel from every game office – on and off the ice, field, or court – could be interconnected cognitively. Additionally, the experiences and knowledge of a long-term athlete could be cognitively connected and utilized by a novice athlete. Or, this technology could be used to improve the officiating of sport.

Not all of the brain linkages will be positive. Athletes may not want to do what the computer-linked messages are telling them. Managing computer instructions in combination with one's thoughts may be a skill that needs to be developed over time. Athletes will have disagreements with the computer – through their thoughts. Further, coaches and other team members may not be welcomed by all athletes in the interconnected brain loop because it may cause stress and upheaval between teammates. Interlinkages between game officials may lead to better officiating during some games and worse in others, depending on the interpretation of the officials' thoughts. Interlinking and enhancing brain capacity may not be a good strategy for humans (Earp et al., 2014) due to the potential implications (Trimper et al., 2014).

When this technology reaches the marketplace and athletes/coaches/officials can begin to utilize it during competitions, they will need to determine if the technology is eligible for use or is prohibited. Rules, regulations, and strategies for ensuring the practices are implemented will be required. Our position is that sport should be proactive and choose strategies that can be put into place long before the technology is used.

To this end, key elements are now outlined for consideration when developing a response strategy for brain technology or any other emerging technology that may come into the marketplace and be utilized within sport. This framework supports a belief that such technologies are part of S&SD, whereby the needs of the current generation in sport are met without hurting the opportunities for the future generations of sporting participants to meet their needs. Additionally, the framework takes into account the two stages of S&SD. The first stage includes the SDoS. The initiatives and progress for the production and consumption of sport products (such as sports equipment and apparel) and services are to be sustainable into the future. The second stage includes S4SD, whereby the contribution of sport aids the viability of our global societies over time – using the analytical concept approach for analyzing sport as a platform "to understand the world as a complex interaction of personal, social, economic, ecological, technological, and political systems" (Sachs, 2015, p. 6). Understandings of the individual parts can be combined to determine the SDoS applied as a microcosm of society.

Additionally, examining sport with the normative concept approach uses sport as a platform "to view the world by defining the objectives of a well-functioning society that delivers well-being for its global citizens today and for future generations. The normative concept urges us to have a universal vision toward a good society" (Sachs, 2015, p. 11).

From a normative perspective, Ulnicane et al. (2021) developed a systematic process for addressing emerging technologies to handle artificial intelligence (AI) concerns and facilitate their development and use in socially beneficial ways. First, rather than focusing on top-down government decisions, consider governance arrangements that bring together government and diverse non-state groups from civil society and the private sector in a balanced and transparent way. Second, rather than assuming the limited role of the state in a market correction, think about the diverse roles of the state in mitigating risks, enabling the participation of diverse groups, and mediating various needs and interests. Third, go beyond traditional goals of technology to support economic growth and productivity and focus on how technology can address societal challenges. Fourth, rather than being a global race where one country wins and others lose, technology development can be based on international research collaboration supported by science diplomacy efforts. Fifth, rather than developing AI ethics based on principles of medical ethics, learn from a related field of computing ethics that has accumulated extensive knowledge on privacy, autonomy, agency, trust, and inclusion. Sixth, one way to go beyond ethical principles is to systematically learn from the responsible innovation approach to address societal needs in developing and using emerging technologies.

Governance of emerging technologies is a highly complex endeavor, and there are no magic solutions. However, to address concerns associated with and to shape its development in socially beneficial ways, recent lessons from other emerging technologies can offer ideas, concepts, and approaches that broaden a range of available options and imagine various ways of achieving desired objectives. Further work should examine governance needs and arrangements of specific AI applications in diverse contexts, different but interconnected levels from technology development projects and laboratories to national policies and international cooperation arrangements (pp. 85–86).

We now hear from an expert in the field of sport concerning emerging technology.

Expert's view: Stefano Gobbi, Project Manager, Sport e Salute Spa, Rome, Italy

On sport technology and innovation

The sport-tech sector is proliferating worldwide. One of the explanations is in response to the crisis caused by Covid-19. In Italy, the group of industrial interlocutors investing in the sport-tech sector is growing, focusing on companies, accelerators, startups, international funds such as venture capital or ethical and private funds, and crowdfunding. For the reasons expressed, these interlocutors' approach to the world of sport is complex despite the growing interest. Much more could be achieved and done if the vision of sport changed.

The first case we discuss is about the world of sport startups. From the perspective of technological innovation, in Italy, WeSportUp is a vertical accelerator created thanks to Cassa Depositi e Prestiti (CDP Venture Capital SGR) and the first European incubator Startupbootcamp. The objectives of this initiative are twofold. The first being "matching," to systematize creativity and innovation with the sports system. The second, to enhance the best, working with ten startups, to make them excellent and scale them. The latter should be achieved working not as a private investor but as a scouting subject to create a stable and effective sport economy that becomes a consolidated and robust industry.

The second case is about online communities. Today the audience of services and activities has grown to dimensions that could not have been imagined. Sports institutions and organizations must understand the need to change their mentality and the way they operate. Staying and living in online communities means changing the language. It needs to build new bridges and channels such as e-sports, video games, new contemporary languages, new services linked to people's needs, creating innovative relationships for enabling activities, reducing spaces, etc.

The third case is about the technological responses of organizations toward the global (Covid-19) pandemic. First, in sport management, scholars and practitioners need to investigate how to optimize communication management that focuses on digital platforms (e.g., Zoom). With the online movement of training sessions and online institutional assemblies, we can observe how a culture of result orientation is spreading. One of the first requirements is to understand the power of the digital medium to extend to an audience of users for services and activities never considered before (e.g., online gymnastics courses for the population).

Moreover, in Italy, it was understood that thanks to the digital tool and the English language (along with online translation services), it is possible to offer training projects and activities on an international level: today, we have participants worldwide. Even if digital tools are not perfect because they have been adapted to these new organizational needs, the offer of services must still be high in number and quality because competition is global.

The administrative staff of the world of sport and associated services now fits into an organizational context that has changed since the pandemic that opens up possibilities such as enhancing the skills of the territory and creating benefits in environmental sustainability and social sustainability. This change is one of the few investments in the future because it produces health benefits, an increasingly valuable and strategic asset – and technology is involved in the transition.

Investments in technology and digital platforms, especially in communication, will become increasingly strategic for the evolution of the sports industry. Technological investments will be the protagonist of important international events in the next five years. These investments will help position sport as an even more strategic asset and tool for developing a new economy, a technology for humans, new training–work models, and new economic models with less impact from the point of view of the environment and increasing benefits for health.

An example is the International Tennis Games in Italy. An event that was traditionally organized as one of the stops of the Association of Tennis Professionals (ATP) tour. That was until the question was asked, how to change? How to enhance a wonderful place like the Foro Italico?

Four innovative axes were the basis for positive change:

1. Fun experience: construction of a tourist village
2. New engagement: development of new contents; visitors as protagonist; new role of sponsors and branding; presence on innovative media such as social media; innovation in event management with professionals and young volunteers who represent new ideas of and for sport at an international level
3. Industry matching: combining the biggest brands in the fashion system and the promotion of "made in Italy."
4. Increases in the value of and reproduction rights for brands, sponsors, and teams

All this over the past 13 years has provided a real benefit to the economic impact on the Italian Tennis Federation, the whole sector, and related services. In particular, it has made it possible to develop and disseminate a successful integrated development sports business model, helping all Italian sport organizations to become a point of reference on a global level as is also the case of "Casa Italia Collection" recently launched in Cortina Casa Italia Collection – Fisi in Cortina for the Alpine Ski World Championships held in Cortina d'Ampezzo. A new format was established to collaborate between the Winter Sports Federation, Coni, Sport e Salute Spa, and the Casa Italia experience at the Olympic Games. An innovative brand designed to support the Federations, through which the strengths of the Olympic project can be expressed on individual international sporting events that will tell the story of Italian excellence, from sport to made in Italy, through art, design, innovation, in unique storytelling. Such an integrated development model arises from a different and innovative idea of sport and sporting event(s) that will create benefits in terms of strategic models and socio-economic impact for the community. Technology is at the foundation of the change. Other countries are also transitioning – what do you see in your region?

Concluding remarks

1. Technology is increasing around the world and is increasingly impacting sport
2. Sport has managed technologies in sport and will need to continue such management into the future
3. Emerging technologies are heading into novel areas, such as advancing brain technology
4. We can build on the experience from previous technologies, such as from the application of AI, and use these foundations to determine how to move forward with novel technologies coming into the marketplace
5. Sport needs people to learn about emerging technologies, consider their potential applications to sport, and guide sport in managing their integration within all aspects of sport
6. Sport needs to be proactive in the management of emerging technologies

Future directions

1. New technologies are being introduced regularly and are being applied to sport
2. This trend will not decrease but will speed up, and sport will have trouble managing all of the technologies to ensure fair and equitable competitions
3. Sport organizations need to team up and work collaboratively to recognize emerging technologies, understand how they work, determine how they apply to sport, including their benefits and detriments, and share strategies for managing them in sport
4. A dedicated body is needed to examine emerging technologies and aid sport in how they can be legally applied to sport. This body may be similar to the World Anti-Doping Agency developed for managing the drug issue in sport

Review questions

1. In your own words, define the technological perspective of S&SD
2. Indicate how technology impacts or relates to the SDoS and S4SD
3. What can the determinist theory tell us about technologies in sport?
4. How do the analytical concept and the normative concept apply to sport and emerging technologies?
5. Are technologies impacting sport? Describe any technological advances in sport that you have noticed. How do they impact S&SD?

Discussion questions

1. What technologies have you noticed have been integrated within sport in the last 5–10 years?
2. Do you think brain-to-brain technology is a possibility?
3. If brain-to-brain technology becomes a reality, what impacts do you predict will occur in sport? What ideas do you have concerning how sport can manage the impacts?
4. What other technologies do you predict will emerge in the next ten years? How could they impact sport?
5. Should sport prohibit an emerging technology beneficial to one's health and well-being if it causes inequities and unfair competition situations? Are one's health and well-being the priority?
6. Conduct debates on emerging technologies – suggested topics include:

   - For example, who is responsible for ensuring sport awareness of emerging technologies before athletes use them in competitions? Who does the surveillance?
   - How can sport become proactive relative to managing emerging technologies?
   - What are the lessons learned concerning managing technologies in sport based on previous issues? For instance, swimming has allowed and then prohibited swimsuit technology. What are the associated impacts on athletes when sport organizations are reactive and need time to make technology decisions?

Class activities

1. Write a S&SD plan for managing emerging technologies as an exercise in critical thinking. Begin with a vision statement that would describe how you envision the technological perspective of S&SD. For example, "Make the world of sport a better place with technology" is considered a vision.
2. Now, outline how you will implement your vision for the technological perspective of S&SD that includes the two stages of SDoS and S4SD.
3. Consider how you will ensure that emerging technologies will be positive for the future of sport? Conversely, how can you eliminate the negative impacts?

Further reading

1. Aggarwal, R. (2011). Developing a global mindset: Integrating demographics, sustainability, technology, and globalization. *Journal of Teaching in International Business*, *22*(1), 51–69. https://doi.org/10.1080/08975930.2011.585920

2. Bai, C., & Sarkis, J. (2020). A supply chain transparency and sustainability technology appraisal model for blockchain technology. *International Journal of Production Research, 58*(7), 2142–2162. https://doi.org/10.1080/00207543.2019.1708989

3. Dao, V., Langella, I., & Carbo, J. (2011). From green to sustainability: Information Technology and an integrated sustainability framework. *The Journal of Strategic Information Systems, 20*(1), 63–79. https://doi.org/10.1016/j.jsis.2011.01.002

4. Ratten, V. (2020). Sport technology: A commentary. *The Journal of High Technology Management Research, 31*(1). https://doi.org/10.1016/j.hitech.2020.100383

5. Vrondou, O. (2020). The integration of technology into the sport tourism experience: From real competition to surreal experiences. In *Cultural and tourism innovation in the digital era* (pp. 219–228). Springer, Cham.

Relevant online resources

1. International Sports Technolgy Association (ISTA): (https://www.istassociation.com

2. International Sports Engineering Association (ISEA): (http://www.sportsengineering.org

3. Global Sports Innovation Center: https://sport-gsic.com

4. Sport Technology and Innovation GroupBankwest Stadium. (2019, August). *Bankwest Stadium: Sustainability case study*. Retrieved from https://bankweststadium.com.au/wp-content/uploads/2019/09/BankwestStadiumSustainability-1.pdf

References

Aljazeera.com. (2019, September). *Football: Roma's online campaign helps find five missing children*. Retrieved from https://www.aljazeera.com/sports/2019/9/20/football-romas-online-campaign-helps-find-five-missing-children

AS Roma. (2020, May). *"Football Cares" missing children campaign deemed an incredible success*. Retrieved from https://www.asroma.com/en/news/2020/5/football-cares-missing-children-campaign-deemed-incredible-success

Bell, J. (2021, February). *Not just a game: Online sports betting and the rise of corrosive technology*. Forbes Technology Council. Retrieved from https://www.forbes.com/sites/forbestechcouncil/2021/02/25/not-just-a-game-online-sports-betting-and-the-rise-of-corrosive-technology/?sh=45757b7970ec

Bliss, N. (2021, February). *Inside Man City's esports team with professional FIFA stars Ryan Pessoa and "Shellzz."* Daily Mirror. Retrieved from https://www.mirror.co.uk/sport/football/news/man-city-fifa-esports-england-23476325

Brown, J. (2020). The creation and regulation of sports equipment: Implications for the future. *Entertainment and Sports Law Journal, 18*(1), 8. 10.16997/eslj.236

Brundtland Commission. (2001). *Climate change 2001: Impacts, adaptation, and vulnerability*. In J.J. McCarthy, O.F. Canziani, N.A. Leary, D.J. Dokken and K.S. White (Eds.), *Contributions of working group II to the third assessment report of the intergovernmental panel on climate change.* Cambridge: Cambridge University Press. Weblink: https://www.ipcc.ch/report/ar3/wg2/

Business Cloud. (2016, August). *Manchester City hackathon won by decision-making algorithm.* Retrieved from https://businesscloud.co.uk/manchester-city-hackathon-won-by-decision-making-algorithm/

Cambridgedictionary.org. (n.d.). *Sustainability: environment,* Cambridge, United Kingdom: Cambridge University Press & Assessment, Retrieved from https://dictionary.cambridge.org/dictionary/english/sustainable

Earp, B., Sandberg, A., Kahane, G., & Savulescu, J. (2014). When is diminishment a form of enhancement? Rethinking the enhancement debate in biomedical ethics. *Frontiers in Systems Neuroscience, 8*(12), 1–8. 10.3389/fnsys.2014.00012

ESPN.com. (2016, September). *76ers acquire esports teams Dignitas and Apex.* Retrieve from https://www.espn.com/esports/story/_/id/17637299/76ers-acquire-esports-teams-dignitas-apex

Fast Company. (2020). *The world's 50 most innovative companies.* Retrieved from https://www.fastcompany.com/90457911/sports-most-innovative-companies-2020

Fisher, E. (2018, April). *Technologies have revolutionized the sports industry.* Sport Business Journal (Digital Edition). Retrieved from https://www.sportsbusinessjournal.com/Journal/Issues/2018/04/30/Technology/Tech-milestone

Gay, J. (2020). *Too much tech might just break sports.* The Wall Street Journal. Retrieved from https://www.wsj.com/articles/too-much-tech-might-just-break-sports-11583870389

Geissdoefer, M., Savaget, P., Bocken, N., Van Hultink, E. (2017). The circular economy – A new sustainability paradigm? *Journal of Cleaner Production, 143*(1), 757–768. 10.1016/j.jclepro.2016.12.048

Gulhane, T. (2014). Various types of advanced technologies in sports. *Journal of Sports and Physical Education, 1*(6), 1–2.

Haake, S. (2009). The impact of technology on sporting performance in Olympic sports. *Journal of Sports Sciences, 27*(13), 1421–1431. 10.1080/02640410903062019

Hasler, J. (2018, March). *Head games: How helmet techn works in 7 different sports.* Popular Mechanics. Retrieved from https://www.popularmechanics.com/adventure/sports/g253/4339919/

Heere, B. (2018). Embracing the sportification of society: Defining e-sports through a polymorphic view on sport. *Sport Management Review, 21*(1), 21–24. 10.1016/j.smr.2017.07.002

Jenmalm, P., & Johansson, R.S. (1997). Visual and somatosensory information about object shape controls manipulative fingertip forces. *Journal of Neuroscience, 17*(11), 4486–4499. 10.1523/JNEUROSCI.17-11-04486.1997

Macovei, S., Tufan, A.A., & Vulpe, B.I. (2014). Theoretical approaches to building a healthy lifestyle through the practice of physical activities. *Procedia-Social and Behavioral Sciences, 117,* 86–91. 10.1016/j.sbspro.2014.02.183

Millington, R., Giles, A.R., van Luijk, N., & Hayhurst, L.M. (2021). Sport for Sustainability? The Extractives Industry, Sport, and Sustainable Development. *Journal of Sport and Social Issues.* 10.1177/0193723521991413

McCullough, B.P., Orr, M., & Kellison, T. (2020). Sport ecology: Conceptualizing an emerging subdiscipline within sport management. *Journal of Sport Management, 34*(6), 509–520. 10.1123/jsm.2019-0294

Muniz-Pardoes, B., Sutehall, S., Angeloudis, K., Guppy, F., Bosch, A., & Pitsiladis, U. (2021). Recent improvements in marathon run times are likely technological, not physiological. *Sports Medicine, 51,* 371–378. 10.1007/s40279-020-01420-7

O'Doherty, J., Lebedev, M., Ifft, P., Zhuang, K., Solaiman, S., Bleuler, H., et al. (2011). Active tactile exploration enabled by a brain-machine-brain interface. *Nature, 479*(7372), 228–231. 10.1038/nature10489

Omoregie, P. (2016, August). *The impact of technology on sport performance.* Proceedings of INCEDI 2016 Conference, Ghana. Retrieved from https://www.researchgate.net/publication/333808384_THE_IMPACT_OF_TECHNOLOGY_ON_SPORT_PERFORMANCE

Pais-Vieira, M., Lebedev, M., Kunicki, C., Wang, J., & Nicolelis, M. (2013). A brain-to-brain interface for real-time sharing of sensorimotor information. *Scientific Reports, 3,* 1319. 10.1038/srep01319

Petrovic, L., Molovanovic, D., & Desbordes, M. (2015). Emerging technologies and sport events: Innovative information and communication solutions. *Innovative Sport Business and Management: An International Journal, 5*(2), 175–190. 10.1108/SBM-06-2012-0021

Ratten, V. (2020). Sport technology: A commentary. *The Journal of High Technology Management Research, 31*(1). 10.1016/j.hitech.2020.100383

Rotolo, D., Hicks, D., & Martin, B. (2015). "What is an emerging technology?" *Research Policy, 44*(10), 1827–1843. 10.1016/j.respol.2015.06.006

Ryan, T., Kling, S., Salata, M., Cupp, S., Sheehan, J., & Voos, J. (2016). Wearable performance devices in sports medicine. *Sports Health, 8*(1), 74–78. 10.1177%2F1941738115616917

Sachs, J.D. (2015). *The age of sustainable development.* Columbia University Press. Retrieved from http://cup.columbia.edu/book/the-age-of-sustainable-development/9780231173155

Scataglini, S., Moorhead, A., & Feletti, F. (2020, June). A systematic review of smart clothing in sports: Possible applications to extreme sports. *Muscles, Ligaments and Tendons Journal, 10*(2), 333–342. 10.32098/mltj.02.2020.19

Schulenkorf, N. (2012). Sustainable community development through sport and events: A conceptual framework for sport-for-development projects. *Sport Management Review, 15*(1), 1–12. 10.1016/j.smr.2011.06.001

Stilgoe, J., Owen, R., & Macnaghten, P. (2013). Developing a framework for responsible innovation. *Research Policy, 42*(9), 1568–1580. Retrieved from https://www.taylorfrancis.com/chapters/edit/10.4324/9781003075028-22/developing-framework-responsible-innovation-jack-stilgoe-richard-owen-phil-macnaghten

Szathmári, A., & Kocsis, T. (2020). Who cares about gladiators? An elite-sport-based concept of Sustainable Sport. *Sport in Society,* 1–19. 10.1080/17430437.2020.1832470

Trimper, J., Wolpe, P., &Rommelfanger, K.S.(2014). When "I" becomes "We": ethical implications of emerging brain-to-brain interfacing technologies. *Frontier Neuroengineering, 7*(4). 10.3389/fneng.2014.00004

Triantafyllidis, S., & Darvin, L. (2021). Mass-participant sport events and sustainable development: Gender, social bonding, and connectedness to nature as predictors of socially and environmentally responsible behavior intentions. *Sustainability Science, 16*(5), 239–253. 10.1007/s11625-020-00867-x

Trimper, J., Wolpe, P., & Rommelfanger, K.S. (2014). When "I" becomes "We": Ethical implications of emerging brain-to-brain interfacing technologies. *Frontier Neuroengineering, 7*(4). 10.3389/fneng.2014.00004

Ulnicane, I., Eke, D., Knight, W., Ogoh, G., & Stahl, B. (2021) Good governance as a response to discontents? Déjà vu, or lessons for AI from other emerging technologies. *Interdisciplinary Science Reviews, 46*(1–2), 71–93. 10.1080/03080188.2020.1840220

University of California Los Angeles (UCLA). (2021). *What is sustainability?* Retrieved from https://www.sustain.ucla.edu/what-is-sustainability/

Vidal, J. (1973). Toward direct brain–computer communication. *Annual. Review of Biophysical and Bioengineering, 2*(1), 157–180.

Weichenberger, M., Schilling-Kässle, V., Mentz, L., Engleder, T., & Hessling, M. (2015). A fencing robot for performance testing in elite fencers. *Sports Technology, 8*(3-4), 95–99. 10.1080/19346182.2015.1108326

10

THE POLITICAL PERSPECTIVE OF SPORT AND SUSTAINABLE DEVELOPMENT

Efthalia (Elia) Chatzigianni

LEARNING OBJECTIVES

Upon completion of this chapter, learners should be able to successfully:

1. Define the political perspective of sport and sustainable development (S&SD)
2. Identify the governmental aspects of S&SD
3. Evaluate the current leadership of S&SD for new policy development
4. Investigate practical cases from the global sport organizations
5. Design sustainable strategic planning process from the political perspective of S&SD

Overview

It is generally accepted that sport is one of the most recognizable endeavors of global human activity. This recognition of sport's unique political power has been used as a platform by several international organizations as a social tool to promote and advance a variety of causes such as global peace and prosperity, social inclusion, education, health, international development, conflict resolution, and environmental sustainability. This chapter focuses on the political perspective of global governance of sport and sustainable development (S&SD). The chapter's

DOI: 10.4324/9781003128953-10

discussion arises from the political theory outlined by Fauziah, Yusoff, and Alhiji (2012) that indicates that appropriate leadership can create good governance and influence decision-making processes and directions. This means that leadership within sport can utilize sport as a social tool, a burgeoning area within sport. The chapter seeks to enhance learners' perspectives on sport governance, illustrate global governance applications within S&SD, and offer multiple examples of sport organizations and their S&SD endeavors. The discussion encourages critical thinking skills concerning the advance of S&SD into the future.

Glossary

Actors

Actors in world politics, states, and non-state actors are entities with the following characteristics: The autonomous capacity to determine their interests and goals, the capability to mobilize material and human resources to accomplish their purposes and activity which are significant enough to exert influence on state-to-state relations or the behavior of non-state actors in the global system (Kan, 2009).

Good governance in sport

Good governance in sport is a condition concerning autonomy and self-regulation of sport organizations. While it is not possible to define a single model of governance in sport across different disciplines and given various national differences, consider that there are inter-linked principles that underpin sport governance, such as autonomy within the limits of the law, democracy, transparency, and accountability in decision-making, and inclusiveness in the representation of interested stakeholders. Furthermore, good governance in sport is a condition for addressing challenges regarding sport and the legal framework. (European Commission, 2018a, para 4.1)

Olympic Movement (OM)

"The Olympic Movement is the concerted, organized, universal and permanent action, carried out under the supreme authority of the IOC, of all individuals and entities who are inspired by the values of Olympism" (International Olympic Committee, n.d.).

Political theory

The political theory supports that organizational leadership can influence governance decision-making and directions (Fauziah et al., 2012).

Sport

"Sport means all forms of physical activity which, through casual or organized participation, aim at expressing or improving physical fitness and well-being, forming social relationships or obtaining results in competition at all levels" (Szathmári & Kocsis, 2020, p. 4).

Sport and sustainable development (S&SD)

S&SD is the process that includes two stages: Sustainable development of sport (SDoS) and sport for sustainable development (S4SD) that, together, enhance the development that meets the needs of current generations without compromising future generations' ability to meet their own needs at the personal, social, economic, ecological, technological, and political levels (Millington et al., 2021; Szathmári & Kocsis, 2020; Triantafyllidis & Darvin, 2021).

Sport for sustainable development (S4SD)

S4SD refers to the contribution of sport to our global societies' viability by encouraging sustainability across the six perspectives of personal, social, economic, ecological, technological, and political worldwide (Macovei et al., 2014; Millington et al., 2021; Schulenkorf, 2012).

Sustainability

The term refers to "the integration of environmental health, social equity, and economic vitality to create thriving, healthy, diverse and resilient communities for this generation and generations to come" (University of California Los Angeles, 2021, para. 2).

The term sustainable development (SD) encompasses the initiatives and progress in pursuit of sustainability. According to the Brundtland Commission (2001), SD is defined as the "development that meets the needs of the present without compromising the ability of future generations to meet their own needs" (p. 82). This includes "the narrow notion of physical sustainability [that] implies a concern for social equity between generations, a concern that must logically be extended to equity within each generation" (p. 82)

Sustainable development of sport (SDoS)

SDoS refers to the sustainable practices taken by sport regarding the management of sport products, services, and sport consumer behaviors to achieve sustainability within the world of sport that encompasses six perspectives including the personal, social, economic, ecological, technological, and political (McCullough et al., 2020; Szathmari & Kocsis, 2020; Triantafyllidis & Darvin, 2021).

Intergovernmental organization (IGO)

The term refers to an entity created by a treaty involving two or more states to work in good faith on common interest issues (Harvard Law School, n.d.).

Non-governmental organization (NGO)

NGOs are typically mission-driven advocacy or service organizations in the non-profit sector. The term, which derives from the United Nations (UN) jargon, aims to delineate between government bodies and private organizations (Harvard Law School, n.d.).

Sui generis

The term means "of its kind" (Cambridge Dictionary, n.d).

Defining the term governance

The term governance has multiple definitions. According to Keohane (2002), governance involves "the processes and institutions, both formal and informal, that guide and restrains the collective activities of a group" (p. 202). Meanwhile, Djelic and Sahlin-Andersson (2006) noted that "governance, in a world where boundaries are largely in flux, is being shaped and pursued in the constellation of public and private actors that include states, international organizations, professional associations, expert groups, civil society groups, and business corporations" (p. 7).

Furthermore, governance is associated with the activity of diverse interests and stakeholders who, in the case of common goals, may work collectively to pursue their interests forming alliances and lobbies at national and international levels (Chatzigianni, 2014, 2018). Additionally, the UN Commission Report on Global Governance (1995) defined global governance as "the sum of the many ways individuals and institutions, public and private, manage their common affairs" (p. 2). Governance today takes place in the framework of globalization, which is defined as the "process whereby goods, information, people, money, communication, sport, fashion, and other forms of culture move across national boundaries" (Eitzen, 2012, p. 210). Therefore, globalization directly impacts governance, such as influencing partnerships.

Global sport governance and sustainable development

Applying political theory means that those in a position to lead sport can choose to govern to contribute to global sustainable development. This type of contribution can involve economic growth, environmental responsibility, and social equity (Hawkins & Wang, 2012; Saha & Paterson, 2008). This can include, for example, a sport organization's awareness of and actions for improving quality of life within society, expanding participation in decision-making, and care for the environment (Wheeler, & Naughright, 2006; Hawkins & Wang, 2012; Jepson, 2019). The correct balance between S&SD initiatives by an organization can be challenging to achieve and quantify – but this difficulty does not diminish the value of such a balance.

As with most aspects of life, global sport governance and sustainable development are open to political maneuvers. These maneuvers can be seen in the actions of sport-related personnel – or actors – within IGOs, NGOs, and private corporations. Political schemes or actions are significant as an actor's motivation and degree of activity can impact decision-making, policy development, relationships, and the strategic planning and implementation of S&SD.

We will identify S&SD directions and initiatives within three sub-sectors involved in S&SD – IGOs, NGOs, and private corporations. It must be noted that the recent intensification of the activity of these organizations in the field of S&SD allows only examples of action to be included in this chapter. It is hoped that readers will further examine the organizations for a full accounting of their S&SD activity. We will begin with IGOs and their S&SD activities. Given the significance of the UN Millennium Development Goals (MDGs) and sustainable development goals (SDGs), the examples will begin presenting the UN activity in sport (Chatzigianni, 2018; Leopkey & Parent, 2012; Ross & Leopkey, 2017; Yélamos et al., 2019). This will be followed by a discussion on NGOs and S&SD, and then other examples from private corporations.

IGOs and S&SD

Three key IGOs and S&SD will be discussed. Examples include the UN, the European Union (EU), and the Council of Europe.

The UN and S&SD

A key IGO involved in S&SD is the UN. This organization has 193 member states and two observer states (Archer, 2001; Bourantonis & Wiener, 1995). The UN, founded in 1945 in San Francisco, United States, aims to maintain international peace and security and strengthen cooperation between its members in issues related to the resolution of international problems and the promotion of respect of human rights and fundamental principles. Its operation is based on the UN Charter, adopted on June 25, 1945 that took effect on October 24, 1945 (Archer, 2001; Bourantonis & Wiener, 1995). The main organs of the UN are: (a) the General Assembly, (b) the Security Council, (c) the Secretariat, (d) the International Court of Justice, (e) the Trusteeship Council, and (f) the Economic and Social Council (ECOSOC). The work of ECOSOC is based on its cooperation with NGOs and the operation of several bodies in the field of economy and society. The UN system also includes several specialized agencies, independent international organizations, programs, and funds, including the UN Children's Fund (UNICEF) and the UN Educational, Scientific, and Cultural Organization (UNESCO).

Notably, the UN General Assembly has granted the observer and permanent observer status to several international organizations – including the EU (with enhanced rights) and the International Olympic Committee (IOC). Their relationship with sport has been evolving based on the two parameters outlined by Chatzigianni (2018). The first parameter is:

a.   The UN and its agencies use sport as a policy tool to promote peace and development worldwide

Even though the international community has used sport as a means to serve its goals on an ad hoc basis since the 1920s, it was only at the beginning of the new millennium and in the framework of the UN MDGs that sport has officially entered the global arena as a formal UN policy tool. The inclusion of sport in the MDGs has resulted in the enhancement of cooperation between the UN, the UN specialized agencies, and the sport governing bodies of the Olympic Movement (OM). This cooperation is further strengthened by the 2015 Sustainable Development Goals (SDGs), a set of universal targets and goals that further pursue and expand the eight Millennium Development Goals. The SDGs represent the UN international development Agenda until 2030, where the contribution of sport to all 17 goals is officially acknowledged in Article 37.

Overall, following the successful use of sport in achieving the MDGs, the SDGs further recognize the significance of sport as an enabler of sustainable development. This achievement has been in the areas of social prosperity, gender equality, social inclusion, health, education, youth empowerment, and the promotion of tolerance and respect to enhance development and peace around the world.

The second parameter, as outlined by Chatzigianni (2018), is:

b.   The UN relates and networks with the global sport governing bodies, mainly the IOC and the International Football Federation (Fédération Internationale de Football, FIFA, 2021).

Sport-related UN documentation and acts prove the significance that the IOC has for achieving UN goals. The relationship between the two global universal organizations, the intergovernmental UN and the non-governmental IOC, started in the 1960s when the IOC attempted to establish a relationship with the UN to recognize its status as the unique international organization representing the Olympic ideal. This recognition was formally achieved in 2009 when the Observer status was awarded to the IOC by the UN. This status provided the IOC with the right to participate in the UN General Assemblies. During the 2015 UN Assembly, whereby the UN SDGs were adopted, the IOC current President, Thomas Bach, praised the inclusion of sport when working to promote peace, education, social inclusion, and healthy lifestyles. Bach stated support of the organization to the UN Agenda for Sustainable Development. He further emphasized that the goals of the Olympic Agenda 2020 are aligned with the 17 SDGs, given that the Olympic Agenda aims to address "progress with regards to sustainability, credibility, and youth in the context of the Olympic Movement" (Bach, 2015, p. 2). He additionally emphasized that "sport is a natural partner when it comes to realizing the ambitious agenda that will guide global development for the next 15 years" (Bach, 2015, p. 1). Bach further stated that

> the IOC shares the ambitious goals of peaceful development of humanity – and based on our shared values of tolerance, solidarity, and peace, we are committed to continued cooperation with the UN and its member states to make the Sustainable Goals a reality. (Bach, 2015, pp. 1–2)

Furthermore, Sport for Development and Peace is an international movement that aims to use sport projects by local, regional, national, and international organizations to promote peacebuilding and achieve specific development goals in various areas and conflict zones worldwide. It started with the UN MDGs (2000–2015) and continues in the SDGs framework (2015–2030). Since 2000, many sport projects have been developed in Asia, Africa, and Latin America, mainly using football (soccer) as sport activity to promote development or peace-related goals (Gadais, 2019).

The EU and S&SD

The EU is an IGO with 27 member states from the European continent. In 1993, the Treaty of Maastricht (1992) came into effect on the European communities' (European Economic Community, European Coal and Steel Community, European Atomic Energy Community). Thus, the EU is a sui generis (one of a kind) political and economic union (Hlavac, 2010).

The EU has involvement in sport policy that is related to its social and economic features. In this framework, given that the EU has a leading role in the global sports market and that traditionally EU states host many mega-sport events, sport-related developments in the EU framework are essential for European and global society. Furthermore, the EU uses sport as a vehicle to advance regional development by promoting innovation, urban regeneration, social cohesion, and sustainable development as well as to enhance physical and mental well-being through projects such as:

- *The Sport and Vitality partnership (ClusSport)*: ClusSport provides support to European regions that aim to create a series of business investment projects in the sector of sport and vitality. To do so, it follows "a bottom-up approach - implemented through interregional cooperation, cluster participation and business involvement as well as aligning specialization profiles of the partner regions" to "turn health care onto proactive care" (European Commission, 2018a, https://epsi.eu/news/clussport-mou-on-smart-sport-innovation-hubs/). In addition, the ClusSport consortium develops smart regional innovation hubs for sports and vitality, which generates data to be used by the sport sector.

- *SportHub: Alliance for regional development in Europe (Share Initiative):* Launched in 2018, the project brings together more than 100 local, regional, and national sport organizations. It aims to bring the sport into policy platforms that are related to regional development.

Furthermore, the EU cooperates with regard to sustainability with European sport governing bodies such as the Union of European Football Associations (UEFA) and the European Non-Governmental Sports Organization (ENGSO). For example, the EU's policy initiator, the European Commission, signed an agreement with UEFA in 2018 to promote sustainable development within the football grounds, sport stadiums, and other sport facilities across Europe (European Commission, 2018b).

Council of Europe (CoE) and S&SD

The CoE is an intergovernmental human rights organization founded on May 5, 1949, with London's Treaty. The CoE has 47 member states, including the Russian Federation and Turkey and five observer states, including the United States of America, Canada, Mexico, Japan, and the Holy See. The CoE has a longstanding relationship with sport best expressed in the European Sports Charter (developed in 1992 revised in 2001), aiming to provide a framework and offers its member states guidance in policymaking and implementation.

The revised European Sports Charter of the Council of Europe (2001) refers to sport and sustainable relationships. Specifically, the Charter emphasizes the need for all sport activities to adjust and be conducted with consideration for the planet's restricted resources to ensure and improve "people's physical, social and mental well-being from one generation to the next" (Council of Europe, 2001, Article 10). Furthermore, the Article provides three principles of sustainable development and considerate management of the environment, which include consideration of nature in the planning and construction of sport facilities, cooperation with sport organizations in the field of conservation of nature and the environment, and support of all their efforts and increase people's awareness and understanding of nature and the relationship between S&SD. The main achievements of the CoE European Sport Charter in the field of S&SD are related to the provision to national governments and NGOs of an efficient and stable common framework to guide them in the formation of related policy and implementation and ensure coordination and complementarity of actions between them.

An example of successful cooperation of intergovernmental and non-governmental factors by the CoE is reflected in initiatives taken by the governing body of the CoE Enlarged Partial Agreement of Sport). This initiative is a pan-

European platform serving as a tool of cooperation and exchange of good practices between intergovernmental and non-governmental sport governing factors, including the OM, all CoE member states, UNESCO and the EU, in the field of socially sustainable development and sport. Further, given the significance that the CoE attributes to the democratic management of cultural diversity in the European continent, as well as the acknowledgment of the contribution that sport may have in the social inclusion of newly arrived migrants, the Enlarged Partial Agreement of Sport EPAS participates in the Activity, Sport, Play for the Inclusion of Refugees in Europe (ASPIRE). The ASPIRE supports sport organizations in their efforts to provide new migrants and refugees with equal participation opportunities in sport by their skills, knowledge, and competencies.

We now move to discuss NGOs and S&SD. The examples include the OM members, starting with its lead, the IOC. This is followed by other OM entities, including World Athletics, the World Taekwondo Federation, and the UEFA. And finally, sport governance and S&SD examples from the civil society and know-how experts are offered.

Non-governmental sport governance: The Olympic Movement (OM) and S&SD

The OM structure is like a pyramid; the head of the pyramid is the IOC. The rest of the components within the OM are the National Olympic Committees (NOCs) – the national representatives of the IOC – the International Federations (IFs), recognized by the IOC as the governing bodies of one or more sport/s at the international level, the National Federations – the IFs national representatives – and the Organizing Committees for the Olympic Games (OCOGs).

The IOC and S&SD

The IOC is the global leader of the OM. As an international NGO of genuine character (Chatzigianni, 2006), the IOC is the leading organization of the OM, with primary responsibility for the Olympic Games organization and related activities. Founded in 1894 in Paris, France, the IOC represents a unique example of a global NGO, granted the authority to act as the OM leader by the Olympic Charter (Chatzigianni, 2006).

In December 2014, the IOC adopted the Olympic Agenda 2020, representing the OM's strategic roadmap (IOC, 2014). The Agenda aimed to strengthen the role of sport in contemporary society and safeguard the future of the OM. This Agenda included 40 recommendations to its members based on the following three pillars: sustainability, youth, and credibility.

Meanwhile, the IOC included a sustainable development strategy in the Olympic framework with two recommendations as stated in the Olympic Agenda 2020 – these are noted as recommendation four and recommendation five. According to recommendation four, the IOC is to "take a more proactive position and leadership role about sustainability and ensure that it is included in all aspects of the planning and staging of the Olympic Games," the IOC will:

1. Develop a sustainability strategy to enable potential and actual Olympic Games organizers to integrate and implement sustainability measures that encompass economic, social, and environmental spheres in all stages of their project
2. Assist newly elected Organizing Committees to establish the best possible governance for the integration of sustainability throughout the organization
3. The IOC ensures post-Games monitoring of the Games legacy with the National Olympic Commitee and external organizations such as the World Union of Olympic Cities (UMVO) (International Olympic Committee, 2017)

Recommendation five of the Olympic Agenda 2020 describes the IOC's sustainability plans in the OM's everyday operations. To do so, the organization has adopted the following principles:

1. The IOC to include sustainability in its day-to-day operations

    *   The IOC has sustainability in its procurement of goods and services and events organization (meetings, conferences, etc.)
    *   The IOC is to reduce its travel impact and offset its carbon emissions
    *   The IOC is to apply the best possible sustainability standards for the consolidation of its headquarters in Lausanne, Switzerland

2. The IOC is to engage and assist OM stakeholders in integrating sustainability within their organization and operations by:

    *   Developing recommendations
    *   Providing tools, for example, best practices and scorecards
    *   Providing mechanisms to ensure the exchange of information between Olympic stakeholders
    *   Using existing channels, such as Olympic Solidarity, to help and assist in implementing initiatives

3. To achieve the above, the IOC cooperates with organizations such as the UN Environment Programme (UNEP) (International Olympic Committee, 2017).

When it comes to the organization of the Olympic Games, the Olympic Agenda 2020 documents explicitly declared that the organizing cities for the Olympic Games must commit to the use of a record number of existing and temporary facilities as means to decrease the cost of the the Games and promote sustainability. This commitment was further expressed in the "New Norm of the Olympic Agenda," a set of 118 reforms related to the organization of future Olympic Games, approved by the 132nd IOC Session held in PyeongChang in February 2018, to allow the Olympic cities to organize the Games based on long-development, sustainable goals

(IOC, 2018). Through the Olympic Agenda 2020 and the New Norm, Tokyo 2020 saved approximately US\$4.3 billion on the organization of the Games: US\$2.2 billion was held as a result of the review of the Venue Master Plan and US\$2.1 billion from cuts from the Games' operational budget (IOC, 2018).

In this strategy for sustainability development, the IOC decided to act in its three-fold capacity: As an organization, as a leader of the OM, and as the owner of the Olympic Games. Further, the IOC has committed to building both the Olympic House and the new IOC headquarters in Lausanne, Switzerland, by the best environmental international and Swiss codes – the Green Building Codes. This is in line with the IOC position following the UN Conference on Environment and Development in 1992, which took place in Rio, at the so-called "Earth Summit," the IOC signed an "Earth Pledge" engaging all sport governing factors to "making the Earth a safe place" and expressed the commitment of the OM to the protection of the planet (International Olympic Committee, 2012, p. 9). Immediately after this pledge was made, strong criticism of the IOC was received due to the environmental degradation caused by the 1992 Winter Olympics. Thus, in 1994, during the Centennial Olympic Congress held in Paris, the OM declared that the environment was "an essential part of Olympism" (International Olympic Committee, 1994). Concern for the environment was expressed as the third pillar of Olympism in the Olympic Charter (Olympic Charter, Chapter 1, Rule 2, para. 13). The IOC was granted the role of Olympic leader in this field with the responsibilities: (a) "to encourage and support a responsible concern for environmental issues, to promote sustainable development in sport and to require that the Olympic Games are held accordingly" (Olympic Charter, Chapter 1, Rule 2, para. 13) and (b) "to promote a positive legacy from the Olympic Games to the host cities and host countries" (Olympic Charter, Chapter 1, Rule 2, para. 14). Since then, environmental governance has become an integral part of the Olympic philosophy.

The IOC influence does not end there. Additionally, the IOC sustainability program involves promoting sustainable development worldwide by forming global partnerships such as the Sport for Hope program to enhance education, sport, and social development in developing countries (International Olympic Committee, 2009). This program is a significant joint initiative by the IOC and many of its partner organizations around the world that participate in global sport governance. Among these organizations lie the following:

- The Confederation of Southern Africa National Olympic Committees
- The Dubai Sports Council
- The National Olympic Committee of the United States
- The National Olympic Committee of Japan
- The International and National Sports Federations
- The UN system

- National governments (as for now the governments of Zambia, France, and Haiti),
- International organizations, such as the Inter-American Development Bank
- The Commonwealth Games Federation, UK Sport
- The International Committee of the Red Cross
- Multinational companies such as Samsung and Merifin Capital
- Other NGOs that offer, among additional, technical expertise and gear
- Local sport associations and foundations

The IOC has played a significant role in the burgeoning area of S&SD. The growth has occurred in NGOs as well. Non-governmental sport bodies that are entities of the OM are now outlined; the three examples include World Athletics, World Taekwondo Federation, and the UEFA. The examples illustrate the political influence of each organization concerning sustainability.

World Athletics and S&SD

Sport governance by World Athletics – previously International Association of Athletics Federation (IAAF) – was founded in 1913 in Berlin, Germany. It is the global governing body for athletics (track and field, race-walking, cross country, road, ultra, and mountain running). World Athletics is an NGO and has 214 Member Federations.

Having recognized the significance of sustainable development, in recent years, World Athletics has been very active in sport and sustainability internationally, establishing new cooperation with other international organizations and launching programs to serve sustainable development. For instance, in 2018, the Federation – then IAAF – teamed up with the UN Environment and the Climate and Clean Air Coalition to tackle air pollution. To this end, the two organizations have established a five-year partnership to monitor air quality at 1000 venues worldwide. Furthermore, in March 2019, at the UN Environmental Assembly in Nairobi, World Athletics presented the Air Quality project, a joint effort of World Athletics with the UNEP to raise awareness about air pollution in the world (World Athletics, n.d.).

Furthermore, in April 2020, World Athletics announced its Sustainability Strategy, which aims to use the popular athletics and political power of athletic sustainability through its network around the world. Its strategy is based on three sustainability pillars, environmental, social, and economic, and consists of the following goals (World Athletics, 2020):

- Leadership in sustainability
- Sustainable production and consumption
- Climate change and carbon
- Local environment and air quality

- Global equality; and
- Diversity, accessibility, and well-being

To achieve the elements above, World Athletics has committed to follow sustainability principles and methods, within any future World Athletics Series event (World Athletics, 2020). It is worth noting that given the background, history, and popularity of World Athletics around the world, its initiatives in the field of sustainability are significant.

World Taekwondo Federation and S&SD

The establishment of the Taekwondo Peace Corps in 2009 and the Taekwondo Humanitarian Foundation in 2019 by the World Taekwondo Federation has provided a means to help young people enhance cross-cultural respect and promote the practice of martial arts in refugee camps globally, while enacting the UN Development Goals (Choue, 2020). The Peace Corps sends coaches and volunteers to various countries around the world in the framework of MDGs, while the Taekwondo Humanitarian Foundation is a clear expression of SDG 3: Ensure healthy lives and promote well-being for all at all ages. According to the President of the Federation, Chungwon Choue, taekwondo requires minimal equipment, can improve the health and conditions of youth, including young refugees and displaced people, and, at the same time, teaches manners, perseverance, self-control, and courage and promotes social values including respect, tolerance, and integrity worldwide (Choue, 2020). The Federation has also established the Taekwondo Cares sport for development program, which aims to develop grassroots and support aid for the 210 national associations members of the federation.

Union of European Football Associations (UEFA) and S&SD

The UEFA is the governing body of football (soccer), futsal, and beach soccer in Europe. It was founded in 1954 (June 15) in Basel, Switzerland, and it is currently the umbrella organization for 55 national associations.

In the past few years, UEFA has been very active in wielding its political power in sustainable development. First, it has introduced strategy priorities that aim to serve human rights, sustainable inclusivity and diversity, gender equality, child safeguarding, and refugee integration – all as part of its corporate responsibility program. Second, it has promoted environmental sustainability in Europe through sport events, competitions, education, and volunteering among football fans. For example, UEFA has launched the PlayGreen project (https://www.playgreenproject.eu) to support the Erasmus+ Programme of the EU (http://www.erasmusprogramme.com) and promote awareness on sport and environmental sustainability in Europe. The program emphasizes the need to volunteer and share good practices among youth and grassroots organizations across Europe. Additional partner organizations of the UEFA include the Malta Football Association, the Estonian Football Federation, the Football

Flanderen, the European Non-Governmental Sports Organizatio, and Ecoserveis, a non-profit consultancy specialized in energy.

Private corporations and experts in S&SD

To a great extent, multinational companies wield political power to encourage change through sport and sustainability with a corporate social responsibility policy framework. Examples of their activity are the following:

Juventus FC as a football company

Following a corruption scandal in 2005, the Agnelli family, owners of the club, have adopted a new corporate approach to the club's management that has incorporated social responsibility principles within the UN SDGs. In this framework, the club has undertaken various projects, including social inclusion, gender equality, waste management, and energy consumption, demonstrating its commitment to a sustainable future. These include the One Tree Planted project (https://onetreeplanted.org), whereby 200 trees are planted for every goal scored by Juventus players; the "Colour? What Colour", a study on discrimination and racism (United Nations Educational Scientific Cultural Organization, 2015), entirely funded by Juventus, and the partnership with Save the Children (since 2014), as means to enhance education, protection, and promotion of sport activities and a healthy lifestyle among children and youth.

Since 2018/2019, Juventus also purchases 100% of its electricity from renewable resources.

Aiming to achieve transparency, one of the main requirements of global sport governance, the club, in the past few years, publishes a report, verified by PricewaterhouseCoopers, that describes all the club activities in sustainability, whether social, financial, or environmental.

The club, along with the IOC, FIFA, UEFA, national NOCs, and other sport teams, have signed the UN Framework Convention on Climate Change – Sport for Climate Action (UNFCCC Sports), which brings together factors of global sport governance to fight climate change by drawing a clear path and setting specific standards to verify emission reporting by the Paris Agreement (2015).

Additionally, several sport-related organizations have been formed that represents the advance of civil and inclusive society through S&SD initiatives. Among these organizations lie Sport and Sustainability International and Green Sports Alliance.

Sport and Sustainability International

Sport and Sustainability International (SansSI) (https:www.sportsustainability.org) is an NGO active in sport and environmental sustainability. Through cooperation with all interested stakeholders and the implementation programs, SanSI aims to advocate for sustainability, educate people and organizations, and create sustainable values using sport (Sport and Sustainability International, n.d.). *SanSI* members include event organizers such as the Formula-E and 11th Hour racing, along with sport leagues including the National Basketball Association, the Major League Soccer, and the National Football League, IFs like the International Volleyball Federation (Fédération Internationale de Volleyball) and the Automobile International Federation (Fédération Internationale de l'automobile), sport clubs, NGOs, private companies as well as (para)athletes, students and other sport professionals (Sport and Sustainability International, n.d.). Among its initiatives lie the following:

SDG Sport Lab

The SDG Sport Lab uses sport as a tool to promote the UN SDG goals. They do so by providing research and practical guidance to sport entities, creating value for innovation in the sport industry, offering communication channels to young decision-makers, elite athletes, and encouraging collective action (SDG Sport Lab, n.d.).

Green Sports Alliance

Green Sports Alliance (https://greensportsalliance.org) is a trade organization that focuses on environmental awareness and promoting a more sustainable future. It was founded in 2010 by Paul G. Allen's Vulcan Inc. The Natural Resources Defense Council and its inaugural members and current partners come from various corporate, collegiate, professional sports organizations, and event and entertainment organizations. Among its initiatives lie valuable resources in the field of S&SD such as the "Guide to Green Teams in Sport Venues," the "Ready to Play Playbook," and the "Fan Engagement Playbook." The Alliance has also supported the "Playing for our Planet: How Sports win from being Sustainable," a joint initiative of UEFA and the World Wildlife Fund that demonstrates to all sport stakeholders the ways to promote sustainable and environmentally friendly performance (Union of European Football Associations, 2018).

Overall, the above examples illustrate the growth of S&SD including sport organizations' awareness of and applying their leadership's political power to direct S&SD initiatives for a sustainable global future.

Concluding remarks

1. Global governance – including global sport governance – involves governmental and non-governmental actors and requires cooperation between international organizations, national governments, the private sector, civil society, and experts
2. Global governance involves an organization's leadership, including its policies, programs, and actions to meet the diverse interests of the stakeholders

3. The political perspective in global governance is founded in political theory that states that leadership has the power to guide the direction of the initiatives; thus, the leadership can use sport as a social tool
4. This chapter offered multiple examples that illustrated that leaders in sport had used their sport governance role to engage with sustainable development
5. Using specific examples of the rising global political awareness of the role that sport can play in sustainable development, diverse S&SD specific and joint initiatives were outlined as offered by IGOs, NGOs, and private corporations
6. The examples illustrated the power of S&SD to address issues within contemporary society
7. An interpretation of the body of examples means that S&SD is now pervasive and a critical aspect of sport. The use of sport as a platform can significantly impact implementing and accelerating sustainability in and through sport
8. A further interpretation is that sport should further promote social goals and enhance environmental sustainability (Triantafyllidis & Darvin, 2021)

It is now up to those in sport to critically evaluate S&SD's impact and determine how to improve the initiatives for effectiveness and efficiency, find the societal gaps, and determine how sport as a platform can aid in filling such gaps.

Strategies for moving forward

Nowadays, it seems necessary that all sport governing bodies are committing themselves to systemic change through intense cooperation and innovation. Consequently, it is essential to note that sustainable development aims to enhance sustainable growth through new initiatives and build coalitions in S&SD. Given the variety of organizations involved in global sport governance, cooperation and combined action are essential elements to raising awareness and tackling S&SD challenges in our contemporary society. The OM worldwide provides an excellent vehicle for all aspects of sustainable development for policymakers and communities to build consensus and achieve progress within this field of S&SD. Additionally, and perhaps most importantly, the UN SDGs offer a significant opportunity for the OM and sport organizations worldwide to use sport to intensify their cooperation with other organizations. Working to achieve progress on the goals will contribute to the further democratization and transparency of global sport governance and increase the impact of sport on global governance.

Review questions

1. What is the definition of the term governance, and what is sport governance? Please provide an example of sport governance in S&SD

2. List the political aspects of S&SD
3. Outline the criteria you would establish so that the political perspective of S&SD can be divided into SD*o*S and S*4*SD
4. Considering the sport of your choice, how would you evaluate the effectiveness of the current leadership of S&SD for policy development in your country? And how for designing sustainable strategic plans critically?

Discussion questions

1. Get familiar with sustainable development initiatives in your region/country. Write a statement to the members of the NOC of your country to ask them to use their sport governance leadership role to engage in some of these regional/national initiatives
2. Discuss the impact of the OM activity in S&SD on sustainable development within the OM
3. Using one of the examples provided in this chapter show how an IGO may use S&SD to promote peace and development worldwide
4. In recent years, we have witnessed many joint initiatives between political actors in the field of S&SD. Consider awareness campaigns for these initiatives. What is your target audience? Athletes, teams, the general public, all of them? What message would you promote? What communication tools would you use?
5. Discuss topics of S&SD to propose a global sport governance joint initiative. Which actors would you choose to bring together and why?

Learning activities

1. Select one IGO and outline its S&SD initiatives. Then, determine the impacts you think the initiatives could have on society
2. Select one non-governmental sport organization and outline their S&SD initiatives. Then, determine the impacts you think the initiatives could have on society
3. Select one private corporation and outline their S&SD initiatives. Then, determine the impacts you think the initiatives could have on society
4. Compare the different S&SD initiatives you have outlined and evaluate how sports contribute to society. What societal priorities do you have that sport could be a platform to promote?
5. Envision and write your perspective concerning what sustainable sport management looks like (your vision of a well-functioning sporting society that possesses the power to offer global sustainability). Outline key steps to make your vision a reality

External online resources

1. Council of Europe: (www.coe.int)
2. EcoServeis: (www.ecoserveis.net)
3. European Union: (www.europa.eu)
4. Juventus Football Club: (www.juventus.com)
5. Green Sports Alliance: (www.greensportalliance.org)
6. Olympic Games: (www.olympic.org)
7. Sport and Sustainability International: (https://www.sportsustainability.org)
8. Union of European Football Associations: (www.uefa.com)
9. World Athletics: (www.worldathletics.org)

References

Archer, C. (2001). *International Organizations*. 3rd edition. London-New York: Routledge.

Bach, T. (2015, September). *Remarks on the occasion of the UN Sustainable Development Goals.* New York: UN Sustainable Summit. Retrieved from https://stillmed.olympic.org/ Documents/IOC_President/UN-SDG-speech-2015.pdf

Baylis, J. (2020). *The globalization of world politics: An introduction to international relations.* USA: Oxford university press.

Bourantonis, D., & Wiener, J. (1995). *The United Nations in the New World Order. The World Organization at Fifty.* Camden, Great Britain: Palgrave MacMillan. Retrieved from https://www.palgrave.com/gp/book/9780312126179

Boykoff, J., & Macarenas, G. (2016). The Olympics, sustainability, and greenwashing: The Rio 2016 Summer Games. *Capitalism Nature Socialism*, 27(2), 1–11. 10.1080/10455752. 2016.1179473

Brundtland Commission. (2001). *Climate change 2001: Impacts, adaptation, and vulnerability. In* J.J. McCarthy, O.F. Canziani, N.A. Leary, D.J. (Eds.), *Contributions of working group II to the third assessment report of the intergovernmental panel on climate change.* Cambridge: Cambridge University Press.

Brundtland, G.H. (1987). *Our common future.* World Commission on Environment and Development, WCED. Retrieved from https://sustainabledevelopment.un.org/ content/documents/5987our-common-future.pdf

Cambridge Dictionary (n.d.). *Sui Generis.* Retrieved from https://dictionary.cambridge.org/ fr/dictionnaire/anglais/sui-generis

Chatzigianni, E. (2006). The IOC as an international organization. *Choregia Sport Management International Journal*, 2(1–2), 91–101.

Chatzigianni, E. (2014). Corporatism and pluralism in European sport interest re-presentation. *International Journal of Sport Policy and Politics*, 6(1), 19–36.

Chatzigianni, E. (2018). Global sport governance: Globalizing globalized. *Sport in Society*, 21(9), 1454–1482. 10.1080/17430437.2017.1390566

Chatzigianni, E. (2020). Sport & environmental policy. In G. Dingle & C. Mallen (Eds.), *Sport and environmental sustainability.* London & New York: Routledge.

Choue, Ch. (2020, September). *THF Chairman delivers powerful speech on Taekwondo for peace at Sport works Talks.* Retrieved from https://thfaid.org/2020/09/17/thf-chairman-delivers-powerful-speech-on-taekwondo-for-peace-at-sportworks-talks/

Commission on Global Governance. (1995). Our global neighbourhood. Oxford, UK: Oxford University Press.

Council of Europe (2001). *European Sports Charter revised*. Retrieved from https://rm.coe.int/16804c9dbb

Djelic, M.L., & Sahlin-Andersson, K. (2006). *Transnational governance: Institutional dynamics of regulation*. Cambridge: Cambridge University Press.

Eitzen, D.S. (2012). Fair and Foul: Beyond the Myths and Paradoxes of Sport. Washington, DC., US: Rowman & Littlefield.

European Commission (2018a). *Smart specialization platform*. Flash News. Retrieved from https://s3platform.jrc.ec.europa.eu/sport

European Commission. (2018b, February). *European Commission and UEFA consolidate co-operation*. European Commission Press Release. Retrieved from https://ec.europa.eu/commission/presscorner/detail/en/IP_18_901

Fauziah, W., Yusoff, W., & Alhaji, A. (2012). Insight of corporate governance theories. *Journal of Business Management, 1*(1), 2–63.

FIFA (2021). UN and FIFA share strategic social goals. Media Release, 9 March 2021. Available at: https://www.fifa.com/about-fifa/president/media-releases/un-and-fifa-share-strategic-social-goals

Gadais, T. (2019). *Sport for development and peace: Current perspectives of research*. Retrieved from https://www.intechopen.com/books/sports-science-and-human-health-different-approaches/sport-for-development-and-peace-current-perspectives-of-research

Harvard Law School (n.d.). *Intergovernmental organizations (IGOs)*. Retrieved from https://hls.harvard.edu/dept/opia/what-is-public-interest-law/public-service-practice-settings/public-international-law/intergovernmental-organizations-igos/

Harvard Law School (n.d.). *Nongovernmental organizations (NGOs)*. Retrieved from https://hls.harvard.edu/dept/opia/what-is-public-interest-law/public-service-practice-settings/public-international-law/nongovernmental-organizations-ngos/

Hawkins, C.V., & Wang, X. (2012). Sustainable development governance: Citizen participation and support networks in local sustainability initiatives. *Public Works Management & Policy*, 17(1), 7–29. 10.1177%2F1087724X11429045

Hlavac, M. (2010). Less than a state, more than an international organization: The Sui Generis nature of the European Union (December 2). Available at SSRN: https://ssrn.com/abstract=1719308 or 10.2139/ssrn.1719308

International Olympic Committee (n.d.). *Leading the Olympic Movement*. Retrieved from https://www.olympic.org/the-ioc/leading-the-olympic-movement

International Olympic Committee (1994). *XII Olympic Congress* - Paris 1994. https://www.olympic.org/paris-1994-olympic-congress

International Olympic Committee (2009). IOC "Sports for Hope Project". *Press release* (23 May). Retrieved from https://www.olympic.org/news/ioc-sports-for-hope-project

International Olympic Committee (2012). *Sustainability through sport: Implementing the Olympic Movement's Agenda 21–2012*. Lausanne: Commission for Sport and Environment. Retrieved from http://www.olympic.org/Documents/Commissions_PDFfiles/SportAndEnvironment/Sustainability_Through_Sport.pdf.

International Olympic Committee (2014). Olympic Agenda 2020: 20+20 recommendations. Retrieved from https://stillmed.olympic.org/Document/Olympic.Agenda/OlympicAgenda_2020-20-20_Recommendations-ENG.pdf

International Olympic Committee (2017, October). *IOC sustainability strategy Executive Summary*. Retrieved from https://stillmed.olympic.org/media/Document%20Library/

OlympicOrg/Factsheets-Reference-Documents/Sustainability/2017-03-21-IOC-Sustainability-Strategy-English-01.pdf

International Olympic Committee (2018). What is the New Norm? Available at: https://olympics.com/ioc/faq/roles-and-responsibilities-of-the-ioc-and-its-partners/what-is-the-new-norm

Jepson, P. (2019). Recoverable Earth: a twenty-first century environmental narrative. *Ambio*, 48, 123–130. https://doi.org/10.1007/s13280-018-1065-4

Kan, H. 2009. "Actors in World Politics." In M. Sekiguchi (Ed.), *Government and politics* (Vol. II, pp. 242–259). Tokyo: Tokyo Metropolitan University.

Karamichas, J. (2012). The Olympics and the Environment. In H.J. Lenskyj, S. Wagg (Eds.), *The Palgrave handbook of Olympic studies*. London: Palgrave Macmillan. 10.1057/9780230367463_24

Keohane, R.O. (2002). *Power and governance in a partially globalized world*. London: Routledge.

Leopkey, B., & Parent, M.M. (2012). The (Neo) institutionalization of legacy and its sustainable governance within the Olympic Movement. *European Sport Management Quarterly*, *12*(5), 437–455. 10.1080/16184742.2012.693116

Macovei, S., Tufan, A.A., & Vulpe, B.I. (2014). Theoretical approaches to building a healthy lifestyle through the practice of physical activities. *Procedia-Social and Behavioral Sciences*, *117*, 86–91. 10.1016/j.sbspro.2014.02.183

Masdeu Yélamos, G., Carty, C. & Clardy, A. (2019). Sport: A driver of sustainable development, promoter of human rights, and vehicle for health and well-being for all. *Sport, Business and Management: An International Journal*, *9*(4), 315–327. 10.1108/SBM-10-2018-0090

McCullough, B.P., Orr, M., & Kellison, T. (2020). Sport ecology: Conceptualizing an emerging subdiscipline within sport management. *Journal of Sport Management*, *34*(6), 509–520. 10.1123/jsm.2019-0294

Millington, R., Giles, A.R., van Luijk, N., & Hayhurst, L.M. (2021). Sport for sustainability? The extractives industry, sport, and sustainable development. *Journal of Sport and Social Issues*. 10.1177%2F0193723521991413

NBA (2015, January). *American Airlines Arena is world's first sports and entertainment facility to achieve LEED ® Gold Recertification*. Press Release. Retrieved from https://www.nba.com/heat/news/americanairlines-arena-worlds-first-sports-entertainment-facility-achieve-leedr-gold

Ross, W.J., & Leopkey, B. (2017). The adoption and evolution of environmental practices in the Olympic Games. *Managing Sport and Leisure*, *22*(1), 1–18. 10.1080/23750472.2017.1326291

Sachs, J.D. (2015). *The age of sustainable development*. New York City, N.Y., US: Columbia University Press. Retrieved from http://cup.columbia.edu/book/the-age-of-sustainable-development/9780231173155

Saha, D., & Paterson, R.G. (2008). Local government efforts to promote the "Three Es" of sustainable development. *Journal of Planning Education and Research*, *28*, 21–37. 10.1177%2F0739456X08321803

Schröder, P., Anggraeni, K. & Weber, U. (2018). The relevance of circular economy practices to the sustainable development goals. *Journal of Industrial Ecology*, *23*(1), 77–95. 10.1111/jiec.12732

Schulenkorf, N. (2012). Sustainable community development through sport and events: A conceptual framework for sport-for-development projects. *Sport Management Review*, *15*(1), 112. 10.1016/j.smr.2011.06.001

Schulenkorf, N. & Siefken, K. (2019). Managing sport-for-development and healthy lifestyles: The sport-for-health model. *Sport Management Review, 22*(1), 96–107. 10.101 6/j.smr.2018.09.003

SDG Sport Lab (n.d). *Racing towards the 2030 Goals.* Retrieved from https:// www.sdgsportlab.org/

Sport and Sustainability International (n.d.). Welcome to Sport and Sustainability International. Retrieved on December 28, from https://www.sportsustainability.org

Szathmári, A., & Kocsis, T. (2020). Who cares about gladiators? An elite-sport-based concept of Sustainable Sport. *Sport in Society*, 1–19. 10.1080/17430437.2020.1832470

Triantafyllidis, S., & Darvin, L. (2021). Mass-participant sport events and sustainable development: gender, social bonding, and connectedness to nature as predictors of socially and environmentally responsible behavior intentions. *Sustainable Science, 16*(1), 239–253. 10.1007/s11625-020-00867-x

United Nations Educational Scientific Cultural Organization (UNESCO). (2015). *Color? What color? Report on the fight against discrimination and racism in football.* Retrieved from https://en.unesco.org/news/unesco-report-racism-and-discrimination-international-football-presented-european-club

Union of European Football Associations (UEFA) (2018). *Playing for our Planet.* Report. Retrieved from: https://www.uefa.com/MultimediaFiles/Download/uefaorg/General/02/55/63/72/2556372_DOWNLOAD.pdf

University of California Los Angeles (UCLA). (2021). *What is sustainability?* Retrieved from https://www.sustain.ucla.edu/what-is-sustainability/

Wheeler, K., & Nauright, J. (2006). A global perspective on the environmental impact of golf. *Sport in Society, 9*(3), 427–443.

World Athletics (n.d.). *IAAF Air Quality project presented at the United Nations Environment Assembly.* Retrieved from https://www.worldathletics.org/news/press-release/air-quality-unea-unep

World Athletics (2020). World Athletics makes commitment to a cleaner, greener, more equitable world. *Press Release* (07 April). Retrieved from https://www.worldathletics.org/news/press-release/sustainability-strategy-2020

World Sailing Federation (2018). World Sailing first international federation to be awarded sustainability standard. Media Release, 14 February, 2018. Available at: https://www.sailing.org/news/86267.php#.YWm_Sy296L0

Yelamos, G., Carty, C., & Aisling, C. (2019). Sport: A driver of sustainable development, promoter of human rights and vehicle for health and well being for all. *Sport, Business and Management, 9*(4), 315–327. doi: 10.1108/sbm-10-2018-0090

Appendix

Sport and sustainable development in the global Olympic policy spectrum

It is important to note that sport policy for Sport and sustainable development is not standardized. Entities of the Olympic Movement, including sport organizations, can implement it in various ways. For example, it can promote environmental awareness and sustainability, enhance respect for human rights and cross-cultural respect, and strengthen equality and diversity.

Organizing committees for the Olympic Games

The Organizing committees for the Olympic Games (OCOGs) are responsible for the Olympic Games organization. According to the Host City Contract, the National Olympic Committee establishes them to deliver an edition of the Olympic Games, and they report directly to the IOC Executive Board. Their creation to their work closely with the IOC, the NOC of the host country, the host city, and all other global and national stakeholders involved in the Olympic Games.

As the Olympic Games owner, the IOC has tried to ensure environmentally sustainable Olympic Games by the Organizing Committee of Olympic Games (OCOGs). Despite prior OCOG failures and criticism in the field of organizing environmentally sustainable Olympic Games (Karamichas, 2012), the more recent OCOGs – London 2012, Rio 2016, PyeongChang 2018, and Tokyo 2020 – have managed to obtain the International Sustainability Organization certification (ISO 20121) which addresses the social, environmental, and economic impacts of events. It must be noted here that ISO 20121 was also awarded in 2018 (February 14) to another significant Olympic Movement member, the *World Sailing Federation*, the first International Federation to obtain it (WSF, 2018).

PART III

The future of sport and sustainable development

11

OUR VISION FOR SPORT AND SUSTAINABLE DEVELOPMENT

Stavros Triantafyllidis and Cheryl Mallen

LEARNING OBJECTIVES

Upon completion of this chapter, learners should be able to successfully:

1. Identify sport and sustainable development (S&SD) as the strategy for global sustainability
2. Discuss Nelson Mandela's vision of sport as a platform for positive global change
3. Recognize that the United Nations (UN) 17 sustainable development goals (SDGs) can guide S&SD toward sustainability
4. Explain the strategic plan that aims to implement our vision for S&SD
5. Develop strategic plans through innovative goals, objectives, strategies, and tactics for achieving your proposed personal vision of S&SD in your community that can also be part of the solution by guiding global organizations toward sustainable development

---

Overview

The world is challenged to find a way to become more sustainable – and sport can be part of the solution. This is because sport and sustainable development (S&SD) can be a platform for guiding society toward global sustainability. This chapter outlines Nelson Mandela's vision of sport as a platform to show how society can be

DOI: 10.4324/9781003128953-11

united for a cause. Next, the UN 17 sustainable development goals (found at https://sdgs.un.org/goals) are endorsed as entities to guide sport to transition to sustainability by 2030. The authors espouse two key strategic stages to move forward to realize this transition, including the sustainable development of sport (SD*o*S) that focuses on adapting sport for sustainability, and sport for sustainable development (S*4*SD) that focuses on how sport can be used as a vehicle to transition society for sustainability. We envision significant contributions to global sustainability through S&SD. Additionally, the donut theory of economics is described as an alternative vision that promotes sustainability. Both visions are open to debate.

Learners are encouraged to critique the proposed visions and strategic directions and determine their proposed way toward S&SD. There is no one right way to transition, and all voices and ideas are important. Debates on the collection of ideas are needed – despite potential difficulties – and, thus, the facilitation skills of the leadership in sport are critical for achieving consensus and progress. In our contemporary era, every individual can make a difference by establishing a positive and open atmosphere for the question: How do you envision S&SD, and how do you propose we get there?

Glossary

Adaption

"A process of deliberate change in anticipation of or reaction to external stimuli and stress" (Nelson et al., 2007, p. 398).

Benchmark

Standards for enacting sport and sustainable development (S&SD); could include standards for policies, procedures, and actions. Benchmarking is "a management approach for implementing best practices at best cost" (Ettorchi-Tardy et al., 2012, p. e101).

Goal

The end toward which an effort is directed (Harms et al., 2010). In strategic management, goal refers to the long-term ends that a person or an organization aims to achieve based on its mission/vision and alignment with its core values (Harms et al., 2010).

Objective

Actions or efforts that aim to accomplish a goal (Harms et al., 2010). In strategic management, an objective is a short-term goal that a person or an organization strives to achieve based on its long-term goals, mission/vision, and alignment with its core values (Harms et al., 2010).

Partnerships

In this chapter, partnerships are voluntary collaborations to deliver messages or services for climate action. Partnerships involve blocks of people/organizations that advance all parties' legitimacy and allow each party to "win" by offering complementary resources (Zeimers et al., 2019). The partnerships can be same-sector or cross-sector collaborations that offer synergies by cooperating for strategy or program development and delivery (Bailey, 2004) and increasing the chances of success than working independently (Wildridge et al., 2004).

Perspicacity

In this chapter, perspicacity includes developing sport management knowledge including quick insights and understandings about sport (Mallen, 2017) concerning the multiple aspects of economic, social, and environmental sustainability and the competence to implement actions to make sport and sustainable development (S&SD) a reality.

Sport

"Sport means all forms of physical activity which, through casual or organized participation, aim at expressing or improving physical fitness and well-being, forming social relationships or obtaining results in competition at all levels" (Szathmári & Kocsis, 2020, p. 4).

Sport and sustainable development (S&SD)

S&SD is the process that includes two stages: sustainable development of sport (SDoS) and sport for sustainable development S4SD) that, together, enhance the development that meets the needs of current generations without compromising future generations' ability to meet their own needs at the personal, social, economic, ecological, technological, and political levels (Millington et al., 2021; Szathmari & Kocsis, 2020; Triantafyllidis & Darvin, 2021).

Sport for sustainable development (S4SD)

S4SD refers to the contribution of sport to our global societies' viability by encouraging sustainability across the six perspectives of personal, social, economic, ecological, technological, and political worldwide (Macovei et al., 2014; Millington et al., 2021; Schulenkorf, 2012).

Sustainability

The term refers to "the integration of environmental health, social equity, and economic vitality to create thriving, healthy, diverse and resilient communities for this generation and generations to come" (University of California, Los Angeles, 2021, para. 2).

The term sustainable development (SD) encompasses the initiatives and progress in pursuit of sustainability. According to the Brundtland Commission (2001), sustainable development is defined as "development that meets the needs of the present without compromising the ability of future generations to meet their own needs" (p. 82). This includes "the narrow notion of physical sustainability [that] implies a concern for social equity between generations, a concern that must logically be extended to equity within each generation" (p. 82).

Sustainable development of sport (SDoS)

SD*o*S refers to the sustainable practices taken by sport regarding the management of sport products, services, and sport consumer behaviors to achieve sustainability within the world of sport that encompasses six perspectives including the personal, social, economic, ecological, technological, and political (McCullough et al., 2020; Szathmari & Kocsis, 2020; Triantafyllidis & Darvin, 2021).

Vision

An imagined future (Polack, 1972) generated with our "ability to perceive something not visual, as through mental acuteness or keen foresight" (Wilson, 1992, p.18) that can offer a coherent and powerful statement of thought concerning what can be in the future (Wilson, 1992).

Sport and sustainable development (S&SD): A "platform" for global sustainability

Sport is embedded within the social fabric of global societies (Kaufman & Wolff, 2010). Specific sports may differ in their appeals – such as the multi-country obsession with rugby and cricket or the limited number of countries conducting hurling matches as played in Ireland or box lacrosse within Canada. Regardless of the specific sport, it can be a regular discussion topic that can build camaraderie or rivals and is at the center of multi-directional debates on rules, contests, players, building teams, and so forth. These debates can appeal to social groups that span multiple socio-economic states (Kaufman & Wolff, 2010). With its wide-ranging social following, this positions sport as a powerful communication vehicle for promoting messages and advocating solutions for achieving global sustainability. This power was harnessed within Nelson Mandela's vision outlined below.

Mandela's vision

In 1995, the National Rugby team of South Africa won the World Cup. One year after this national achievement, Nelson Mandela was elected as South Africa's president. Mandela's (2000) speech indicated how S&SD could have an integrated vision for a peaceful and equitable world when he stated:

> *Sport has the power to change the world. It has the power to unite people in a way that little else does. It speaks to youth in a language they understand. Sport can create hope where once there was only despair. (YouTube, 2020)*

As the president of South Africa, Mandela repeated those words over and over in his public speeches. He emphasized that sport was a platform for positive change – and his words were heard throughout our global societies. Mandela's power as a political leader prioritized sport because he knew it could contribute significantly to global sustainable development. Now, it is time to illustrate how his vision became a reality with sport leading by example concerning S&SD.

Embracing Mandela's vision with S&SD

Sport has proven to be a powerful platform for pursuing several sustainable development undertakings including the economic, social, and environmental aspects. For instance, sport has been employed to support a number of social change concepts (Kaufman & Wolff, 2010). The concepts for social change aim to build bridges for social transformation that support conflict resolution (Lyras & Welty Peachey, 2011), global peace (Svensson & Loat, 2019), the promotion of public health (Hills et al., 2019; Sherry et al., 2015), the development of community leadership (Edwards, 2015), and social justice with "the social inclusion of the disadvantaged" (Lyras & Welty Peachey, 2011, p. 311).

Athletes have used their sport podium to advocate for political and social justice through "activism to foster progressive social change" (Kaufman & Wolff, 2010, p. 154). Athletes have shone a spotlight on society's inequities concerning racism, sexism, and homophobia and have illustrated their social consciousness as well as their responsibilities as citizens (Kaufman & Wolff, 2010). Further, athletes and sport organizations have promoted awareness and a call for environmental sustainability within sport and society. Significantly, Sartore-Baldwin and McCullough (2018) positioned sport as sharing overall responsibility for safeguarding the natural environment with the incorporation of principles and practices that ensure sport becomes "more ecologically just" (p. 391). Their vision was positioned as being acquired through:

> An equity-based perspective, recognizing the interdependent relationships between humans and the natural environment, and acknowledging how sport organizations hinder the natural environment's opportunities to thrive,

sport organizations can contribute to the planet's health and its inhabitants through their organizational practices (p. 391).

Additionally, Mallen and Chard (2011) offered a debate framework that encouraged the advancement of environmental sustainability within sport, and Mallen and Chard (2012) put forward a vision of "what could be" in environmental sustainability at sport facilities. Additional strategies promoted the advance of environmental performance measurement tools and models (Boggia, et al., 2018; Collins et al., 2007; Genovese et al., 2014; McCullough et al., 2020); advancing the environmental communications promoted by sport (Ciletti et al., 2010; Spector, 2017; Spector et al., 2012;); considering the legal system and the law as a means to regulate advancements in sport's sustainability actions (Schmidt, 2018); and frameworks such as "the Climate Vulnerability of Sport Organizations framework by building on—and linking—concepts of climate vulnerability, exposure, sensitivity, and adaptive capacity in the context of sport organizations" (Orr & Inoue, 2018, p. 391).

There has been initial progress toward a transition of sport to sustainable development. But sport can do more! Our vision involves significant contributions to global sustainability through S&SD.

Sustainability directives

The UN 17 sustainable development goals (SDGs) (https://www.un.org/sustainabledevelopment/) have been put forward to transform our world by 2030. Scientists from a plethora of countries have agreed to a vision of eliminating poverty and hunger; advancing good health and well-being; quality education; gender equality; ensuring all communities have clean water and sanitation, affordable and clean energy; along with decent work and economic growth; the advance of industry, innovation, and infrastructure; reduce inequalities; sustainable cities and communities; responsible consumption and production; climate action; support for life below water and on land; peace and justice, strong institutions; and finally, partnerships to achieve the goals. These established SDGs mean that we can move past generating goals for sustainability within sport. Accordingly, SDGs should be adopted to guide sustainability within sport. It is proposed that sport should make this adoption to avoid spending time developing goals – when they have already been set with the collaboration of multiple countries within the UN. It is instead time to move to act on becoming sustainable.

Embedding sustainability goals within the sport realm is supported by Szathmari (2017), who encouraged sport to be rebuilt specifically with sustainability entrenched within every policy, procedure, and program. To move forward in this transition, Orr et al. (2020), along with Campbell (2018), promoted transformative learning as a critical element for generating momentum. This means that sport must learn how to embed sustainability. Envisioning this movement to sustainability is part of the rebuilding process.

Envisioning the rebuilding of sport for sustainability through S&SD

Establishing "visions" of what sport will look like in its sustainable future is presented as a strategy to set a direction and increase the momentum toward such a future. The use of visions for this purpose was established by Polack (1972) and his research on the historical use of imagining one's future as influential in achieving a set direction. Applying this concept means that those in the sport industry and sport management academia, including students, faculty and researchers, need visions of a sustainable future for the sport industry. Further, it is important to note that our human "potential [for] adaptive capacity is high but rarely achieved." (World Health Organization WHO: Western Pacific Region, 2018, p. 75). This implies a belief that we can adapt to ensure a transition to sustainable development must be accompanied by efforts to diligently implement strategies to ensure such capacity is reached – for the sake of the future of sport and our global society. Accordingly, we developed the following vision for S&SD for debate:

Our vision for S&SD

We envision significant contributions to global sustainability through SSD; we illustrate our strategic plan in Figure 11.1.

Our vision's mission statement

To establish one's S&SD perspicacity that encompasses the ability to develop one's knowledge, with associated quick insights and understandings of S4SD and SDoS, along with the competence to implement actions for fully embedding S&SD in sport by 2030, and the capacity to guide world societies to also transition.

Our vision's strategic initiatives

1. To embed S&SD into every sport policy, procedure, and program in all aspects of sport (including manufacturing, sales, organizations, events, and so forth)
2. To continuously elucidate examples of successful S&SD. This includes highlighting SDoS and S4SD examples in sport that can be applied for global societal sustainability
3. To constantly share best practices in S&SD policy, procedures, and programs to advance learning that accelerates implementation

Strategies for meeting our S&SD goal and objectives

Many leaders of sport organizations, leagues, facilities, events, and manufacturing have exhibited acts supporting personal, social, economic, ecological, technological, and political sustainability. These examples of S&SD can be elucidated to advance

---

Our Vision

We envision significant contributions to global sustainability through sport and sustainable development (S&SD).

Mission Statement

To establish S&SD perspicacity that encompasses the ability to develop one's knowledge of S&SD, with associated quick insights and understandings of *S4SD* and *SDoS*, along with the competence to implement actions for fully embedding S&SD in sport by 2030, and the capacity to guide world societies to also transition.

Achieving
Sport and Sustainable Development (S&SD)

Sport and sustainable development (S&SD) is the process that includes two stages: sustainable development of sport (SDoS) and sport for sustainable development (S4SD) that, together, enhance the development that meets the needs of current generations without compromising future generation's ability to meet their own needs at the personal, social, economic, ecological, technological, and political levels (Millington et al., 2021; Szathmari & Kocsis, 2020; Triantafyllidis & Darvin, 2021).

Strategic Initiatives

1. To embed S&SD into every sport policy, procedure, and program in all aspects of sport (including manufacturing, sales, organizations, events, and so forth);
2. To continuously elucidate examples of successful S&SD. This include highlighting SDoS and S4SD examples in sport that can be applied for global societial sustainability.
3. To constantly share best practices in S&SD policy, procedures, and programs to advance learning that accelerates implementation.

FIGURE 11.1 Strategic plan for implementing our vision for sport and sustainable development (S&SD)

awareness of actions being instituted to meet the vision outlined above. Notably, however, such actions are not consistently embedded within every aspect of the sport; instead, S&SD has been applied intermittently.

The authors of this chapter propose that accelerating S&SD throughout sport involves championing and embedding sustainability into every aspect of sport. Accordingly, a multi-pronged strategy promoted is comprised of renewing sport management education, establishing linkages between sport management education and practitioners, and establishing a shared knowledge database through collaborative partnerships between sport management researchers and practitioners in the field.

Renewing sport management education for the transition to a sustainable future

We begin with education as a critical component in realizing sports transition for perspicacity in S&SD. Our transformative educational focus has multiple parts – and all must be completed concurrently.

First, a separate course is proposed for higher education programs that promote visions of the future of S&SD and strategies for reaching such visions. This course involves debates on the personal, social, economic, ecological, technological, and political aspects of S&SD and the various topics intertwined within each (i.e., social justice, gender equality, etc.). A plethora of debates is necessary to build consensus within sport on visions, roles, and strategies for "what could be" in the future. Such debates are critical in setting directions, overcoming arising issues during the transitional process, and finalizing solutions. The inclusion of practitioners from sport organizations in the debates can help develop future visions and establish the way forward. This educational setting is ideal for coordinating such debates critical for covering the diverse range of sport management topics, generating consensus on goals and objectives, setting specific strategic directions, and determining the key actions for the way forward.

A number of visions can be proposed and debated (including the multiple parts in the visions outlined in this chapter). Participants learning to facilitate small group debates while keeping the atmosphere positive, moving forward to achieve a consensus, and seeking solution-based implementation strategies are important aspects of the course. What visions will be predominant by the end of the semester? And, how are they proposed to be implemented by 2030?

Second, it is proposed that every higher education institution embeds S&SD into all aspects of sport management education to advance insight on the topic because it is critical for the concept of S&SD to be integrated within all aspects of sport. For instance, S&SD can be inserted into discussions on the various topics within finance and economics courses, along with marketing and sponsorship, facility and event management, globalization, law, and so forth. Such knowledge is the nexus for acting with competence in embedding sustainability and transitioning sport. Faculty can be guided by the UN 17 SDGs. When embedded, the topic gains priority status, which advances the hope that S&SD can be realized by 2030.

Third, sport practitioners working hand-in-hand with educators at higher education institutions are proposed to share quick insights to become competent in knowledge and action for S&SD. This strategy sets up what has been called for by Peachey et al. (2019) as "durable bridges between theory and practice" (p. 375) with a conduit for learning from experience concerning change in sport, including best practices on overcoming barriers to change.

Fourth, that sport management faculty exhibit sustainability in their daily actions – teaching through action. Sport management educators are positioned to guide students to act as the future leaders of change for S&SD. An essential aspect of this leadership role in developing a culture that fully embraces S&SD. In turn, this culture aids in building the need for policies and procedures that promote the tenants of sustainability in all aspects of sport. This culture is a key component when seeking to realize what Kellett and Turner (2011) stated was sport's ability to "be a model for self-regulatory institutions" (p. 155); as well as to generate what

Mandela envisioned was the power of sport to unite − in this case, unite in a movement for S&SD.

Much work is needed to develop visions concerning the leadership role, renewing educational programs, and seeking strategies for transitioning for S&SD. Another group is brought into our vision to aid in the transition − sport researchers.

Educators require support for the integration of S&SD. This support can be acquired through knowledge disseminated by researchers in the field of sport management. The researchers can reveal gaps and trends in the transition to S&SD.

Fifth, our vision includes developing an open-access database to disseminate knowledge that aids the global sport community transition for S&SD. The database is stocked with knowledge from a cooperative partnership between global sport academic research centers and sport management educators and practitioners. A collaborative partnership can generate, amalgamate, and disseminate an ever-growing database of knowledge on S&SD. The aim is to support sport transitioning toward sustainability quickly − not in a piecemeal fashion, but for a complete rebuild of sport for sustainability. The database is positioned to continuously build on a foundation of knowledge for use by sport teams, leagues, organizations, manufacturers, etc., and other industries, so they do not start from scratch as they learn to transition to S&SD. The intention is to have the current knowledge available and to build upon such a body of knowledge as quickly as possible.

Each research center and the associated sport management researchers plays its part as they cooperatively work with those in the industry and consider the range of topics within S&SD and advance knowledge focusing on nine key areas, including

  i. Ensuring sport policy is congruent to support S&SD(Lindsey & Darby, 2018)
 ii. Benchmarks for S&SD
iii. Trends in S&SD
 iv. Partnerships to advance S&SD
  v. Lessons learned (including what went well and what went wrong) for good governance for S&SD (for example, in policy development, procedures, programs, and financial implications)
 vi. A collection of best practices S&SD
vii. Barriers/challenges to S&SD in practice
viii. Strategies for overcoming obstacles, and the sharing of "hindsight," and finally
 ix. The advance of comprehensive and comparable S&SD reports from the field

This proposed dedicated database offers a synthesis of knowledge on S&SD that can advance what Funk (2019) proposed as an essential aspect − the speed of dissemination of knowledge. Thus, such academic and practical expertise can spread throughout the global sporting community − including researchers,

practitioners, faculty members, students, those at sport organizations, manufacturers, etc., as well as those interested in society at large. Notably, the database
offers a historical record. It generates a timeline that illustrates changes in the
baseline of knowledge in advance of the transition in sport to S&SD. This data can
aid in adapting visions by academics and practitioners concerning where sport
could be for sustainability in the short, medium, and long terms.

In this scenario, knowledge sharing is critical in S&SD and generates an academic and industry network linking research and practice. Additionally, challenges
in practice and how they were overcome can be illustrated – and in particular, the
current challenges can be outlined at every stage along the way with a related call
for research that aids in finding solutions for each obstacle.

Overall, a vision was posed that included a rebuild of sport management
education for S&SD, linkages to those in practice, and a database of knowledge
developed by academic research centers and sport management practitioners to
build momentum in S&SD. The interconnectiveness of education, research, and
practice is critical to the success of S&SD. Progress in each of these areas has
begun, but they are not in the advanced stages.

The focus now needs to be a move from an inconsistent smattering of actions
to embedding S&SD within all aspects of sport. The elements in our vision posed
above are building blocks promoting quick advances in a transition of S&SD by
2030. Ours is not the only vision. Another vision can be seen through the donut
theory of economics. This theory offers a vision of the future that can be applied
to sport to advance sustainable development.

Developing S&SD with the donut theory of economics applied to sport

It is important to note a trend emerging with a new economic strategy tested in
cities worldwide – such as Amsterdam, Netherlands; Copenhagen, Denmark;
Brussels, Belgium; Dunedin, New Zealand; Nanaimo, Canada; and Portland,
United States (Nugent, 2021). Instead of focusing on a pattern of continuous
economic growth, there is a move to implementing the "donut theory of economics" (Raworth, 2012), "where everyone has what they need to live a good
life" (Nugent, 2021, para. 3). The donut theory consists of three parts: (1) the
donut itself, (2) inside the donut hole, and (3) outside the exterior perimeter of the
donut. We will now describe the three parts, and then questions will be posed to
decide if this theory can provide a direction for society into the future – and a role
for sport.

Part 1: The donut itself

The ultimate goal is to live on the donut, as this is noted as "the environmentally
safe and socially just space for humanity to thrive in" (Raworth, 2012, p. 4). In this
place, there is a focus on some elements that you have access to, including the

following: "water; food; health; education; income/work; peace/justice; political voice; social equality; gender equality; housing; networks; and energy" (Raworth, 2012, p. 4). Additionally, living on the donut is where S&SD efforts impact sporting opportunities for health, enjoyment, and achievement.

Part 2: Inside the donut hole

Many individuals/communities/nations today do not have access to the elements of life listed above. They are living inside the donut hole. This area has a "shortfall" (Nugent, 2021, para. 3) of the elements. Thus, life basics are not accessible, and support conditions are missing to allow community members to thrive. The donut hole has been noted as generally occurring "in poorer countries [that] often fall below the social foundation" (Nugent, 2021, para. 3). The efforts concerning S&SD have an impact. Such efforts seek to aid those inside the donut hole to move toward being on the donut through, for example, sport for social justice, sport for social and gender equality, and the sharing of sport facility generated renewable energy with local communities.

Part 3: Outside the donut

If you are outside the donut, then you can be considered to have taken a bite out of the donut itself – impacting the safe place for humanity. A bite includes contributing to actions that generate "climate change, ocean acidification; chemical pollution; nitrogen and phosphorus loading; freshwater withdrawals; land conversion; biodiversity loss; air pollution; and ozone layer depletion" (Raworth, 2012, p. 4). Being outside the donut implies living beyond the ceiling of ecological boundaries that exploit our Earth to its detriment. It has been noted that "by and large, people in rich countries live above the environmental ceiling" (Nugent, 2021, para. 3). S&SD could have a role here too, for example, increasing awareness and education concerning the adverse environmental conditions; to push for climate action, reduction of chemical use in sport manufacturing and grass-based sport fields.

Moving forward

Consider if having your community utilize the donut theory of economics is a worthwhile endeavor? If so, no matter where you are currently positioned within the three aspects of the theory, each community seeking to implement the theory must set their goals and strategic directions for moving to – and maintaining a position on – the donut.

Now, consider the role of sport in aiding communities with their pursuit of being on the donut. Sport is a powerful body for lobbying for change – so, is this a role for sport?

Concluding remarks

1. The time to transition sport for S&SD is now – this encompasses a sustainable sporting society embedded with the associated social, economic, environmental, technological, and political aspects
2. There is no need for sport to spend time developing their goals for sustainability as the UN 17 SDGs are available for application. This means that sport can move forward implementing such goals by 2030
3. Our proposed vision of how to move forward in S&SD is open for debate. Our vision included areas such as a separate higher education course in S&SD to generate a space for debate and advance visions for the way forward; embedding S&SD in all sport management courses; generating partnerships to aid the advance of perspicacity (including partnerships between higher education sport management educators, their students, researchers, research centers, and practitioners). A database to disseminate knowledge that can aid sport and society to transition as quickly as possible
4. A vision using the donut theory of economics was outlined as an alternative strategy when applied to S&SD. This vision is also open for debate
5. Further visions of the future are needed. We need visions of what sport and society will look like when embedded with the UN 17 SDGs – along with strategies for reaching proposed visions by 2030
6. There is an emphasis on debates related to proposed visions. These debates are critical to generating consensus, the specific strategic directions, and actions needed to move forward. Much work is required to develop the leadership to frame and conduct such debates within sport. Educational institutions are excellent spaces to house such debates – and to extend these debates into general society
7. Embedding specific sustainability principles and practices within sport is still in the development stage. Much work has yet to be completed to bring visions of a sustainable future into reality

Future directions

1. Develop visions of sport's future in terms of: "What could be" in S&SD?
2. Debate the arising visions and build consensus for the way forward in S&SD for global sustainability
3. Generate perspicacity for transitioning for S&SD (including quick insights and understandings of S&SD for use in practice)
4. Determine the leadership requirements that underscore the transition to S&SD. Further, determine where this leadership will come from and the skills required
5. Embed, personal, social, economic, environmental, technological, and political aspects of sustainability within all aspects of sport in your community, and then show your local community your best practices in transitioning for S&SD

Review questions

1. How can S&SD be used as a platform for global sustainability?
2. Nelson Mandela used sport as a platform for a particular purpose … what was the purpose?
3. Outline how the UN 17 SDGs can guide sport toward sustainability?
4. What is the vision posed by the authors? Do you agree or disagree with heading toward this vision? Why?
5. In your own words, outline the donut theory of economics and indicate how it applies to sport

Discussion questions

1. What is the role of Nelson Mandela in S&SD?
2. Can visions of the future aid in achieving such visions?
3. Should the UN 17 SDGs guide sport to a sustainable future, or should sport develop their own sustainability goals?
4. If the athletes worldwide signed the pact to adopt the donut theory of economics globally – as an athlete – would you sign the contract?
5. Now, non-athletes follow suit and have developed a pact that indicates that they will not work in a community that does not support efforts to ensure their community members are on/in the donut portion of the theory. Would you sign the pact knowing that you may have to give up a future career opportunity to ensure the pressure encourages a movement that aids society's environmental and social development as a whole?

Learning activities

1. Record which elements of the proposed vision of S&SD with which you agree. Next, adapt the vision to include your ideas. Include a minimum of five key steps for implementing such as vision
2. Benchmarks for S&SD need to be broken into segments, such as benchmarks for sustainable sport equipment manufacturing, sport facility management, sport event management, sport organizational management of athletes, leagues, teams, etc. Select one area and establish initial benchmarks that can guide the transition to S&SD
3. If a database of knowledge were developed to support S&SD:

    • Who could set up such a database? And be responsible for updating it? For example, should current bodies, such as the North American Society for Sport Management, or European Association for Sport Management, or the Sport Management Association of New Zealand and Australia be involved in the development of a database? Or should an independent body be developed that focuses specifically on communication for S&SD?

- Should the data be set up with a focus on positive directives for moving forward? (Or should negative aspects also be included?)
- Who would own the data?
- How could the knowledge from so many avenues within economic, social, and environmental sustainability be organized to facilitate educators' and practitioners' easy access?

4. What type of leadership is needed to aid sport to transition to being sustainable?
5. What type of system can be established so practitioners can report their innovations and other sustainable development strategies to educate others?
6. There is a place for you in sport management ... aiding the advance of S&SD! How will you get involved and make strides in heading toward an envisioned future?

Further reading

1. Moustakas, L., & Işık, A.A. (2020). Sport and sustainable development in Botswana: towards policy coherence. *Discover Sustainability*, *1*(1), 1–12. https://doi.org/10.1007/s43621-020-00005-8
2. Yélamos, G., Carty, C., & Clardy, A. (2019). Sport: A driver of sustainable development, promoter of human rights, and vehicle for health and well-being for all. *Sport, Business and Management: An International Journal*, *9*(4), 315–327. https://doi.org/10.1108/SBM-10-2018-0090
3. UCLA Sustainability (2021). What is sustainability? Retrieved from https://www.sustain.ucla.edu/what-is-sustainability/
4. Coakley, J. (2015). Assessing the sociology of sport: On cultural sensibilities and the excellent sport myth. *International Review for the Sociology of Sport*, *50*(4–5), 402–406. https://doi.org/10.1177%2F1012690214538864
5. Thibault, L. (2009). Globalization of sport: An inconvenient truth. *Journal of Sport Management*, *23*(1), 1–20. https://doi.org/10.1123/jsm.23.1.1
6. Morodi, L. (2011). The reconstruction, development, and transformation of South African diversified society through sport: Cherished ideals of Nelson Mandela and their challenges. *International Journal of Sport & Society*, *2*(3), 11–20. https://doi.org/10.18848/2152-7857/CGP/v02i03/53875

Relevant online resources

1. How Nelson Mandela united South Africa during the Rugby World Cup – The power of sport: https://sunilsharmauk.medium.com/how-nelson-mandela-united-south-africa-during-the-rugby-world-cup-the-power-of-sport-4a9cbd865fb6
2. ESPN: https://www.espn.com/espn/story/_/id/10085352/nelson-mandela-impact-world-sports

3.   USA Today: https://www.usatoday.com/story/sports/2013/12/05/nelson-
     mandela-death-soccer-rugby-sports-impact-appreciation/2432659/
4.   United Nations Environment: https://www.unep.org/news-and-stories/
     press-release/nelson-mandela-champion-sustainable-development-dies-95
5.   United Nations: https://www.un.org/en/exhibits/page/building-legacy-nelson-
     mandela
6.   World Economic Forum: https://www.weforum.org/agenda/2016/12/
     heres-what-nelson-mandela-can-teach-us-about-modern-sustainability/
7.   Nelson Mandela University: https://sustainability.mandela.ac.za

References

Bailey, N. (2004). Toward a research agenda for public-private partnerships in the 1990s. *Local Economy: The Journal of Local Economy Policy Unit, 8*(4), 292–306. 10.1080/0269094 9408726205

Boggia, A., Massei, G., Paolotti, L., Rocchi, L., & Schiavi, F. (2018). Research article: A model for measuring the environmental sustainability of events. *Journal of Environmental Management, 206*, 836–845. 10.1016/j.jenvman.2017.11.057

Brundtland Commission. (2001). *Climate change 2001: Impacts, adaptation, and vulnerability.* In J.J. McCarthy, O.F. Canziani, N.A. Leary, D.J. Dokken and K.S. White (Eds.), *Contributions of working group II to the third assessment report of the intergov*ernmental panel on climate change. Cambridge: Cambridge University Press. Retrieved from https://www.ipcc.ch/report/ar3/wg2/

Campbell, M. (2018). Can sport help the public understand the effects of climate change? *Sport Sustainability Journal*, Published Sept 28 Online https://sportsustainabilityjournal.com/analysis/can-sport-help-the-public-understand-the-effects-of-climate-change/

Ciletti, D., Lanasa, J., Ramos, D., Luchs, R., & Lou, J. (2010). Sustainability communication in North American professional sports leagues: Insights from website self-presentations. *International Journal Sport Communi*cation, *3*, 64–91. 10.1123/ijsc.3.1.64

Collins, A., Flynn, A., Munday, M., & Roberts, A. (2007). Assessing the environmental consequences of major sporting events: The 2003/04 FA Cup Final. *Urban Studies, 44*(3), 457–476. 10.1080%2F00420980601131878

Edwards, M. (2015). The role of sport in community capacity building: An examination of sport development research and practice. *Sport Management Review, 18*(1), 6–19. 10.101 6/j.smr.2013.08.008

Ettorchi-Tardy, A., Levif, M., & Michel, P. (2012, May). Benchmarking: A method for continuous quality improvements in health. *Health Policy, 7*(4), e101–e119.

Funk, D. (2019). Spreading research uncomfortably slow: Insight for emerging sport management scholars. *Journal of Sport Management, 33*(1), 1–11. 10.1123/jsm.2018-0315

Genovese, A., Koh, L., Jumar, N., & Tripathi, P. (2014). Exploring the challenges in implementing supplier environmental performance measurement models: A case study. *Production Planning & Control, 25*(13–14), 1198–1211. 10.1080/09537287.2013.808839

Harms, R., Reschke, C.H., Kraus, S., & Fink, M. (2010). Antecedents of innovation and growth: Analyzing the impact of entrepreneurial orientation and goal-oriented management. *International Journal of Technology Management, 52*(1/2), 135–152. 10.1504/IJTM.2010.035859

Hills, S., Walker, M., & Barry, A. (2019). Sport as a vehicle for health promotion: A shared value example of corporate social responsibility. *Sport Management Review, 22*(1), 126–141. 10.1016/j.smr.2018.10.001

Kaufman, P., & Wolff, E. (2010). Playing and protesting: Sport as a vehicle for social change. *Journal of Sport & Social Issues, 34*(2), 154–175. 10.1177%2F0193723509360218

Kellett, P., & Turner, P. (2011). CSR and water management in the sport sector: A research agenda. *International Journal of Sport Management and Marketing, 10*(1–2), 142–160. 10.1504/IJSMM.2011.043616

Lindsey, I., & Darby, P. (2018). Sport and the sustainable development goals: Where is the policy coherence? *International Review for the Sociology of Sport, 45*(3), 295–314. Retrieved from 10.1177/1012690217752651

Lyras, A., & Welty Peachey, J. (2011). Integrating sport-for-development theory and praxis. *Sport Management Review,* 14, 311–326. 10.1016/j.smr.2011.05.006

Macovei, S., Tufan, A.A., & Vulpe, B.I. (2014). Theoretical approaches to building a healthy lifestyle through the practice of physical activities. *Procedia-Social and Behavioral Sciences, 117,* 86–91. 10.1016/j.sbspro.2014.02.183

Mallen, C. (2017). Chapter 2: The concept of knowledge in event management. In C. Mallen and L. Adams (Eds.), *Event management in sport, recreation and tourism: Theoretical and practical dimensions.* London, England: Routledge.

Mallen, C. & Chard, C. (2012, May). "What could be" in Canadian sport facility environmental sustainability. *Sport Management Review, 15,* 230–243. 10.1016/j.smr.2011.10.001

Mallen, C., & Chard, C. (2011). A framework for debating the future of environmental sustainability in the sport academy. *Sport Management Review, 14*(4), 424–433. 10.1016/j.smr.2010.12.002

Mallen, C., Stevens, J., & Adams, L.J. (2011). A content analysis of environmental sustainability research in a sport-related journal sample. *Journal of Sport Management, 25*(3), 240–256. 10.1123/jsm.25.3.240

McCullough, B.P., Orr, M., & Kellison, T. (2020). Sport ecology: Conceptualizing an emerging subdiscipline within sport management. *Journal of Sport Management, 34*(6), 509–520. 10.1123/jsm.2019-0294

McCullough, B.P., Orr, M., & Watanabe, N.M. (2020). Measuring externalities: The imperative next step to sustainability assessment in sport. *Journal of Sport Management, 34*(5), 393–402. 10.1123/jsm.2019-0254

Millington, R., Giles, A.R., van Luijk, N., & Hayhurst, L.M. (2021). Sport for Sustainability? The Extractives Industry, Sport, and Sustainable Development. *Journal of Sport and Social Issues.* 10.1177/0193723521991413

Nelson, D., Adger, W., & Brown, K. (2007). Adaption to environmental change: Contributions of a resilience framework. *Annual Review of Environment and Resources, 32,* 395–419. 10.1146/annurev.energy.32.051807.090348

Nugent, C. (2021, January 22). Amsterdam is embracing a radically new economic theory to help save the environment. Could it also replace capitalism? *Time Magazine.* Retrieved from https://time.com/5930093/amsterdam-doughnut-economics/

Orr, M., & Inoue, Y. (2018). Sport versus climate: Introducing the climate vulnerability of sport organizations framework. *Sport Management Review, 21*(4), 391–402. 10.1016/j.smr.2018.09.007

Orr, M., McCullough, B.P., & Pelcher, J. (2020, July). Leveraging sport as a venue and vehicle for transformative learning. *Journal of Sustainability in Higher Education, 21*(6), 1071–1086. 10.1108/IJSHE-02-2020-0074

Peachey, J., Schulenkorf, N., & Spaaij, R. (2019). Sport for social change: Bridging the theory-practice divide. *Journal of Sport Management 33*(5), 366–378. 10.1123/jsm.2019-0291

Polack, F. (1972). *The image of the future.* San Francisco: Jossey-Bass.

Raworth, K. (2012, February). A safe and just space for humanity – Can we live within the donut? Oxfam Discussion Papers. Retrieved from https://www-cdn.oxfam.org/s3fs-public/file_attachments/dp-a-safe-and-just-space-for-humanity-130212-en_5.pdf

Sachs, J.D. (2015). *The age of sustainable development*. New York City, New York, US: Columbia University Press. Retrieved from http://cup.columbia.edu/book/the-age-of-sustainable-development/9780231173155

Sartore-Baldwin, M., & McCullough, B.P. (2018). Equity-based and ecocentric management. Creating more ecologically just sport organization practices. *Sport Management Review*, *21*(4), 391–402. 10.1016/j.smr.2017.08.009

Schmidt, R. (2018). Protecting the environment through sports? Public-private cooperation for regulatory resources and international law. *The European Journal of International Law*, *28*(4), 1341–1366. 10.1093/ejil/chx063

Schulenkorf, N. (2012). Sustainable community development through sport and events: A conceptual framework for sport-for-development projects. *Sport Management Review*, *15*(1), 1–12. 10.1016/j.smr.2011.06.001

Sherry, E., Schulenkorf, N., & Chalip, L. (2015). Managing sport for social change: The state of play. *Sport Management Review*, *18*(1), 1–5. 10.1016/j.smr.2014.12.001

Spector, S., (2017). Environmental communications in New Zealand's skiing industry: Building social legitimacy without addressing non-local transport. *Journal of Sport & Tourism*, *21*(3), 159. 10.1080/14775085.2017.1298461

Spector, S., Chard, C., Mallen, C., & Hyatt, C. (2012, November). Socially constructed environmental issues and sport: A content analysis of ski resort environmental communications. *Sport Management Review*, *15*, 416–433. 10.1016/j.smr.2012.04.003

Svensson, P., & Loat, R. (2019). Bridge-building for social transformation in sport for development and peace. *Journal of Sport Management*, *33*(5), 426–439. 10.1123/jsm.2018-0258

Szathmari, A. (2017). Building sustainability in sport: A clear offside or chance for a "slow" rebirth. *Budapest Management Review*, *48*(11), 33–40. 10.14267/VEZTUD.2017.11.04

Szathmári, A., & Kocsis, T. (2020). Who cares about gladiators? An elite-sport-based concept of Sustainable Sport. *Sport in Society*, 1–19. 10.1080/17430437.2020.1832470

Triantafyllidis, S., & Darvin, L. (2021). Mass-participant sport events and sustainable development: gender, social bonding, and connectedness to nature as predictors of socially and environmentally responsible behavior intentions. *Sustainability Science*, *16*(5), 239–253. 10.1007/s11625-020-00867-x

University of California, Los Angeles (UCLA). (2021). *What is sustainability?* Retrieved from https://www.sustain.ucla.edu/what-is-sustainability/

Wilson, I. (1992). Realizing the power of strategic vision. *Long Range Planning*, *25*(5), 18–28. 10.1016/0024-6301(92)90271-3

Wildridge, V., Childs, S., Cawthra, L., & Madge, B. (2004). How to create successful partnerships – A review of literature. *Health Information and Libraries Journal*, *21, Suppl 1*, 3-19. Doi: 10.1111/j.1740-3324.2004.00497.x

World Health Organization (WHO): Western Pacific Region. (2018). *Drinking water, sanitation, and hygiene in the Western Pacific Region: Opportunities and challenges in the SDG era*. Retrieved from https://apps.who.int/iris/bitstream/handle/10665/274719/97892 90618614-eng.pdf?sequence=1&isAllowed=y

YouTube. (2020, February 9). *Mandela's iconic speech*. Retrieved from https://www.youtube.com/watch?v=y1-7w-bJCtY

Zeimers, G., Anagnostopoulos, C., Zintz, T., et al. (2019). Examining collaboration among nonprofit organizations for social responsibility programs. *Nonprofit and Voluntary Sector Quarter*, *48*(5), 953–974. 10.1177/0899764019837616

12

STUDENT PERSPECTIVES ON SPORT AND SUSTAINABLE DEVELOPMENT: TEACHING AND LEARNING APPROACHES

Stavros Triantafyllidis

LEARNING OBJECTIVES

Upon completion of this chapter, learners should be able to successfully:

1. Define sport and sustainable development (S&SD) from a student's perspective
2. Identify the critical aspects for studying S&SD from a students' perspective
3. Examine how students believe S&SD can contribute to global sustainability
4. Investigate the role of sustainable development of sport (SDoS) and sport for sustainable development (S4SD) stages from a student perspective
5. Recognize the educational needs that require academic attention for moving forward and achieving global sustainable outcomes through S&SD

Overview

This chapter provides a synopsis of undergraduate and graduate students' perspectives concerning sport and sustainable development (S&SD). Students' perspectives were collected through two focus groups. Students' responses were primarily from the Generation Z (Gen Z) age group and pertained specifically to the analytical and normative concepts of S&SD across the two stages of sustainable development of sport ((SDoS) and sport for sustainable development S4SD). The qualitative investigative findings facilitated the conclusions

DOI: 10.4324/9781003128953-12

about the definition of S&SD, along with future directions in academia and practice on studying S&SD for educational purposes, protecting our natural environment, and moving forward as humankind that lives in harmony among us and with our planet.

Glossary

Digital age

The digital age is the period starting in the 1970s with the introduction of the computer combined with the significant growth of the internet in the 1990s and the fast-paced increase of smartphones in the 2010s (Sachs, 2020).

Discussion boards

A discussion board is a term for any online forum and discussions where people post their opinion about a topic, and they expect to view others' responses with a critical perspective on their initial response (Smith et al., 2006).

Focus groups

An investigation technique is used to collect data through a group of people, usually a small number of carefully selected individuals who discuss a given topic. The focus groups are conducted to identify how people think and behave on specific concepts and help investigators to answer why people believe and act in those manners (Creswell & Creswell, 2017).

Generation Z

Gen Z is the demographic group that follows Millennials and precedes Generation Alpha (Mijatovic, 2020). Mijatovic (2020) noted that this group includes individuals born between 1997 and 2015 and began to reach adulthood just prior to the second decade of the 21st century.

iGen

iGen describes young Americans born between 1995 and 2012 and considers it the largest and most influential age in history (Twenge, 2017).

Sport

"Sport means all forms of physical activity which, through casual or organized participation, aim at expressing or improving physical fitness and well-being, forming social relationships or obtaining results in competition at all levels" (Szathmári & Kocsis, 2020, p. 4).

Sport and sustainable development (S&SD)

S&SD is the process that includes two stages: SDoS and S4SD that, together, enhance the development that meets the needs of current generations without compromising future generations' ability to meet their own needs at the personal, social, economic, ecological, technological, and political levels (Millington et al., 2021; Szathmári & Kocsis, 2020; Triantafyllidis & Darvin, 2021).

Sport for sustainable development (S4SD)

S4SD refers to the contribution of sport to our global societies' viability by encouraging sustainability across the six perspectives of personal, social, economic, ecological, technological, and political worldwide (Macovei et al., 2014; Millington et al., 2021; Schulenkorf, 2012).

Sustainability

The term refers to "the integration of environmental health, social equity, and economic vitality to create thriving, healthy, diverse and resilient communities for this generation and generations to come" (University of California Los Angeles, 2021, para. 2).

The term sustainable development (SD) encompasses the initiatives and progress in pursuit of sustainability. According to the Brundtland Commission (2001), SD is defined as "development that meets the needs of the present without compromising the ability of future generations to meet their own needs" (p. 82). This includes "the narrow notion of physical sustainability [that] implies a concern for social equity between generations, a concern that must logically be extended to equity within each generation" (p. 82).

Sustainable development of sport (SDoS)

SDoS refers to the sustainable practices taken by sport regarding the management of sport products, services, and sport consumer behaviors to achieve sustainability within the world of sport that encompasses six perspectives including the personal, social, economic, ecological, technological, and political (McCullough et al., 2020; Szathmári & Kocsis, 2020; Triantafyllidis & Darvin, 2021).

The analytical concept applied to S&SD

A theoretical approach for analyzing sport as a platform to understand the world as a complex interaction of personal, social, economic, ecological, technological, and political systems. Understandings from the individual parts' can be combined to determine the level of S&SD that can be considered a microcosm of society (Millington et al., 2021; Szathmári & Kocsis, 2020; Triantafyllidis & Darvin, 2021).

The normative concept applied to sport and sustainable development (S&SD)

Examinations are completed using sport as a platform to view the world by defining the objectives of a well-functioning society that delivers well-being for its global citizens today and for future generations. The normative concept urges us to have a universal vision toward a good society. These examinations lead to understandings of where we are currently and the gaps that need to be addressed moving into the future based on the six perspectives of S&SD (Millington et al., 2021; Szathmári & Kocsis, 2020; Triantafyllidis & Darvin, 2021).

The teaching and learning process

An educator assesses learning needs and wants, establishes learning objectives, develops teaching and learning strategies to implement a work plan (curriculum and syllabus), and evaluates the instruction outcomes (Lawrence & Tar, 2018).

Qualitative investigation

The term involves collecting and analyzing qualitative data such as text, video, or audio, to explore in-depth people's opinions, perceptions, and experiences on specific concepts (Creswell & Creswell, 2017).

Leaders of our future and S&SD

The world is changing rapidly with global pandemics, social inequalities, climate change, economic crises, technological advances, and political transformations (Ferdig, 2007; Sachs, 2015; 2020). Investigative discussions have focused on the evidence regarding these critical issues and have implored that adaptations be made for the sake of the future of humanity and the planet (Ferdig, 2007; Sachs, 2015, 2020). In this chapter, the focus is on adaptations that involve transitioning for S&SD that includes two stages: The SDoS and S4SD.

This chapter sought to obtain student perspectives concerning S&SD, including the demographic cohort's opinions, thoughts, feelings, and behaviors that will take over the leadership of sport in a few years. The student perspectives are considered socially constructed and cognitively influenced by individual viewpoints (Richards, 2010). Further, students' perspectives are important as newcomers to a field can encourage change as they see old process-oriented systems but are not entrenched within them (Kuhn, 1970). The change agent power of students means that current learners, or newcomers to the field of sport management, can more easily reconfigure or transform (Gersick, 2020) an organization through reinterpretations, reimagining, and establishing directions for renewal of a field (Kuhn, 1970). Accordingly, students can be considered optimistic future leaders who guide humanity and global society to live and function in harmony with our planet's resources. A few years from now, Millennials, Gen Z, and Generation Alpha will be voting on the leadership or will be the leaders of our world (Gersick, 2020).

In this chapter, S&SD was examined to identify student's perceptions of sustainability. Now, let's look at their input.

Influences on current generations

There have been several vital influences on current generations. Technologically, the most recent generations have grown up with electronic devices, increasingly advancing technology for computers, fast internet, a wide variety of social media, advanced and direct communication, and have had the opportunity to be part of many global online communities. Several common traits and experiences characterize the IGen, and Gen Z. First, they have been raised and taught by millennial parents (mostly) (Jiménez & Glater, 2020). Second, they have learned to be independent, are more educated, well-behaved, and are more concerned about societal issues (compare to previous generations) (Jiménez & Glater, 2020). Additionally, many current generations have been affected by debts, such as student loans (Jiménez & Glater, 2020). They have faced a growing income gap, a shrinking middle class, and financial independence from a very young age (Jiménez & Glater, 2020).

Interestingly, iGen includes individuals (born between 1995 and 2012), have been characterized by their lifestyles that include the technological and digital evolution (Twenge, 2017). For example, they grew up with smartphones, social media accounts, and pages (i.e., Facebook, Instagram, and Snapchat). Essentially, they were born with the internet and during the fastest technological growth in the world's history. The digital age is the era whereby technological changes have been dramatically shaping today's world (Sachs, 2020). The digital age's key elements include the considerable amount of information shared across the globe daily. For example, in 2020, globally, there were transmitted 44 zettabytes (44,000,000,000,000,000,000,000 bytes) of data per day (Sachs, 2020). Accordingly, in the digital age, we should realize that the teaching and learning methods and tools used in educating the arising generations need to change to recognize technological advancements. We will now examine educational processes.

Educating our emerging leaders

Due to the digital age's impacts, Lawrence and Tar (2018) investigated changing educational processes. In particular, they focused on integrating Information

Communication Technology (ICT) in teaching and learning processes. The ICT is an increasingly valuable teaching tool that colleges and universities use to motivate contemporary students' learning practices (Lawrence & Tar, 2018). Specifically, the ICT encompasses communication and the associated technologies that support such communication in our modern educational settings (Lawrence & Tar, 2018). Advanced technology supports educators in accessing stored data, controlling the possible manipulations, and disseminating data to generate a conduit to understanding concepts and addressing associated issues. The innovative techniques available through ICT can allow for efficient classroom, online and pedagogical activities (Lawrence & Tar, 2018). ICT is the new trend as we move forward to educate the current generations. For teachers and learners, the adaptation of ICT methods in teaching and learning environments and institutions have been found to work in our modern digital world (Twenge, 2017).

But what topics are critical for the future based on the perspectives of students? Is S&SD a critical education topic to access younger generations' thoughts and beliefs for making the world a better and more sustainable place for future generations, our planet's ecosystems, and global society?

We will now examine their perspectives concerning S&SD. Accordingly, we will use the term "current generations" to refer to the collective of Millennials, Gen Z, and iGen.

Learning process: Acquiring new knowledge related to S&SD

A series of discussions on S&SD and focus groups were conducted to acquire the reflective narratives of the future leaders for S&SD. The underlying purpose of this examination is to optimize our teaching, learning, and assessing methods used in our curricula, and view how sustainable development can be better applied for educational purposes with the application of primarily sport management student perspectives. To advance understanding of S&SD perspectives held by some members within this group, undergraduate and graduate program students were investigated. The following sections illustrate the process and outcomes of the discussions, forums, and focus groups undertaken through several semesters to come to our conclusions.

Exploring students' perspective on S&SD: Qualitative investigation

A semester long project of capturing students' perspectives in undergraduate and graduate sports management programs offered a crucial synopsis on the term of S&SD and its future directions. Qualitative data were collected from students through a series of discussion boards to guide researchers to determine the focus groups' key topics and questions. Finally, two focus groups were employed to explore in-depth students' perceptions of S&SD (Creswell & Creswell, 2017). Initially, a series of discussion boards was conducted as a pilot project that helped determine the focus groups' key topics and questions. The discussion boards were completed across one academic semester (Fall 2020). From the series of discussion boards, the responses of students were recorded and represented 78.3% of the students majoring in a higher education sport management program. All four years were represented. Further, respondents were graduate students from a master's in sport management program. They represented 100% of the graduate program student body.

Examination objectives

The method used for investigating students' perspectives on S&SD was a qualitative approach for understanding their in-depth thoughts, beliefs, and opinions. The guiding question for this examination was:

Project's central question: Why is it essential to study S&SD?

Accordingly, the following objectives were established to answer the project's central question and achieve a vision on an effective S&SD educational endeavor.

Examination objective 1: To identify students' thoughts and beliefs on studying S&SD.
Examination objective 2: To generate a definition for S&SD as perceived by the higher education students.

Participants and procedures

After collecting students' perceptions through the discussion boards, two focus groups were held with the same student population as the discussion boards. The first focus group was held with only undergraduate students and the second one with only graduate students. At the beginning of the focus groups, students were provided with the following definitions of sport, as well as sustainable development:

- Sport: "All forms of physical activity that aim to optimize people's athleticism, active living, mental well-being, spiritual health, social relationships, connectedness to nature, and quality of life" (Pitts & Danylchuk, 2007).
- Sustainable development: "The development that meets the needs of the present without compromising the ability of future generations to meet their own needs" (Brundtland Commission, 2001).

Focus groups topics

The question posed to the participants of the focus groups were developed based on the guiding statement outlined earlier (why is it essential to study S&SD and the development of a definition for S&SD) (Sachs, 2015; Triantafyllidis & Darvin, 2021). Accordingly, the questions posed to students were:

Topic #1: General views on S&SD

- Connection and differences between the concepts of "sport" and of "sustainable development"
- Studying S&SD – essential or not important
- Definition for S&SD – How would you define S&SD?
- Connection and differences between the SDoS and the S4SD

Topic #2: Perspectives on SDoS

- Thoughts, feelings, beliefs, and opinions on the ways sport can become sustainable in the next ten years and across the six perspectives – personal, social, economic, ecological, technological, and political
- Sustainable strategic management of sport for becoming sustainable – sustainable sport management

Topic #3: Perspectives on S4SD

- Thoughts, feelings, beliefs, and opinions on the ways sport can enhance sustainable development outcomes for six perspectives – personal, social, economic, ecological, technological, and political
- Sport as a strategy for implementing the global sustainable development goals (SDGs) by 2030

Process for analyzing students' responses on S&SD topics

The focus groups enabled researchers to capture data regarding the importance of S&SD by collecting qualitative data from seniors (undergraduate) and graduate students (Creswell & Creswell, 2017). Qualitative data refers to the words, comments, and non-numerical information provided through the discussion boards and focus groups (Creswell & Creswell, 2017). The criteria for recruiting participants included, but were not limited to, their age, previous experiences with sport, both academic (sport management) and on-field (athletes, etc.). The focus groups were conducted through the online communication platform Zoom. Each focus group lasted approximately 60 minutes.

All participants' comments were combined. For data confidentiality, personal identifiers were removed, and we used pseudonyms, such as participant-1 was noted as P-1, and so forth (until P-14) (Creswell & Creswell, 2017). It is essential to mention students' attitudes and opinions are the key aspects that helped determine their overall perceptions of S&SD. Students' views were considered to include "an attitude [that] is a psychological tendency that is expressed by evaluating a particular entity with some degree of favor or disfavor" (Eagly & Chaiken, 1993, p. 1). Further, their shared opinion was considered a collection of thoughts or beliefs that a group of people has toward a particular entity (Cambridge Dictionary, 2021).

Results and discussion on students' perspectives on S&SD

The investigation offered critical insights on student perspectives concerning S&SD. First, the focus groups provided consistency for responses on the S&SD role in education. The responses reflected students' attitudes and opinions that S&SD in educational programs plays a role in achieving sustainability outcomes. Students valued S&SD courses as contributing to the quality education of current and future generations, especially in cultivating leadership and communication skills for S&SD.

Three themes and six sub-themes arose from students' responses that reflected on both the SDoS and S4SD. Each theme and sub-theme will now be reviewed.

Theme 1: S&SD and global leadership

Students revealed that sport could be a critical component of the global leadership for S&SD. Responses highlighted that sport could contribute to global leadership in S&SD by educating those within sport on the topic (P-1). Those educated can then use the power of sport to influence action for S&SD. An example offered by a student involved educating

> star athletes on sustainable development ... [as] athletes have become the face of anything that's gone on in the world and what needs to be changed ... [and] can only improve knowledge and help ... focusing on how we can do what we love and use it to help others. (P-1)

A further example noted that coaches had a role in inspiring and using their leadership talent for advancing S&SD (P-2; P-5).

Additionally, the education of sports leadership, including future leaders, was found to be "crucial ... because our future leaders must know what can be done and implement those plans to achieve an excellent global society" (P-3; P-8). The education can result in "a positive network that is supportive and can enhance the creation of a world that would be better than the one we are living in now" (P-4; P-6).

Theme 1 had two sub-themes that included (a) the star power of athletes and coaches and (b) communication effectiveness and leadership. Students reported that sport was influential in S&SD as it has the power to influence public perceptions positively.

Sport has the power to cultivate opinions and positive attitudes of the general public toward sustainable development and global sustainability. The support and action for S&SD is based on its professional capability to communicate messages worldwide very effectively (P-1; P-5; P-7; P-10; P-14). Students noted that sport and society are interconnected through social media, including multiple social media platforms, television radio, and so forth (P-4; P-6; P-11; P-13). "Therefore, messages ... can be promoted and publicized to these large audiences to spread awareness" (P-8), and "It is a great way to communicate ideas" (P-9).

Theme 2: S&SD and empowerment

Students confirmed that sport could empower those in society to think and act for sustainability.

Responses positioned the topic as necessary. It was stated that "it is critical to think about sustainability" (P-12).

Theme 2 had two sub-themes that included (a) sustainable community development and (b) strong social networks.

"From a community development standpoint, sport-related activity groups (SDoS) and sport as a platform (S4SD) can both (S&SD) help create a positive environment for underprivileged youth and those looking to become part of a team" (P-1). Essentially, S&SD (both SDoS and S4SD) can help to provide opportunities and positivity within the community by acting as an outlet for impoverished individuals who may feel left out or excluded due to their disadvantages. As students stated:

> SDoS and S4SD can offer these individuals chances to play their capabilities and talents in a safe and stable environment. Often they are not given opportunities and guidance to become a part of something; they can make adverse decisions that impact their lives in harmful ways. Utilizing sport to learn and grow can be a very appealing vehicle, especially to the younger generation. (P-1; P-3; P-5)

"Sustainable development as far as the rise of S4SD can be enhanced through sport because of the influence of sports in communities" (P-3).

> Sport is a globally known platform and top-rated attractions to a large variety of people worldwide. There are philanthropists outside of the world of sport that like the idea of sport because they see it as a way to facilitate positive community outcomes associated with sport activities. (P-5)

"From a social network perspective, students purported that networks can be generated through sport. These networks can include individuals and groups within society that can work toward S&SD" (P-1; P-5; P-7; P-8; P-13). This includes, for instance, "underprivileged youth and those looking to become part of a team" (P-9) as sport can provide opportunities for these individuals to use their capabilities with guidance to act. "The opportunities, including education in the principles of S&SD, can "reinforce social networks" (P-10; P-12). Additionally, the social networks for S&SD can aid in bringing those within society together to act for a sustainable future because the networks

> can instill social trust among a group, cooperation, coordination, and collaboration on ideas to fulfill mutual goals. S&SD can contribute to the development of a group coming together under one collective identity in which the group represents something larger than themselves. (P-14)

Theme 3: S&SD and climate resilience

Students' responses highlighted the role of S&SD in cultivating an environmental consciousness and building the foundations for generating climate resilience. Students' positions supported with answers stated that "sport can provide funding toward environmental action" (P-6; P-10; P-11) and showcase technologies that can assist in the fight against climate change (P-9; P-13; P-14). "One example would be Formula-E has showcased new battery technology and advancements in electric car motors. In that way, it becomes a way to increase the exposure and image of electric cars" (P-1; P-4; P-12).

Theme 3 had two sub-themes that included (a) environmental consciousness and (b) climate action. Sport was noted as being able to use its power to educate and communicate to generate consciousness and climate action. These actions encompass many avenues such as the multiple aspects of "the whole communities' welfare" (P-12), including human, flora, fauna, and overall environmental health. Sport can be part of our actions for "environmental change" (P-12) or safeguards.

Defining S&SD

An exciting task was the focus group question about how students would define S&SD. Accordingly, responses regarding the appropriate term for S&SD definition as reported by the student included:

- "Being able to build sport without damaging future generation's ability to do the same" (P-9)
- "I believe it is the concept of using principled leadership through sports to create a better understanding of sustainable development and to improve the health, society, and environment for our communities" (P-12)

Additionally, students discussed the potential definition of S&SD from a more S4SD perspective. For example:

- "S&SD is the positive development of communities, ecosystem, and healthy lifestyles through sport" (P-14)

- "Utilizing sport as a way to promote important and powerful messages including sustainability, healthy lifestyle choices and unity within the community" (P-9)
- "Using sport as a vehicle to influence and promote people to make conscious choices about their health, society, and the environment to create sustainability for years to come" (P-8)

Using the input from students on the qualitative investigation and support of the current literature and concepts of S&SD (Heere, 2018; Sachs, 2015; Szathmári & Kocsis, 2020), the following definition of S&SD was developed:

S&SD can be viewed as the direct connection between SDoS and S4SD that, together, encourage the world to meet the needs of current generations without compromising future generations' ability to meet their own needs at the personal, social, economic, ecological, technological, and political levels (Heere, 2018; Sachs, 2015; Szathmári & Kocsis, 2020).

But, as there is no definitive definition of S&SD in sport management, this definition is, thus, open for debate. How would you adapt it to represent the term best?

So, what did we learn about the study of S&SD and its importance?

The focus groups helped us to answer our investigation question as follows:

S&SD is a quality educational endeavor to cultivate strong-minded leaders in our world. It is also a platform for encouragement, inspiration, and unity for our planet and its current and future generations to continue learning to make the world a better and safer place where humans live in harmony with our planet.

Concluding remarks

1. There were three themes and six sub-themes that arose from the student's perspectives. S&SD and global leadership: (a) sustainable community development and (b) solid social networks; S&SD and empowerment: (c) sustainable community development and (d) strong social networks; S&SD and climate resilience: (e) environmental consciousness and (f) climate action
2. Students' responses reflected an overall contribution of S&SD as a critical component of the transition to global sustainability. Accordingly, students' perspectives expressed that it is important to study S&SD because sport has the power of influence. Therefore, by sport being sustainable and sport leaders advocating the positive impacts of sustainable development on global society, S&SD is privileged to contribute significantly to sustainability outcomes worldwide
3. Students highlighted the importance of SDoS for making S4SD viable and credible
4. S&SD as a concept that integrates SDoS and S4SD is the ultimate platform for implementing sustainable development goals (SDGs) such as the 17 SDGs of the Agenda 2030 and the United Nations.

Future directions

1. S&SD is an avenue for global sustainability
2. Build a strong foundation in sport educational programs for sustainability
3. Embrace sport and society with S&SD and sustainability
4. Develop leadership programs for S&SD in academia and practice
5. Design implementation strategies for the S&SD goals to achieve global sustainability
6. Embrace sustainability in quality education to build academic curriculums for teaching and learning excellence
7. Continuously work to define S&SD
8. Research should continue to examine factors that could make the sport more sustainable and advocate sustainable development worldwide efficiently

Review questions

1. How did students perceive the field of study in S&SD, and how does the theory of teaching and learning support it?
2. What are the top three definitions that you believe best fit the term S&SD?
3. How do you believe that S&SD can contribute to the global SDGs and sustainability worldwide? Please provide three methods
4. What is the difference between SDoS and S4SD for shaping the contribution of S&SD on global sustainability?
5. What are the top three needs or wants of your generation for adapting its lifestyle toward the principles and practice of S&SD and achieving global sustainable outcomes and sustainability?
6. What is a method you would propose for effectiveness in teaching and learning S&SD?
7. What do you think are the top three key strategic future directions for S&SD?

Discussion questions

1. Do you consider it important to study S&SD? Yes or no? Please explain why
2. How can sport as a platform enhance sustainability outcomes worldwide?
3. How sport empowers people in your local community?
4. What future hope do you have for your generation in terms of aiding developing countries? Does sport have a role within your hopes? How?
5. What trends have you noticed in terms of how your generation perceives developing nations? What do you think is the role of sport in this perspective?
6. How can leaders inspire your generation to aid developing countries and the world toward sustainability?
7. Can sport become an ultimate strategy for implementing the 17 Global SDGs 2030?

8. What are your perspectives (thoughts, feelings, beliefs, and opinions) on how sport can contribute to our lives in sustainable development over the next 5–10 years?

Learning activities

1. For this activity, you should write your perspective for the future of S&SD in both academia (as an educational endeavor) and practice (as an industrial approach in the sport sector). For both academia and practice, you should also view S&SD through the two stages of SDoS and S4SD
2. Develop an S&SD curriculum that could be taught (a) at the undergraduate level and (b) at the graduate level
3. Create a visual, conceptual map that would illustrate the interconnections of the six perspectives of S&SD (personal, social, economic, ecological, technological, and political) across the two stages of SDoS and S4SD

Further readings

1. Dale, A., & Newman, L. (2005). Sustainable development, education, and literacy. *International Journal of Sustainability in Higher Education*, 6(4), 351–362. https://doi.org/10.1108/14676370510623847
2. O'Flaherty, J., & Liddy, M. (2018). The impact of development education and education for sustainable development interventions: A synthesis of the research. *Environmental Education Research*, 24(7), 1031–1049. https://doi.org/10.1080/13504622.2017.1392484
3. Shulla, K., Filho, W.L., Lardjane, S., Sommer, J.H., & Borgemeister, C. (2020). Sustainable development education in the context of the 2030 Agenda for sustainable development. *International Journal of Sustainable Development & World Ecology*, 27(5), 458–468. https://doi.org/10.1080/13504509.2020.1721378
4. Lawson, H. A. (2005). Empowering people, facilitating community development, and contributing to sustainable development: The social work of sport, exercise, and physical education programs. *Sport, Education and Society*, 10(1), 135–160. https://doi.org/10.1080/1357332052000308800
5. Ličen, S., & Jedlicka, S. R. (2020). Sustainable development principles in US sport management graduate programs. *Sport, Education and Society*, 1–14. https://doi.org/10.1080/13573322.2020.1816541

Relevant online resources

1. United Nations Educational, Scientific, and Cultural Organization (UNESCO): https://en.unesco.org/themes/education-sustainable-development
2. Educational for Sustainable Development (ESD): https://esd-expert.net/files/ESD-Expert/pdf/Was_wir_tun/Lehr-%20und%20Lernmaterialien/What_is_Education_for_Sustainable_Development.pdf

3. Sustainability in Schools: https://sustainabilityinschools.edu.au/what-is-efs
4. Education for Sustainable Development Strategy: https://unece.org/esd-strategy
5. United Nations (UN): https://www.un.org/en/chronicle/article/role-sport-achieving-sustainable-development-goals
6. Sustainability Curriculum Colloquium: https://www.curriculumforsustainability.org/2021-sustainability-curriculum-colloquium/
7. The Association for the Advancement of Sustainability in Higher Education (AASHE): https://www.aashe.org
8. The Sport Ecology Group (SEG) – Sustainability Education: https://www.sportecology.org/research/categories/sustainability-education

References

Brundtland Commission (2001). Climate change 2001: Impacts, adaptation, and vulnerability. In McCarthy, J.J., Canziani, O.F., Leary, N.A., Dokken, D.J. & White, K.S. (Eds.), Contributions of Working Group working group II to the Third Assessment Report third assessment report of the Intergovernmental Panel intergovernmental panel on Climate Change climate change. Cambridge: Cambridge University Press. Weblink: https://www.ipcc.ch/report/ar3/ wg2/

Cambridge Dictionary. (2021, April). *Opinion.* Retrieved from https://dictionary.cambridge.org/us/dictionary/english/opinion

Creswell, J.W., & Creswell, J.D. (2017). *Research design: Qualitative, quantitative, and mixed methods approach.* Thousand Acres, California, US: Sage publications.

Eagly, A.H., & Chaiken, S. (1993). *The psychology of attitudes.* New York City, N.Y., US: Harcourt Brace Jovanovich College Publishers.

Ferdig, M.A. (2007). Sustainability leadership: Co-creating a sustainable future. *Journal of Change Management, 7*(1), 25–35. 10.1080/14697010701233809

Gersick, C. (2020). Reflections on Revolutionary Change, *Journal of Change Management, 20*(1), 7–23. 10.1080/14697017.2019.1586362

Heere, B. (2018). Embracing the sportification of society: Defining e-sports through a polymorphic view on sport. *Sport Management Review, 21*(1), 21–24. 10.1016/j.smr.2017.07.002

Jiménez, D., & Glater, J.D. (2020). Student debt is a civil rights issue: The case for debt relief and higher education reform. *Harvard Civil Rights- Civil Liberties Law Review, 55,* 131. Retrieved from https://harvardcrcl.org/wp-content/uploads/sites/10/2020/09/Jimenez-Glater.pdf

Kuhn, T.S. (1970). *The structure of scientific revolution* (2nd ed.). Chicago: University of Chicago Press.

Lawrence, J.E., & Tar, U.A. (2018). Factors that influence teachers' adoption and integration of ICT in teaching/learning process. *Educational Media International, 55*(1), 79–105. 10.1080/09523987.2018.1439712

Macovei, S., Tufan, A.A., & Vulpe, B.I. (2014). Theoretical approaches to building a healthy lifestyle through the practice of physical activities. *Procedia-Social and Behavioral Sciences, 117,* 86–91. 10.1016/j.sbspro.2014.02.183

Macovei, S., Tufan, A.A., & Vulpe, B.I. (2014). Theoretical approaches to building a healthy lifestyle through the practice of physical activities. *Procedia-Social and Behavioral Sciences, 117,* 86–91. 10.1016/j.sbspro.2014.02.183

McCullough, B.P., Orr, M., & Kellison, T. (2020). Sport ecology: Conceptualizing an emerging subdiscipline within sport management. *Journal of Sport Management*, *34*(6), 509–520. 10.1123/jsm.2019-0294

McCullough, B.P., Orr, M., & Kellison, T. (2020). Sport ecology: Conceptualizing an emerging subdiscipline within sport management. *Journal of Sport Management*, *34*(6), 509–520. 10.1123/jsm.2019-0294

Mijatovic, I. (2020). Teaching standardization to Generation Z–learning outcomes define teaching methods. In *Sustainable development* (pp. 191–208). Cham: Springer.

Millington, R., Giles, A.R., van Luijk, N., & Hayhurst, L.M. (2021). Sport for sustainability? The extractives industry, sport, and sustainable development. *Journal of Sport and Social Issues*. 10.1177%2F0193723521991413

Pitts, B.G., & Danylchuk, K.E. (2007). Examining the body of knowledge in sport management: A preliminary descriptive study of current sport management textbooks. *Sport Management Education Journal*, *1*(1), 40–52.

Richards, S. (2010, March). Reflections: The past and future of research on institutions and institutional change. *Journal of Change Management*, *10*(1), 5–21. 10.1080/1469701 0903549408

Sachs, J.D. (2015). *The age of sustainable development*. New York City, N.Y., US: Columbia University Press. Retrieved from http://cup.columbia.edu/book/the-age-of-sustainable-development/9780231173155

Sachs, J.D. (2020). *The sges of globalization: Geography, technology, and institutions*. New York City, N.Y., US: Columbia University Press. Retrieved from http://cup.columbia.edu/book/the-ages-of-globalization/9780231193740

Schulenkorf, N. (2012). Sustainable community development through sport and events: A conceptual framework for sport-for-development projects. *Sport Management Review*, *15*(1), 1–12. 10.1016/j.smr.2011.06.001

Smith, A.F., Goodwin, D., Mort, M., & Pope, C. (2006). Adverse events in anesthetic practice: A qualitative study of the definition, discussion and reporting. *BJA: British Journal of Anaesthesia*, *96*(6), 715–721. 10.1093/bja/ael099

Szathmári, A., & Kocsis, T. (2020). Who cares about gladiators? An elite-sport-based concept of Sustainable Sport. *Sport in Society*, 1–19. 10.1080/17430437.2020.1832470

Triantafyllidis, S., & Darvin, L. (2021). Mass-participant sport events and sustainable development: gender, social bonding, and connectedness to nature as predictors of socially and environmentally responsible behavior intentions. *Sustainability Science*, *16*(5), 239–253. 10.1007/s11625-020-00867-x

Twenge, J.M. (2017). *iGen: Why today's super-connected kids are growing up less rebellious, more tolerant, less happy--and completely unprepared for adulthood--and what that means for the rest of us*. New York City, N.Y., US: Simon and Schuster.

University of California Los Angeles (UCLA). (2021). *What is sustainability?* Retrieved from https://www.sustain.ucla.edu/what-is-sustainability/

13

ADVANCING SPORT AND SUSTAINABLE DEVELOPMENT

Stavros Triantafyllidis and Cheryl Mallen

LEARNING OBJECTIVES

Upon completion of this chapter, learners should be able to successfully:

1. Determine the role sport can play in advancing sustainability within both sport and our global society through sport and sustainable development (S&SD)
2. Define the need for a robust body of S&SD leadership to guide sport and society to transition for sustainability and antifragility
3. Identify the concept of congruence and recognize that congruence is needed to advance efficient and effective policy development, programming, and implementation strategies that can aid in leading sport and society into a sustainable future through S&SD
4. Define policy and policy development to better comprehend S&SD policy and its connection with congruence
5. Explain the benefits of moving forward to a sustainable future with effective policy development in S&SD
6. Identify the key elements of policy development and how it can be applied to S&SD
7. Create an innovative policy brief for S&SD

DOI: 10.4324/9781003128953-13

Overview

There is a need to move all aspects of life and work – including sport – into action to support sustainability for the long-term survival of society and human life. This need arises from a plethora of unprecedented challenges impacting our world's personal, social, economic, ecological, technological, and political aspects. These challenges have left society – including the society of sport – in need of antifragility or needing to ensure their systems are robust and capable of thriving despite unpredictable, unstable, and fickle times and stressors (Taleb, 2012).

First, this chapter offers conclusions that encapsulate the work in the previous chapters. Next, the discussion sets the foundation for moving forward in sport and sustainable development (S&SD), emphasizing congruence. This means all plans for achieving S&SD need to be coordinated within each sport organization, between organizations, and society to make swift and efficient progress in achieving sustainability. Moving forward in tandem with other sport leaders and those in our greater society, navigating the multifaceted aspects of sustainability is essential. Such navigation is complex. It is proposed that achieving congruence begins with policy development that guides formulated strategies and implementation to achieve sustainability and antifragility successfully.

Glossary

2030 Agenda for Sustainable Development

The 2030 Agenda is a plan of action for people and society, economy, natural environment, technology, and politics. The purpose of the 2030 Agenda is to enhance universal peace and eradicate poverty in all its forms and dimensions. This 2030 Agenda includes the 17 sustainable development goals (SDGs) and 169 targets established by the United Nations (UN). The SDGs and targets seek to build on the previous Millennium development goals and complete what these have not yet achieved (United Nations, 2021).

Adaptive capacity

"The combination of the strengths, attributes, and resources available to an individual, community, society, or organization that can be used to prepare for and undertake actions to reduce adverse impacts, moderate harm, or exploit beneficial opportunities" (International Panel on Climate Change, 2012, p. 556).

Antifragility

The pursuit of robust systems that help increase the capability of individuals and organizations to thrive despite stressors, shocks, volatility, noise, mistakes, faults, attacks, or failures (Taleb, 2012).

Congruence

Congruence is defined as "the suitability or appropriateness of the chosen policy given the external and internal operating pressures experienced by the company" (Ghobadian et al., 2001, p. 387). Accordingly, the term refers to the state of agreeing or corresponding in a decision–making process, discussion, or debate (Dictionary, 2021). It involves considering other perspectives and working in tandem to achieve a goal.

Leadership

The term leadership has been discussed in depth in the literature, but there are still arguments concerning what constitutes leadership. Accordingly, for this chapter, the term we adopted is the following: "the capacity to translate vision into reality" (Forbes, 2021, p. 2).

Partnerships

In this chapter, partnerships are voluntary collaborations to deliver messages or services for climate action. Partnerships involve blocks of people/organizations that advance all parties' legitimacy and allow each party to "win" by offering complementary resources (Zeimers et al., 2019). The partnerships can be same-sector or cross-sector collaborations that offer synergies by cooperating for strategy or program development and delivery (Hermens et al., 2019) and increasing the chances of success compared to working independently (Wildridge et al., 2004).

Perspicacity

In this chapter, perspicacity includes developing knowledge and quick insights and understandings in sport (Mallen, 2017). Further, the knowledge, insights, and understandings are applicable to the six perspectives of S&SD including the personal, social, economic, ecological, technological, and political aspects.

Policy

Policy refers broadly to a set of actions designed to address an issue or achieve specific outcomes (Bacchi, 2009).

Policy development is a process that can include several stages, that can range from three to seven (Wu et al., 2017). According to the literature, a typical policy development process often reflects the following five stages (Howlett & Giest, 2012; Wu et al., 2017). They include (1) agenda setting (this stage identifies the issue to be addressed by the proposed policy), (2) policy formulation, (3) policy adoption, (4) policy implementation, and (5) policy evaluation (Howlett & Giest, 2012).

Sport

"Sport means all forms of physical activity which, through casual or organized participation, aim at expressing or improving physical fitness and well-being, forming social relationships or obtaining results in competition at all levels" (Szathmári & Kocsis, 2020, p. 4).

Sport and sustainable development (S&SD)

S&SD is the process that includes two stages: Sustainable development of sport (SDoS) and sport for sustainable development (S4SD) that, together, enhance the development that meets the needs of current generations without compromising future generations' ability to meet their own needs at the personal, social, economic, ecological, technological, and political levels (Millington et al., 2021; Szathmári & Kocsis, 2020; Triantafyllidis & Darvin, 2021).

Sport for sustainable development (S4SD)

S4SD refers to the contribution of sport to our global societies' viability by encouraging sustainability across the six perspectives of personal, social, economic, ecological, technological, and political worldwide (Macovei et al., 2014; Millington et al., 2021; Schulenkorf, 2012).

Sustainability

The term refers to "the integration of environmental health, social equity, and economic vitality to create thriving, healthy, diverse and resilient communities for this generation and generations to come" (University of California Los Angeles, 2021, para. 2).

The term sustainable development (SD) encompasses the initiatives and progress in pursuit of sustainability. According to the Brundtland Commission (2001), sustainable development is defined as the "development that meets the needs of the present without compromising the ability of future generations to meet their own needs" (p. 82). This includes "the narrow notion of physical sustainability [that] implies a concern for social equity between generations, a concern that must logically be extended to equity within each generation" (p. 82).

Sustainable development goals (SDGs)

The UN SDGs include a set of 17 goals. Each SDG sets its plans based on its national issues, and each goal has a targeted that focus on national circumstances (United Nations, 2021).

Sustainable development of sport (SDoS)

SD*o*S refers to the sustainable practices taken by sport regarding the management of sport products, services, and sport consumer behaviors to achieve sustainability within the world of sport that encompasses six perspectives including the personal, social, economic, ecological, technological, and political (McCullough et al., 2020; Szathmári & Kocsis, 2020; Triantafyllidis & Darvin, 2021).

The analytical concept applied to sport and sustainable development (S&SD)

A theoretical approach for analyzing sport as a platform to understand the world as a complex interaction of personal, social, economic, ecological, technological, and political systems. The individual parts' understanding can be combined to determine the S&SD and applied as a microcosm of society (Millington et al., 2021; Szathmari & Kocsis, 2020; Triantafyllidis & Darvin, 2021).

The normative concept applied to sport and sustainable development (S&SD)

Examinations are completed using sport as a platform to view the world by defining the objectives of a well-functioning society that delivers well-being for its global citizens today and for future generations. The normative concept urges us to have a universal vision toward a good society. These examinations lead to understandings of where we are currently and the gaps that need to be addressed moving into the future based on the six perspectives of S&SD (Millington et al., 2021; Szathmari & Kocsis, 2020; Triantafyllidis & Darvin, 2021).

Summarizing the conclusions for S&SD

S&SD, including its two stages of SD*o*S and S4SD of society, has been noted as a conduit to a new world order of sustainability. Sport has been recognized as a fundamental and strategic enabler for sustainable development at the UN since 2015.

This role uses the power of sport to influence members of society in many ways, including shifting perspectives on issues.

Sport is challenged, however, to ensure mechanisms are in place that advance sustainability into the future. It is proposed that reaching the capacity of sport for sustainability, and guiding society to transition to sustainability, can be achieved through S&SD. A call for leadership in sport is made to generate momentum toward sustainability to build antifragility. Accordingly, a robust future for sport and society can be established by ensuring systems are healthy and capable of thriving despite unpredictable, unstable, and fickle times and stressors (Taleb, 2012). This chapter stresses that a robust future includes implementing the 17

SDGs outlined by the UN by the deadline established in the 2030 Agenda. This Agenda asks for governments, private organizations, and citizens for immediate coordinated action. Sport must do their part to achieve these goals.

Due to the existence of the SDGs, sport does not need to spend time developing their own sustainability goals. Instead, sport can be guided by the established SDGs and can move to act now to advance sustainability as the deadline of 2030 is approaching. Time is critical – sport must determine the way forward quickly if there is the hope of meeting the time frame established. The time to transition for S&SD is now.

The transition for S&SD will not be easy as the breadth and scope of sustainability in sport are complex and diverse. S&SD extends to a vast array of initiatives from impacting economic growth and the need for investments that advance how sport manages the efficiency and effectiveness of sustainability through financial transparency, accountability, and innovations. Additionally, there are concerns with raising awareness and action for social development and the impacts of behavior for sustainability stemming from sociodemographic factors, including age, race; along with social justice factors that promote equality, diversity, and inclusion. Also, there is a need to resolve the climatic issues that impact sport and society with the advance of sustainable infrastructures, safeguards for our natural resources, sustainable production, and consumption. In the following paragraphs, we outline the momentum that S&SD can gain as we move forward, and we discuss the critical role of appropriate S&SD leadership.

Currently, S&SD is gaining momentum and is now pervasive – but generally, in the primary stages of development. Still, much work remains to be done to reach our adaptive capacity for sustainability in both sport and society. It is now up to those in sport to critically evaluate S&SD's impact, determine how to improve the initiatives for effectiveness and efficiency, find the societal gaps, and determine how sport as a platform can aid in filling such gaps. For S&SD leadership, we use the supportive quote by Warren Bennis: "Leadership is the capacity to translate vision into reality" (Forbes, 2021, p. 2). Accordingly, we aim to promote the development of effective plans with strategies, tactics, action plans, and policies that could turn visions for S&SD into reality. We envision significant contributions to global sustainability through S&SD.

Overall, a robust body of S&SD leadership is a critical element for the success of the transition. S&SD leadership needs to prioritize the advance of visions of S&SD, encourage and facilitate debates that lead to a consensus on the selected vision(s) for moving forward. This movement includes embedding S&SD in all sport management courses; generating partnerships to aid the advance of perspicacity (including partnerships between higher education sport management educators, students, researchers, research centers, and practitioners). A database to disseminate knowledge that can aid sport and society to transition as quickly as possible and ensure sport builds antifragility within the system. Finally, appropriate leadership in S&SD can position sport as a catalyst for efficient and effective actions that result in sustainability.

Leadership does not exist without teamwork, collaborations, and partnerships. Accordingly, much can be done with partnerships – but these take time and effort to cultivate and manage. The time and effort stem from the number of potential partnerships needed to achieve sustainability from governmental actors on the international, national, regional, and local levels, along with non-governmental actors. These partnerships can include, for example, international sport organizations, the private sector, civil society, and experts in the multiple areas of focus within sustainability. It seems implausible that one sport and one leader can manage the transition of sport toward sustainability. However, sports various leaders and organizations are well-positioned to jointly transition to address demands concerning issues and outline solutions within society. Accordingly, S&SD leadership needs to be guided with the core concept of congruence.

Congruence: A critical aspect for achieving sustainability

This chapter emphasizes that congruence is a critical element when transitioning to achieve sustainability. Congruence infers transitioning in a coordinated manner that aids in reaching the sport world's adaptive capacity. Such congruence involves determining "the suitability or appropriateness of the chosen policy given the external and internal operating pressures experienced by the company" (Ghobadian et al., 2001, p. 387). Moreover, congruence promotes "strategic capability to be more clearly understood before a policy is defined" (James et al., 1999, p. 346). Thus, the application of congruence to S&SD involves working in a coordinated manner within each sport and also within the society of sport as a whole.

Grant (1998) noted that four conditions are needed to achieve congruence. First, goals need to be stated simply and be utilized over the long term – and in this case, the SDGs are indicated by the UN and are already available to guide sport. Second, decisions by the leadership are based on a thorough understanding of the context – and in sport, this context is complex and diverse within and between sports. Third, the necessary resources must be available to support the pursuit of sustainability. The resources include, for example, personnel, financial, and technological, along with educational resources. And fourth, that the organization is capable of implementing the determined policies within their practice (Grant, 1998), including managing conflicts in the pursuit of congruent sustainability practices.

We will now examine S&SD policy and its role in the pursuit of congruence and how it connects with policy development by defining the term policy, describing the key stages of policy development, and the areas of focus in S&SD policy.

Achieving congruence through S&SD policy

In general terms, policies are commitment statements that also provide direction to organizations (Bacchi, 2009). Further, a policy is a management or procedural method for moving forward with its strategic planning (Bacchi, 2009). The UN position is that: "An integrated policy maximizes benefits to the three dimensions of sustainable development – economic, social and environmental – not as a sum, but each in its own right" (sportanddev.org, 2021). Organizations can, thus, be guided with a policy framework that enables actions for transitioning to sustainable practices.

Due to the complexity and diversity of S&SD, multiple policies are needed to reflect the six perspectives of S&SD – including the personal, social, economic, ecological, technological, and political aspects. In addition, such policy can be applied to regional, national, and international levels of sport, where governments make decisions, sport federations, leagues, and so forth (sportanddev.org, 2021). For SDoS, policies for sustainability are needed in the critical areas of the administration of sport. Examples include, but are not limited to, human resources, finance, operations, facilities, events, equipment, marketing, community relations, risk management, services, etc. In S4SD, sport organizations and entities that utilize the power of sport as a vehicle for positive societal changes can establish policies that support specific codes of conduct such as eliminating racial discrimination, ensuring gender equality, etc. A staged policy development strategy is now outlined for the multiple types of policy needed for S&SD.

Policy development in S&SD

Similar to congruence noted above, policy development is also a process that can include several stages. The stages have been noted as ranging from three to seven stages (Wu et al., 2017). In this chapter, we follow the Howlett and Giest (2012) five-stage process that includes (1) agenda setting (this stage identifies the issue to be addressed by the proposed policy), (2) policy formulation, (3) policy adoption, (4) policy implementation, and (5) policy evaluation.

Based on the staged model outlined in Figure 13.1, the development of policies is a linear process and starts with the agenda-setting stage (Howlett & Giest, 2012). Stage one identifies the issue that the proposed approach aims to address. For S&SD and stage one of the policy development, there are plenty of problems that can be addressed within SDoS and S4SD that reflect on the six perspectives of personal, social, economic, ecological, technological, and political. Accordingly, there are multiple policies to be developed. First, the areas relating to sustainability within each perspective should be identified. Next, data should be collected indicating the context and the magnitude of the issues. Finally, evidence that supports the development of policy or policies as a solution is needed and should be added to the agenda of S&SD for discussion by policymakers. For example, policy development for the perspectives of S&SD can target each of the 17 SDG goal issues such as physical inactivity, mental health issues, poverty, unemployment, environmental pollution, and so forth.

Stage two involves policy formulation. This stage is comprised of processes whereby existing policies can be refined, or new policy approaches should be created to improve the condition of the identified issue. This stage focuses on

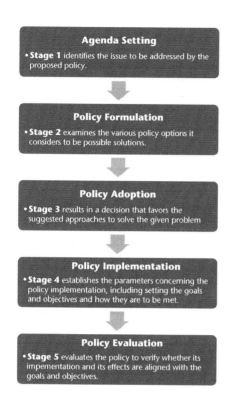

FIGURE 13.1 Policy development process in sport and sustainable development (S&SD) with the Howlett and Giest (2012) staged framework.

forecasting – or making predictions concerning the issue – to develop the best policy. Stage three involves the decision pertaining to the adoption of the policy or policies by the policymakers. A final decision made in this third stage establishes the selected direction that will be taken for managing the issue. Stage four includes establishing the parameters regardingthe policy implementation, including setting the goals and objectives and how they are to be met. The parameters outline the limits of who, what, where, when, and how the policy is implemented. These boundaries impact the potential success of a policy in achieving its goals and objectives. Before establishing limitations, policymakers and governmental actors can closely monitor and document the issue, and if possible, the consequences of previously adopted policies; they can analyze the magnitude of the expected impact of the adopted approach and then monitor the human and financial re-sources. Such data can provide feedback on the best practices that should continue and the gaps that need to be filled within a policy. The final stage is policy eva-luation, whereby policymakers evaluate the proposed policy and verify if the adopted policy is aligned with the goals and objectives set during the implementation stage.

Concluding remarks

Overall, there is a need to move all aspects of life and work – including sport – to actions that support sustainability for the long-term survival of sport, society, and human life. Policy development is a key strategy for achieving antifragility and congruence during a transition to global sustainability through S&SD. Antifragility involves ensuring systems within sport and society are robust and capable of thriving despite unpredictable, unstable, and fickle times and stressors (Taleb, 2012). Additionally, achieving congruence builds a force of change that ensures sport and society are heading in the same direction during a transition to become sustainable. There is a critical need for leadership to advance policymaking for S&SD to manage a plethora of unprecedented challenges impacting our world's personal, social, economic, ecological, technological, and political perspectives.

The key outcomes of this chapter:

1. S&SD, including the two stages (SDoS and S4SD) across the six perspectives (personal, social, economic, ecological, technological, and political), is integral for the transition of sport for sustainability
2. Congruence in S&SD is needed to ensure a fast and coordinated transition to sustainability
3. S&SD policy is a crucial component underscoring how we move forward to a more sustainable future
4. The policy development process in S&SD encompasses five stages, including (1) agenda setting (this stage identifies the issue to be addressed by the proposed policy), (2) policy formulation, (3) policy adoption, (4) policy implementation, and (5) policy evaluation (Howlett & Giest, 2012)

Future directions

1. The generation of leadership for S&SD is a priority in the process of achieving the necessary understandings concerning the current state of SDoS and S4SD; for advancing visions of S&SD; for managing debates that lead to a consensus on the selected vision(s) for moving forward; for working to ensure sport building antifragility within the system; and for achieving congruence for sustainability in sport and society
2. The promotion of S&SD and learning to implement the concept is needed for its success into the future.
3. It is now up to those in sport to give rise to the necessary leadership, to promote and encourage the current and next generation of sporting participants to ensure a movement toward a sustainable future in sport and society
4. Monitoring and evaluation strategies are needed to continuously express the progress being made (or not made) to pursue sustainability in sport and society
5. Recommendations stemming from monitoring and evaluation activities can aid to keep moving forward in achieving sustainability

Learning activities

The following paragraphs define a policy brief and indicate how you can create one for S&SD. Based on this chapter's discussion, further reading, and relevant online resources (please see the following two sections), you should be able to synthesize the current knowledge and use the readings to support the development of your policy brief on S&SD.

Developing a policy brief for S&SD

A policy brief is usually generated and then provided to an informed and active public audience – including decision-makers and citizens who participate in the public sphere. However, the audience may not have the technical expertise or extensive prior knowledge about the policy's problem, issue, or need. Moreover, many of these individuals are very busy – elected officials, local citizens who take time from family and work to contribute to the public good, or professionals whose work in the public or private sphere makes enormous demands on their time. In short, policy briefs are for busy people with many responsibilities, little time to waste, and for whom the problem, issue, or need of interest is only one of many they are trying to address.

Your task is to prepare a policy brief that would provide decision-makers in sport with three contrasting strategies to address the threat of not transitioning for sustainability or to take advantage of opportunities to enhance sustainability. First, select a problem, issue, or need you have identified concerning sustainability in SDoS (i.e., a lack of clean energy at sport facilities) or S4SD (i.e., a lack of gender equality). Do not confuse the policy brief with a short-term plan or a planning process. Instead, you are trying to provide sport leaders with a synopsis of the issue and alternative strategies for the issue that a community, or a group of communities, can pursue into the future.

The purpose of this learning activity aims to cultivate your skills for building a policy brief for S&SD. Accordingly, students should explore the complex interactions between personal, social, economic, ecological, technological, and political elements of S&SD. Further, review the conclusions outlined above, along with the future directions. Findings across the two S&SD stages (SDoS and S4SD) and the six perspectives allow you to expand your analytical, critical, and creative thinking skills. Accordingly, be sure to identify the factors that affect problems or issues for SDoS and S4SD.

Your goal in this learning activity is to prepare a short policy brief (i.e., 3–5 pages in length) that would convince sport policymakers and government officials to follow a specific strategy for addressing an issue or threat to sustainability that you have identified. Accordingly, you are trying to convince your audience to adopt an overall strategy that the global society and the world leaders can pursue over the next decade to achieve global sustainability by 2030.

Consider the following:

- How will you get the leaders of your local community and beyond to adopt an overall strategic approach that will inform or guide specific decisions toward the adoption of S&SD elements and implementation of our vision for S&SD (our vision: We envision significant contributions to global sustainability through S&SD)

- The people you are trying to convince with your policy brief are sport leaders at either the regional, national, or international levels, or the government counterparts. Please make sure your policy brief draws attention to the factors driving change today, shows that the threat or challenge is a serious one with major causes and potential severe implications for the future of the world, and illustrates divergent approaches to reducing the danger

- Design an effective policy brief for S&SD utilizing the following sections in your assignment:

  - A Title Page: A compelling title of a paper should give readers a quick overview of the subject and problem addressed in the policy paper. A reader may use the title in deciding whether to read the paper or not

  - An Executive Summary: This synopsis on the topic aims to raise readers' interest in wanting to read more about the topic. The primary goal of the executive summary is to satisfy the needs of those readers who will not read the entire paper and readers whose main interest is in the key proposed policy recommendations. The executive summary represents the whole paper by providing a synopsis of all principal parts and findings

  - An Introduction: This sets the scene by presenting the context for the threat or challenge and linking this to the specific focus of the policy paper. Describe the setting and the nature of the communities that are the strategy's objective. The introduction demonstrates that an urgent threat exists and that your essay is worth reading because it will offer possible solutions. The opening will include a statement about the purpose of the policy paper. Most policy papers also have a brief overview of the methodology for data collection and the kinds of resources used in its construction, but this will be limited in your case to describing the sources of data you have used to construct your recommendations

  - Identified Problem Description: The problem description identifies, defines, and elaborates the nature of the threat or challenge under discussion. This may include background information about the history of the threat, its causes, who is affected, descriptions of previous policies aimed at addressing the threat, and the outcomes of implementing those policies

  - Policy Alternatives: This section outlines, evaluates, and compares the possible policy alternatives. Remember, you are focusing on overall strategic policymaking, not developing a plan of action. You should present all the approaches or strategies that you think are potentially useful for addressing the threat. Offering the full range of options helps you build a comprehensive and convincing case. For example, you should explain how it strengthens your final position because it shows that you have carefully considered several vital alternatives. The focus is on evaluating how each option compares to reducing the threat. Based on this evidence, an argument is made for the preferred policy alternative. Your policy options should reflect the critical differences in strategic frameworks that we have discussed in this class. Be sure to state your recommendations concerning the policy alternatives

- Conclusions and Future Direction: This section presents the case for your preferred alternative strategy to decision-makers. This section provides a concise synthesis of significant findings. However, this is more than a summary of the main conclusions. You should explain how your strategy will lead to and inform policy recommendations relevant to your tackling issue

Further reading

1. Keepnews, D.M. (2016). Developing a policy brief. *Policy, Politics, & Nursing Practice, 17*(2), 61–65. https://doi.org/10.1177%2F1527154416660670
2. Wong, S.L., Green, L.A., Bazemore, A.W., & Miller, B.F. (2017). How to write a health policy brief. *Families, Systems, & Health, 35*(1), 21. https://psycnet.apa.org/doi/10.1037/fsh0000238
3. Schwach, V., Bailly, D., Christensen, A.S., Delaney, A.E., Degnbol, P., Van Densen, W.L., ... & Wilson, D.C. (2007). Policy and knowledge in fisheries management: A policy brief. *ICES Journal of Marine Science, 64*(4), 798–803. https://doi.org/10.1093/icesjms/fsm020

Relevant online resources

1. IDRC – CRDI: https://www.idrc.ca/en/how-write-policy-brief

   a. https://www.icpolicyadvocacy.org/sites/icpa/files/downloads/icpa_policy_briefs_essential_guide.pdf

2. Guidelines for writing a policy brief: https://www.pep-net.org/sites/pep-net.org/files/typo3doc/pdf/CBMS_country_proj_profiles/Philippines/CBMS_forms/Guidelines_for_Writing_a_Policy_Brief.pdf
3. Preparing policy briefs: http://www.fao.org/3/i2195e/i2195e03.pdf
4. Research to action: https://www.researchtoaction.org/wp-content/uploads/2014/10/PBWeekLauraFCfinal.pdf
5. American Public University System: https://apus.libanswers.com/writing/faq/228884

References

Bacchi, C. (2009). *Analyzing policy*. Pearson Higher Education AU: Melbourne, Australia

Brundtland Commission. (2001). Climate change 2001: Impacts, adaptation, and vulnerability. In McCarthy, J.J., Canziani, O.F., Leary, N.A., Dokken, D.J. & White, K.S. (Eds.), Contributions of Working Groupworking group II to the Third Assessment Report third assessment report of the Intergovernmental Panelintergovernmental panel on Climate Change climate change. Cambridge University Press: Cambridge. Weblink: https://www.ipcc.ch/report/ar3/wg2/

Dictionary (2021). *Congruence*. Retrieved from https://www.dictionary.com/browse/congruence

Forbes. (2021, June). *What is leadership?* Retrieved from http://www.professorpeaches.com/wp-content/uploads/2015/02/What-is-leadership-Forbes.pdf

Ghobadian, A., Viney, H., & Holt, D. (2001). Seeking congruence in implementing corporate environmental strategy. *International Journal Environmental Technology and Management*, *1*(4), 384–401. 10.1504/IJETM.2001.000771

Grant, R. (1998). *Contemporary strategic analysis* (3rd ed.). Oxford: Blackwell.

Howlett, M., & Giest, S. (2012). The policy-making process. In *Routledge handbook of public policy* (pp. 35–46). Routledge: Oxon, England.

Hermens, N., Verkooijen, K. T., & Koelen, M. A. (2019, February). Associations between partnership characteristics and perceived success in Dutch sport-for-health partnerships. *Sport Management Review*, *22*(1), 142–152.

International Panel on Climate Change (IPCC). (2012). *Annex 11 Glossary of terms*. In *Managing the risks of extreme events and disasters to advance climate change adaptation*. Retrieved from https://archive.ipcc.ch/pdf/special-reports/srex/SREX-Annex_Glossary.pdf

James, P., Ghobadian, A., Viney, H., & Liu, J. (1999). Addressing the divergence between environmental strategy formulation and implementation. *Management Decision*, *37*, 4, 338–347. Retrieved from https://www.emerald.com/insight/content/doi/10.1108/00251749910269384/full/html

Macovei, S., Tufan, A.A., & Vulpe, B.I. (2014). Theoretical approaches to building a healthy lifestyle through the practice of physical activities. *Procedia-Social and Behavioral Sciences*, *117*, 86–91. 10.1016/j.sbspro.2014.02.183

Mallen, C. (2017). The concept ofknowledge in event management. In Mallen, C. & Adams, L. (Eds) Event management in sport, recreation and tourism. New York, NY: Routledge

McCullough, B.P., Orr, M., & Kellison, T. (2020). Sport ecology: Conceptualizing an emerging subdiscipline within sport management. *Journal of Sport Management*, *34*(6), 509–520. 10.1123/jsm.2019-0294

Millington, R., Giles, A.R., van Luijk, N., & Hayhurst, L.M. (2021). Sport for sustainability? The extractives industry, sport, and sustainable development. *Journal of Sport and Social Issues*. 10.1177/0193723521991413

Sachs, J.D. (2015). *The age of sustainable development*. Columbia University Press: New York City, N.Y, US. Retrieved from http://cup.columbia.edu/book/the-age-of-sustainable-development/9780231173155

Schulenkorf, N. (2012). Sustainable community development through sport and events: A conceptual framework for sport-for-development projects. *Sport Management Review*, *15*(1), 1–12. 10.1016/j.smr.2011.06.001

Sport and Development. (2021, May). *Introduction to sport and development policy*. Retrieved from https://www.sportanddev.org/en/learn-more/sport-and-development-policy/introduction-sport-and-development-policy

Szathmári, A., & Kocsis, T. (2020). Who cares about gladiators? An elite-sport-based concept of Sustainable Sport. *Sport in Society*, 1–19. 10.1080/17430437.2020.1832470

Taleb, N. N. (2012). *Antifragile: Things that gain from disorder* (Vol. 3). Random House Incorporated.: New York City, N.Y., US.

Triantafyllidis, S. & Darvin, L. (2021). Mass-participant sport events and sustainable development: gender, social bonding, and connectedness to nature as predictors of socially and environmentally responsible behavior intentions. *Sustainable Science, 16(5)*, 239–253. 10.1007/s11625-020-00867-x

University of California Los Angeles (UCLA). (2021). *What is sustainability?* Retrieved from https://www.sustain.ucla.edu/what-is-sustainability/

Welzand, H., Schindler, L., Puls-Elvidge, S., & Crawford, L. (2015). Definitions of quality in higher education: A synthesis of the literature. *Higher Learning Research Communications, 5*(3), 4–13. 10.18870/hlrc.v5i3.244

Wildridge, V., Childs, S., Cawthra, L., & Madge, B. (2004, June). How to create successful partnerships- A review of literature. *Health Information Library Journal*, 21 Supplement 1, 3–19. 10.111/j.1740-3324.2004.00497.x

Wu, X., Ramesh, M., Howlett, M., & Fritzen, S.A. (2017). *The public policy primer: Managing the policy process*. Routledge: New York City, N.Y., US.

Zeimers, G., Anagnostopoulos, C., Zintz, T., & Willem, A. (2019). Examining Collaboration Among Nonprofit Organizations for Social Responsibility Programs. *Nonprofit and Voluntary Sector Quarterly, 48*(5), 953–974. 10.1177/0899764019837616.

INDEX